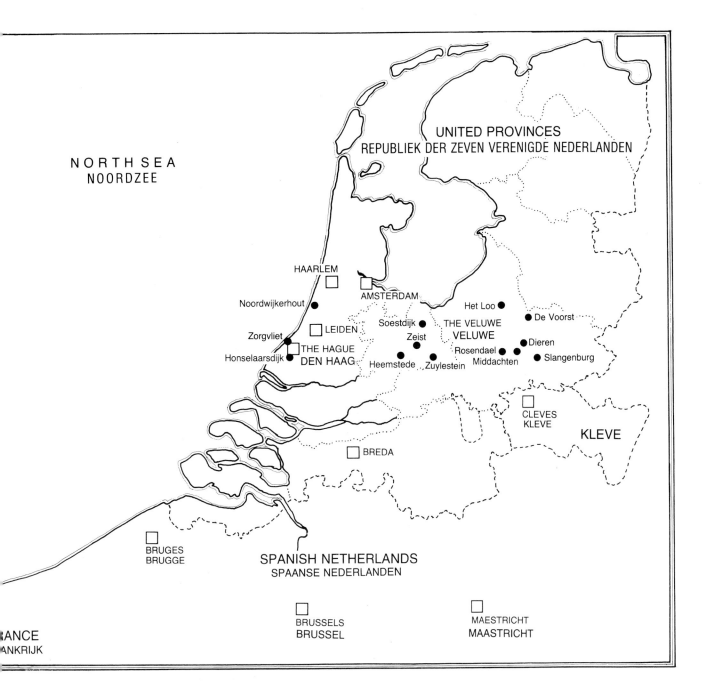

NORTH SEA
NOORDZEE

UNITED PROVINCES
REPUBLIEK DER ZEVEN VERENIGDE NEDERLANDEN

HAARLEM

AMSTERDAM

Noordwijkerhout

Het Loo

De Voorst

Soestdijk   THE VELUWE
VELUWE

Zorgvliet   LEIDEN   Zeist   Dieren
THE HAGUE   Rosendael
Honselaarsdijk   DEN HAAG   Middachten   Slangenburg
              Heemstede   Zuylestein

CLEVES
KLEVE

KLEVE

BREDA

BRUGES
BRUGGE

SPANISH NETHERLANDS
SPAANSE NEDERLANDEN

BRUSSELS
BRUSSEL

MAESTRICHT
MAASTRICHT

FRANCE
FRANKRIJK

THE GARDENS OF

WILLIAM AND MARY

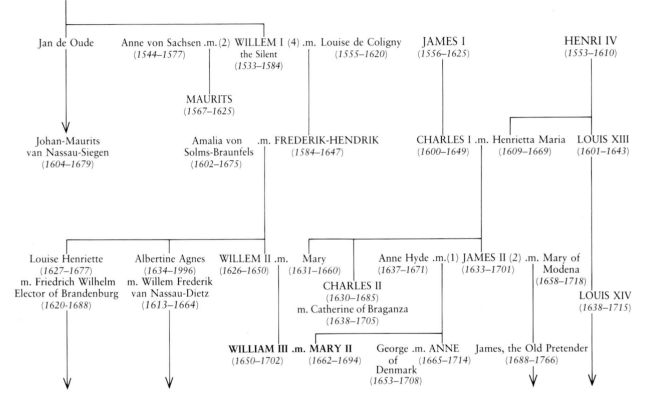

HOUSE OF ORANGE | ENGLAND, IRELAND AND SCOTLAND | FRANCE

Counts of Nassau

Jan de Oude

Anne von Sachsen .m. (2) WILLEM I (4) .m. Louise de Coligny
(1544–1577) the Silent *(1555–1620)*
(1533–1584)

MAURITS
(1567–1625)

JAMES I
(1556–1625)

HENRI IV
(1553–1610)

Johan-Maurits
van Nassau-Siegen
(1604–1679)

Amalia von .m. FREDERIK-HENDRIK
Solms-Braunfels *(1584–1647)*
(1602–1675)

CHARLES I .m. Henrietta Maria
(1600–1649) *(1609–1669)*

LOUIS XIII
(1601–1643)

Louise Henriette
(1627–1677)
m. Friedrich Wilhelm
Elector of Brandenburg
(1620-1688)

Albertine Agnes
(1634–1996)
m. Willem Frederik
van Nassau-Dietz
(1613–1664)

WILLEM II .m. Mary
(1626–1650) *(1631–1660)*

Anne Hyde .m.(1) JAMES II (2) .m. Mary of
(1637–1671) *(1633–1701)* Modena
(1658–1718)

CHARLES II
(1630–1685)
m. Catherine of Braganza
(1638–1705)

LOUIS XIV
(1638–1715)

WILLIAM III .m. MARY II
(1650–1702) *(1662–1694)*

George .m. ANNE
of *(1665–1714)*
Denmark
(1653–1708)

James, the Old Pretender
(1688–1766)

William's and Mary's
combined family trees,
showing descents from the
royal houses of England
and France, and from the
Counts of Nassau

THE GARDENS OF
WILLIAM
AND MARY

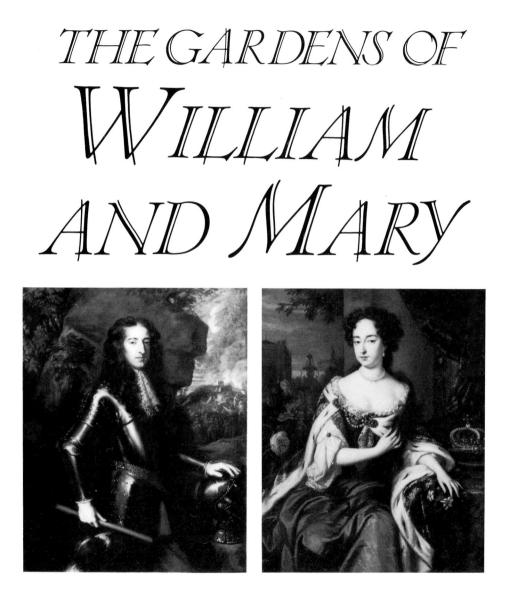

David Jacques and Arend Jan van der Horst
assisted by Helen Allan and Ar Koppens

Contributions from Mavis Batey, Susan Campbell, Ruth Duthie, Peter
Goodchild, John Harris, John Harvey, David Jacques, Ar Koppens,
Ian McNeil, Carla Oldenburger-Ebbers, Jean O'Neill, Willem
Overmars, Donald Pigott, Edward Saunders, Arend Jan van der Horst,
Rudolf Vosteen, Onno Wijnands and Jan Woudstra.

Christopher Helm
London

© 1988 David Jacques and Arend Jan van der Horst
Christopher Helm (Publishers) Ltd, Imperial House,
21–25 North Street, Bromley, Kent BR1 1SD

ISBN 0–7470–1608–9

A CIP catalogue record for this book is available from the British Library

Typeset by Opus, Oxford
Printed and bound in Great Britain
By Butler and Tanner, Frome

CONTENTS

PART TWO: A TOUR OF THE GARDEN

Contents

Note on Contributors

Mavis Batey is President of the Garden History Society and the author of many books about Oxford and eighteenth-century gardening; she has contributed to Chapter 5, particularly on Celia Fiennes.

Susan Campbell is a freelance writer with a particular knowledge of British kitchen gardens; she has contributed most of Chapter 12.

Ruth Duthie is an authority on British florists' flowers and has contributed most of Chapter 11.

Peter Goodchild is a lecturer at the Centre for the Conservation of Historic Parks and Gardens at the University of York; he has contributed to Chapter 5, particularly on the topographical artists in England.

John Harris is an architectural historian and author of many books on seventeenth- and eighteenth-century garden design; he has contributed to Chapters 2, 4 and 5.

John Harvey is an architect specialising in medieval archecture; he is also an authority on the history of the English nursery trade and a past President of the Garden History Society; he has contributed to Chapters 2, 6, 10 and 12.

David Jacques is the Inspector of Historic Parks and Gardens at the Historic Buildings and Monuments Commission for England; he has contributed most of Chapters 2 and 4 as well as editing and making additions to the other chapters.

Ar Koppens is an historian who wrote a thesis on the restoration of the Het Loo gardens when at the University of York; he has contributed Chapters 1 and 3 and helped with Chapter 5.

Ian McNeil is a technical and general author and journalist, and a member of the Newcomen Society; he has contributed part of Chapter 8.

Carla Oldenburger-Ebbers is the Conservator of the Library at Wageningen Agricultural University and an authority on seventeenth-century Dutch horticulture; she has contributed to Chapters 7, 11 and 12.

Jean O'Neill has researched Hans Sloane and the Duchess of Beaufort for many years; she has contributed part of Chapter 10.

Willem Overmars works at the Staatsbosbeheer (State Forestry Service) and with the Stichting voor het Beheer van Particuliere Historische Buitenplaatsen (Foundation for the Preservation of Private Historical Country Houses); he has contributed part of Chapter 6.

Donald Pigott is Director of the University Botanic Garden at Cambridge and has a particular interest in early British avenues; he has contributed Appendix A and part of Chapter 6.

Edward Saunders is an architect whose projects include Melbourne Hall, Derbyshire, and who has a special interest in ironwork; he has contributed on ironwork to Chapter 6.

Arend Jan van der Horst is a landscape architect and author from Amsterdam; he has acted as joint editor and made contributions to many of the chapters.

Rudolf Vosteen is an engineer at the Rijksgebouwendienst who was largely responsible for the restoration of the waterworks at Het Loo; he has contributed part of Chapter 8.

Onno Wijnands is a lecturer at Wageningen Agricultural University, and is an authority on the introduction of exotics to the Netherlands; he has provided Appendix C, and has helped with Appendix B, as well as contributing on the collection of exotics to Chapter 10.

Jan Woudstra is a horticulturalist and garden historian who researched wildernesses when at the University of York; he has contributed Chapter 9 and Appendix B.

Responsibility for the final form of the text rests with the editors.

Acknowledgements

Original material is reproduced by kind permission of the following (colour plate numbers are in bold):

Algemeene Rijksarchief, The Hague 3.9, 3.12.
Trustees of the British Library **9, 10**.
Trustees of the British Museum 4.14.
Canaletto 3.8, 3.10.
Trustees of the Will of Major Peter George Evelyn 11.6.
Gemeentearchief, The Hague **1, 4, 11, 21**; 1.1, 1.4, 1.5, 1.6, 1.7, 3.2, 3.3, 3.4, 3.5, 7.4, 7.9, 7.11, 7.13, 8.1, 8.5, 11.4.
Iconographisch Bureau 5.5.
Institut de France, Bibliothèque 2.4.
J.T.L. Jervoise, Esq. 12.7.
Leiden University 1.2.
Her Majesty Queen Beatrice, Royal Collection, Koninglijke Huisarchief **3**; 3.1, 3.6, 7.5, 7.14, 8.3, 8.6, 8.8, 9.10, 9.11, 12.3, 12.5, 12.6.
Museum Boymans-van Beuningen, Rotterdam 4.3.
Trustees of the National Gallery **2, 15**.
National Portrait Gallery Portraits of William and Mary, 2.8.
Duke of Northumberland 2.5.
Property Services Agency 4.13, 7.12, 10.9.
Her Majesty Queen Elizabeth, Royal Library, Windsor Castle 2.10.
Rijksbureau Kunsthistorische Documentatie 3.7, 3.11, 3.13, 3.15 (Private Collection).
Royal Institute of British Architects, Drawings Collection 2.6, 2.7, 4.2, 4.12, 9.7.
The Trustees of Sir John Soane's Museum **8, 19**.
Statens Konstmuseer, Stockholm 4.10.
Travers Morgan Planning 2.2, 4.4, 7.3.
The Library, Wageningen Agricultural University 6.9, 7.1, 7.2, 7.6, 7.8, 7.10, 8.2, 9.3, 9.8, 10.2, 10.8, 11.1, 11.2, 12.1, 12.2, 12.5.
Yale Centre for British Art 5.3.
Stedelijk Museum, Zutphen 3.14.

Photography is reproduced by kind permission of the following:

Fiona Cowell 6.1.
Ruth Duthie **23**; 10.4, 10.6, 10.7, 10.10, 11.3, 11.5, 11.6.
Photo Holland — Aerial Photography **5**.

ACKNOWLEDGEMENTS

Hampshire County Council 12.7

John Harris 2.1, 2.8, 2.9, 2.11, 2.12, 2.13, 2.14, 2.15, 4.1, 4.6, 4.8, 4.9, 5.2, 5.4, 8.4, 10.1.

Land Use Consultants 2.3, 2.5.

National Trust Photographic Library **20, 22**; 4.7, 4.11.

Willem Overmars 1.3, 6.2, 6.3, 6.4, 6.5, 6.6, 6.7.

Gordon D. Rowley 10.5.

Edward Saunders **14**; 6.8.

Alan C.B. Urwin 2.5.

Rudolf Vosteen **18**; 8.7.

John Wilson 2.2, 4.4, 7.3.

Jan Woudstra 9.1, 9.2, 9.4, 9.6, 9.9.

Foreword

The Garden History Society is very pleased to be associated with the Dutch Garden Society in the production of this book as part of the William and Mary Tercentenary celebrations at a time when the importance of garden history is increasingly being understood and valued. To have the Dutch and English gardens of the reign of William and Mary described together in one book will add a new dimension to garden history in both countries.

From our point of view we are able to learn not only much that is new about horticultural skills in the Netherlands but to increase our knowledge of a period of English garden history that has been little studied. The English garden had not yet found its own style and was very receptive to European ideas and we can now recognise, not only Dutch influences, but common sources of inspiration in the gardens of our two countries. A closer study of the periods following the reign of William and Mary shows us, however, that what came to be described as a 'Dutch garden' in England was not necessarily like anything that was seen in Holland.

Mavis Batey
President, the Garden History Society

Part of the glorious past of the garden history of my country comes to life in this book, that has been compiled under the auspices of the Garden History Society and De Nederlandse Tuinenstichting (The Dutch Garden Society). In the Netherlands as well as in many other countries, gardens have very often been lost by neglect, change of interest and shortage of money. It is therefore necessary that information about the most important gardens of a country is published.

We are very happy to present this interesting book about one of the most important periods of the Dutch and English garden history which links our two countries closely together.

Baroness H.L.M. van Verschuer-d'Yvoy van Mijdrecht
President of De Nederlandse Tuinenstichting

WILLIAM AND MARY

1688   1988

ANGLO-DUTCH CELEBRATION

Introduction

'What a pitch the Practice and Esteem of Gard'ning is within these thirty Years last past arrived' remarked Stephen Switzer in 1715. Daniel Defoe agreed, commending William III for having revived 'the love of gardening' in his kingdom

> with the particular judgement of the king, all the gentlemen in England began to fall in; and in a few years, fine gardens, and fine houses began to grow up in every corner; the king began with the gardens of Hampton Court and Kensington, and the gentlemen followed every where, with such a gust that the alteration is indeed wonderful throughout the whole kingdom.

Yet this is the period, when William, Mary and Anne reigned, that was so decisively rejected by the protagonists of the English landscape garden. There were even complaints about the 'Dutch style'. This was unfair. The Dutch were certainly the leaders in horticulture, but, while both countries were within the European tradition led by France, topography and tradition gave quite distinct characteristics to each nation's garden design. The only English gardens for which the epithet 'Dutch' was at all justified were the Royal Gardens.

The Netherlands was small, and good land scarce and hard-won, so Dutch gardens tended to be compact. Except for the heathy Veluwe Forest in the east, it was also mostly flat. Yet the Dutch achievement in gardens was certainly not contemptible. Indeed in their consistently high standards of organisation and use of mathematical form they equalled, even perhaps surpassed, any formal garden tradition anywhere. The poor reputation of Dutch gardens in England was very largely the fault of English writers, who badly maligned them in the eighteenth century for English national interests, and then, in the nineteenth century, misunderstood them as having been a tradition merely in flower gardens.

When we look at the wonderful engravings of Dutch and English gardens of William's time, we would be blind not to recognise the skill and expense with which these gardens were made. If tourists like Celia Fiennes and Daniel Defoe didn't share later concepts of Taste, and of the need to work with Nature, they evidently regarded and admired gardens as the receptacles of arts such as ironworking, fountaineering, the making of *parterres* and topiary. All these arts were lost from the landscape garden, only to be revived in the nineteenth century.

The tercentenary of William and Mary's accession to the throne gives an opportunity to recall to memory the gardens that were amongst the wonders of their age. While politically the Glorious Revolution of 1688/9 finally laid to rest the doctrine of the 'divine right' of kings, and established a constitutional monarchy ruling by consent of Parliament, in gardening it meant a spell of Dutch skill and practice in the Royal Gardens, as William's and Mary's interests were transplanted to England. This book principally concerns the gardens of the royal couple and of their court.

The theme could have been merely a general history of the greater gardens, but this would have denied us half the pleasure. Much of the interest is in the several arts such as those mentioned above. Material on these specialist arts, both from the Netherlands and from Britain, is displayed in the same order that the visitor would have seen them on a visit to a palace. The result, we feel, was worth the trouble. The book has become more than just a recital of the works of the famous; it is a celebration of those many artists, gardeners and collectors who, through their diverse contributions, brought the gardens of the day to their state of glory.

Part II of this book thus commences with the axial avenue of elm or lime leading to the ironwork gate at the forecourt, where culminated the grand approach to the impressive front façade. Behind the house the *parterres* in intricate patterns of different coloured materials, with statues, trellis, and fountains, make a great display. Canals around the garden or in line with the axis form reflective surfaces and might have some lively waterfowl. Enclosing the garden would be *bosquets* and wildernesses, bringing shelter to the tender plants that grow in the *plates-bandes* around the *parterre de broderie*, and providing the owner with some private retirements where nothing more intrusive than bird song would disturb his contemplation.

In the more horticultural areas of the garden pride of place was given to the collection of tender exotics housed in heated greenhouses. Nearby would be the flower garden where the highly-prized florists' flowers could be displayed and perhaps cut for bouquets to be brought into the house. It would be easy to forget, after all the decorative splendours of the *parterre*, that gardens are places to grow fruit and vegetables. Every large house at least had a kitchen garden and orchard, and indeed these largely became the *parterre* and *bosquet* in certain places.

The pleasures of these gardens are simple and enduring. The exquisite florists' flowers still interest some discerning gardeners, who collect them in preference to their overblown modern relatives. Many other elements are frequently revived for present-day gardens, like trellis, pots for flowers, clipped hedges and topiary. These are suitable for small gardens, where they are again gaining in popularity. Conservatories are built once again, partly as extra living space and partly for the opportunity they give to grow exotic plants.

The illustrations in this book revive the former appearance of grand formal gardens, and archives and descriptions complete the picture. After comparing their former state with the present, it is sad to relate that amongst the palaces Hampton Court is unique in having retained its grand layout, though even there the details have changed considerably.

The rest have long since been altered, vanished or remain as vestiges. Kensington Gardens, for example, was transformed by Charles Bridgeman, and the present 'Dutch garden' dates only from the 1900s. Of the great southern garden only the grassed platform survives. The huge layouts by George London – Burghley, Longleat and Chatsworth – were transformed by Capability Brown in the 1750s and 1760s. What remained of the gardens of Dyrham was landscaped in the 1800s when Humphry Repton provided a Red Book. There are still the outlines of smaller gardens which the fluctuations of taste have passed by, kept up by successive generations of gardeners for the sake of the plants they contain, but this too is rare.

Amongst the Dutch palaces, Rijswijk was neglected by William III's heirs and demolished later in the eighteenth century. Honselaarsdijk was demolished in 1815 and is now a scrapyard. Fate has been kinder to the Noordeinde Palace, though the gardens were landscaped in 1787 by P. W. Schonk. Under Louis Napoleon, Het Loo and the southern garden at Huis ten Bosch were landscaped by Alexandre Dufour in 1807, whilst a new landscape garden was added on the north side of Huis ten Bosch by J. D. Zocher senior. Zocher worked at Soestdijk from 1815, and later his son, J. D. Zocher junior, took over there, and at Zeist in 1830, Clingendaal in 1834 and Rosendael in 1836. The other great formal layouts mentioned in this book, such as Dieren, Zorgvliet, and De Voorst, also succumbed to the landscape style later in the nineteenth century.

The growing interest in historic gardens to both academics and an increasingly knowledgeable and concerned public has provoked a fresh look at the seventeenth-century gardens in Britain and the Netherlands. The traditional derision of the Dutch gardens of William and Mary's time, taught to us by our forefathers in their excessive zeal for picturesque taste, has prevented us appreciating their virtues. We have only to accept them on their own terms to gain enormous pleasure from them.

Perhaps the first restoration of an historic garden in Britain was that of Westbury Court carried out by the National Trust between 1967 and 1970. Much has been made of the supposed Dutchness of this small formal garden made between 1696 and 1705, but these speculations are secondary to the enjoyment that the public clearly derives from the curious canals and topiary of the place. Another National Trust restoration of a formal garden to have survived in outline was that of Erddig, in Wales, carried out between 1975 and 1977. The Dutch have restored only one great formal garden, but this is Het Loo, the palace upon which William III lavished most expenditure. Just over the German border, the Corporation of Cleves started in 1978 on the renovation of the amphitheatre and surrounding areas originally laid out by Count Johan-Maurits in the 1650s.

The Tercentenary is a chance for English and Dutch garden enthusiasts to get together, and to explore what other restoration work may be feasible. The renovation of Hampton Court has so far consisted only of the replanting of the lime semicircle in the Great Parterre, now called the Fountain Garden, which badly needed attention anyway. Clearly further possibilities there are enormous.

Before passing on to some remarks about dates and spelling, the editors want to thank the many contributors, each of whom provided fresh and stimulating material on their own subject. It was, though, not easy to edit material from so many specialists, each with his or her special concerns and style, and much of the success in doing so is due to their forbearance in accepting and commenting on changes. Special thanks go to Helen Allan, whose considerable work in translation and picture-researching eased the passage of the book at its most crucial periods.

Until the middle of the eighteenth century the year started on 25 March. To avoid confusion, a date between 1 January and 24 March, which would have been in, say, 1696 at the time, but 1697 by modern reckoning, is written '1696/7'. Spellings of personal names and places are in the form recognised now (hence Le Nôtre not Le Nostre, Zorgvliet not Sorgvliet). Quotations in the original language are, though, given verbatim.

Measurements at places in Britain are given in imperial and at places in the Netherlands in metric (three feet make one yard or 0.91 metres). Units of currency are those obtaining at the period in question.

PART ONE
THE GARDENS

The Dutch Classical Garden

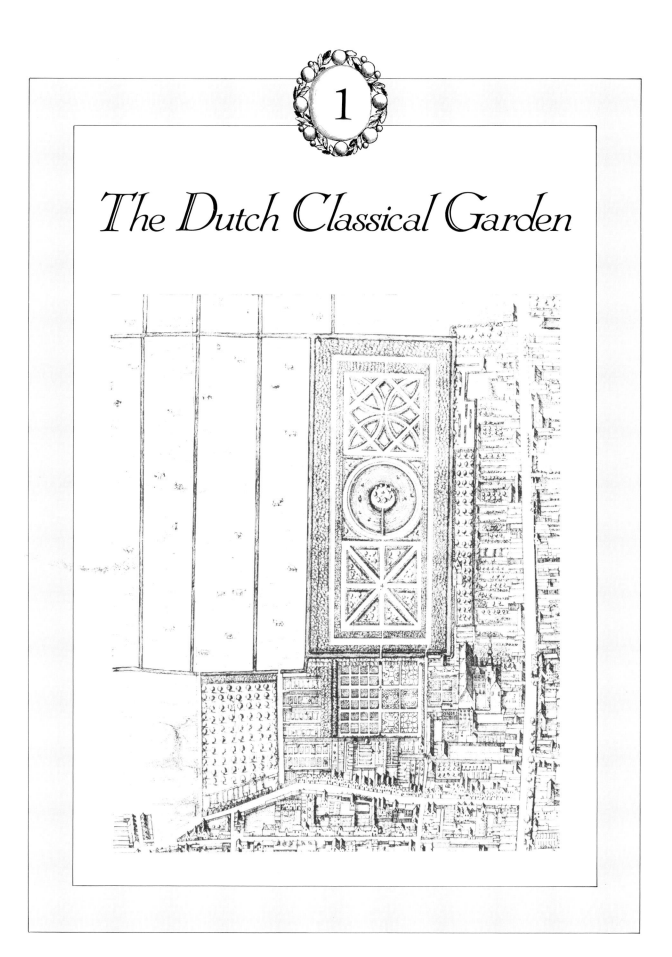

1.1 *Previous page*: Princess's Garden at the Noordeinde Palace, in The Hague, from a map by Bos and Van Harn (1616). This garden was made for his mother, the dowager Princess of Orange, by Frederik-Hendrik about 1610

The House of Orange

William III was by coincidence not just the third king of England of this name, but was also the third head of the House of Orange by this name. His father, who died in 1650, had been the second, and the first had been his great-grandfather, Willem the Silent, the founder of the Dutch House of Orange. This first Willem was a Count of Nassau, whom Philip II, King of Spain, had made Stadholder, or governor, of the Netherlands. He inherited extensive properties in the Netherlands and the principality of Orange in the south of France from his cousin René de Chalons. However Willem the Silent will always be chiefly remembered for joining in the fight for the liberation of the Netherlands from the Spanish which began in 1568.

This led to the proclamation in 1581 of an independent Republic consisting of a federation of seven Dutch provinces, each with its own government. The assembly of representatives from each state was the 'States-General', which met at the Binnenhof Palace in The Hague. The States retained the important constitutional rights of the legislature, foreign policy and the treasury, while Willem the Silent was made the first independent stadholder in several of the provinces, as well as captain-general of the army and admiral-general of the navy.

As the young republic grew in wealth and power, the republican leanings of the wealthy merchant classes were continually at odds with the monarchical tendencies of the House of Orange. Because of the great achievements of Willem the Silent, and his sons' fight for freedom, they felt themselves to be the born national leaders who had a birthright to be elected as stadholders. The common people too came to regard the Princes of Orange as the symbols of the new state. Perhaps in the Europe of the time it was easier to identify with princes than with the more anonymous representatives of the States who in theory were the holders of sovereign power.

However, the underlying strength of the republic was the enormous wealth generated by the merchants. The Dutch were becoming Europe's carriers and merchants, with ships plying the known world. The Dutch East India Company was founded in 1602, and the Dutch West India Company in 1621. Soon the Netherlands outstripped Venice as the leading mercantile republic in Europe, and by mid-seventeenth century it was the world's leading commercial power. Prosperity spread over the country, and this led to a flowering of the arts of painting, architecture and gardening. This was the age of Rubens, Van Dyck, Frans Hals, Ruysdael, Vermeer, and Rembrandt.

The military strength required to keep the Netherlands free continued to be provided by the House of Orange. Willem the Silent married several times. His son Maurits from his second marriage was elected stadholder after Willem's assassination in 1584 and carried on his struggles. In the year of his death Willem had another son, Frederik-Hendrik, by his fourth wife, Louise de Coligny, the daughter of the prominent French Huguenot, Admiral Coligny. Like their father, these two sons proved to be able generals and statesmen. When Frederik-Hendrik was made stadholder at the death of his brother Maurits in 1625, he had already established a reputation as a brilliant general, with a great talent for diplomacy.

Largely due to the continual fighting, the courts of Willem the Silent and Maurits had been strong in military architecture and engineering, but modest in the pacific arts such as domestic architecture. However, Frederik-Hendrik and his wife Amalia von Solms lived in less turbulent times. Although

Frederik-Hendrik took to the field of battle most years, with his secretary Constantijn Huygens at his side, the Court in The Hague had enough leisure to develop into one of splendour and elegance. Frederik-Hendrik could indulge in architecture and gardening; indeed the letters that Huygens sent to Amalia from the battlefield show that even when on campaign the prince was absorbed with plans for the construction of his palaces and gardens at Honselaarsdijk and Huis ter Nieuwburg at Rijswijk.

The Princess's Garden, Maurits's Garden and Honselaarsdijk

After Willem the Silent's death, Louise, the dowager Princess of Orange, lived at Het Oude Hof, later called the Noordeinde Palace. In 1609 Frederik-Hendrik purchased land behind the palace in order to lay out a large garden for his mother. A canal and rows of lime trees surrounded it, and paths divided it into three squares, the outer ones being orchards and the middle one containing a circular pond with a central island reached by a bridge. Throughout the gardens stood large pots with orange trees, fig trees, olives, bays and flowers.

About ten years later Prince Maurits built himself a garden in the Buitenhof, an area adjacent to the stadholder's residence at the Binnenhof Palace in The Hague. The shape was a double square, 60 by 30 m, totally enclosed with a crenellated brick wall and a canal. Each square had a circular arbour and corner arbour pavilions, while there was a built pavilion with a ceiling painted to simulate the blue sky at the point where the two circles touched. Inside the circles were *parterres de broderie*, perhaps the earliest in the Netherlands, each consisting of four letters 'M', and at the centres were fountains. Around and at the centres of the circles were bronze flower pots, and under the walls outside the arbours were pots containing orange trees, apples, figs, olives and bays. All these perhaps went into the pavilion in winter.

1.2 Prince Maurits's garden at the Buitenhof, in The Hague, from Henric Hondius's *Institutio Artis Perspectivae* (c. 1630)

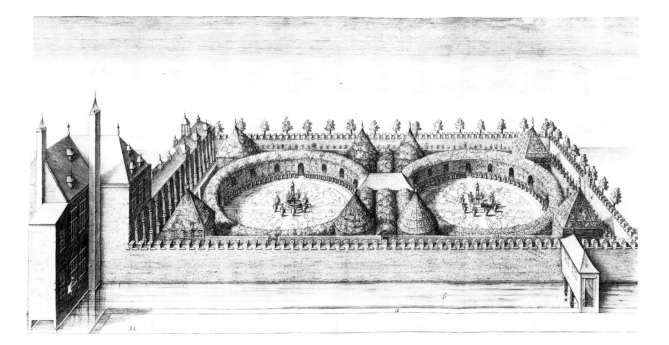

According to an epigram by Constantijn Huygens, the two circles of the Buitenhof garden were a reference to Alexander the Great's regret that there was only one world to conquer. Military aspirations were thus not far below the surface of the garden, and not surprisingly Maurits employed the mathematics and Italian theories of proportion with which he was familiar through his military architecture. Frederik-Hendrik's highly mathematical layout at the Noordeinde Palace was perhaps also derived from such sources.

When Frederik-Hendrik came to lay out new gardens for the mansion at Honselaarsdijk about 1621 the overall design was once again on mathematical lines, with canals defining three rectangles one within the other. The innermost was the house with its forecourt, set within the gardens and orchards, the heart of which were two *bosquets* laid out in double circles and corner pavilions, very reminiscent of the Buitenhof. Outside the gardens was an area of agricultural improvement divided into square parcels by paths flanked by lime trees, and in front of the mansion a semicircle at the termination of a processional avenue.

Interchange with French garden design

It is clear that when the Huis ter Nieuwburg at Rijswijk was being constructed in about 1630 Frederik-Hendrik was keen to vie with the French in their achievements in garden design. Without losing the highly mathematical Dutch approach to the overall layout, the Rijswijk Palace was a clear use of French skills in the details. With its hedged *parterres de broderie* and river gods, Rijswijk was highly evocative of Salomon de Caus's work at Heidelberg between 1615 and 1619, though the careful division of the layout into a grid of rectangles, and the surrounding raised walk, lines of limes and canal mark Rijswijk out as Dutch.

In 1633 André Mollet, a member of a prominent French gardening family, was invited to superintend the prince's gardens. Mollet had already been in Charles I's service and, later, was to be employed by Henrietta Maria, Charles's queen. Shortly after his appointment to Frederik-Hendrik's service, Mollet provided designs for the *parterres* flanking the mansion at Honselaarsdijk. On the right was a highly intricate *parterre de broderie*, and on the left was a *parterre à l'Angloise* with contrasting colours of gravel and box hedges in a background of grass and with an heraldic lion at its centre.

These designs were engraved for Mollet's *Le Jardin de Plaisir* (1651), and one of Mollet's designs for a garden layout was clearly his version of how he would have completed Honselaarsdijk, including these two *parterre* designs, a design for replacing the two circular *bosquets* by further *parterres*, and a revision of the orchard area with a *patte d'oie* of hornbeam hedges lined with cypress trees. Interestingly, though, he kept the overall structure of the garden, with its surrounding avenues and canals, corner pavilions, and avenue approach with half-moon termination which had been planted sometime before 1625. The mathematical organisation of Honselaarsdijk thus became of international significance and indirectly influenced garden layouts in many parts of northern Europe.

Dutch classicism

At the same time that work on the Rijswijk Palace was underway the court of Frederik-Hendrik began to learn of an architecture founded more directly

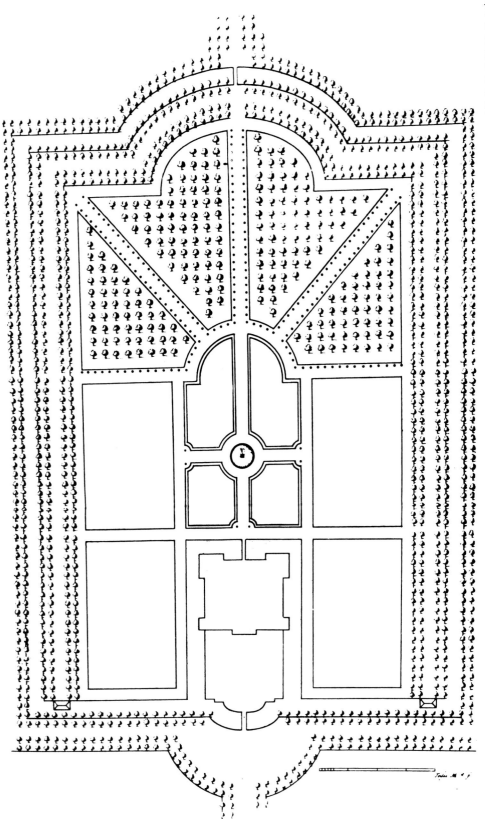

1.3 Plan of an ideal garden, from André Mollet's *Le Jardin de Plaisir* (1651). Mollet described how some of the blank spaces on this plan could be filled with the *parterres* that he had made at Honselaarsdijk in 1633, and so this ideal layout seems to have been based on that place

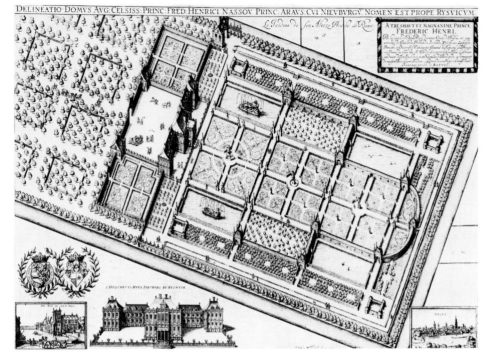

1.4 Huis ter Nieuwburg, Rijswijk, by J. Julius Milheusser (1644). Made about 1630, this layout combined recent Italian and French fashion with Dutch concern for an ordered layout

1.5 *Below*: Hofwijk, from Constantijn Huygens's *Hofwijk* (1653). Made by Frederik-Hendrik's secretary about 1640, this country estate was a forerunner of the more complex canal gardens such as Clingendaal

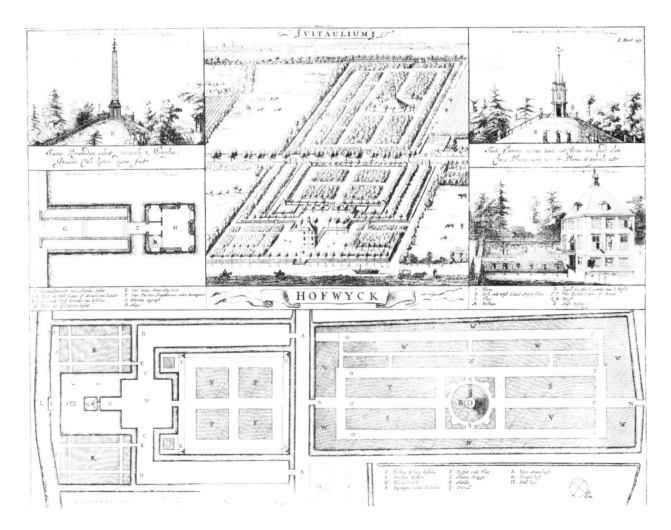

upon classical principles. Jacob van Campen was the principal architect to espouse the new style, attempting much the same as Inigo Jones at the English court. Van Campen's most influential early patrons at Frederik-Hendrik's court were Constantijn Huygens and Johan-Maurits, Count of Nassau-Siegen, a cousin of Frederik-Hendrik. Van Campen assisted with town houses in The Hague for both Huygens and Johan-Maurits from about 1633. When the latter went to Brazil in 1637 for seven years Huygens probably supervised the *Mauritshuis* in his stead. In 1639 Huygens purchased a country estate which he called Hofwijk, and Van Campen was engaged as the architect.

One of Van Campen's draughtsmen for Hofwijk was Pieter Post, who a few years later was put in charge of Huis ten Bosch, a retreat for Frederik-Hendrik's wife Amalia. When Frederik-Hendrik died in 1647, leaving his son Willem II to take up the reigns of power, Amalia turned Huis ten Bosch into a sort of memorial for her husband. The house was at the centre of a rectangle surrounded by a wall and a drainage canal. Small private gardens were placed to the sides of the house, and to the north a square forecourt in grass and to the south a large *parterre de compartiment*. In the spaces to either side of the forecourt were placed the stables and offices, and to either side of the *parterre* were kitchen gardens. The cross-axes, of the *parterre* were terminated by octagonal, heavily-foliaged, pavilions raised on bases from which views of the *parterre* could be obtained.

Count Johan-Maurits, back from Brazil, and Stadholder of Cleves for the

1.6 Zorgvliet, engraving by J. van den Aveele 'De groene Parnassus-Berg' (c. 1690). The poet Jacob Cats had filled the gardens of his retreat (Zorgvliet means 'flight from woe') with symbolic and curious features such as this mount in the 1650s

13

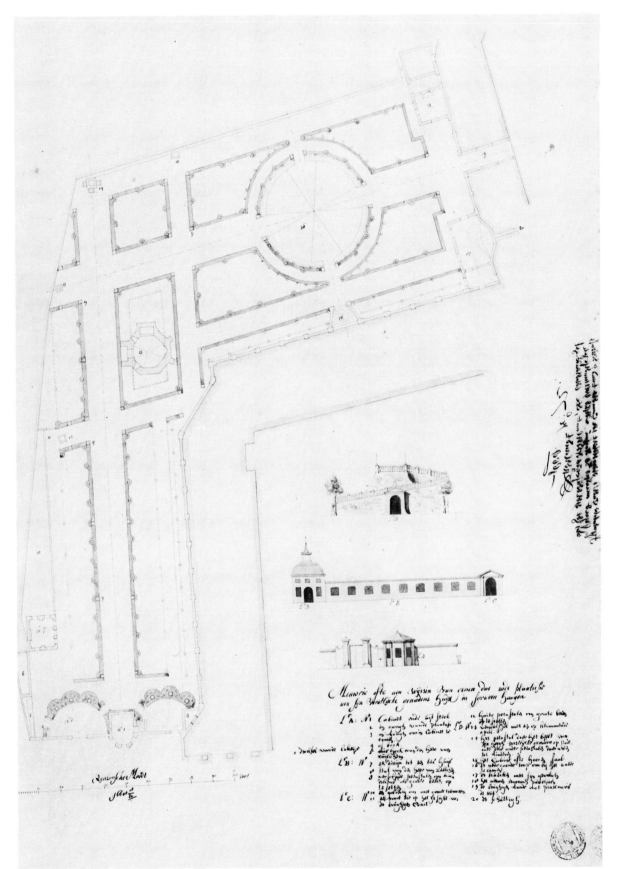

Elector of Brandenburg from 1647, built himself a series of parks and gardens at Cleves. One of these, built in 1653, was called the Springenberg. His architect was the ageing Van Campen, who recalled the villas on the Veneto in building a Palladian semicircular amphitheatre. However Palladian the Springenberg amphitheatre appeared, it was full of diverse symbolism and imagery. The series of descending ponds contained statues of various subjects, and in other sections of the garden could be found rare plants such as the monkey-puzzle (*Araucaria araucana*), a display of military trophies such as cannonballs and mortars, and a high pillar surmounted by a suit of armour.

Perhaps, then, the layout of Zorgvliet, the home of the Grand Pensionary of Holland and Calvinist poet, Jacob Cats, need not seem so incongruous. Built in about 1651, it too was full of symbolism and had such old-fashioned elements as mounts and a huge statue of a reclining Neptune. Cats's poems about Zorgvliet were likewise full of traditional Calvinist imagery, such as the toil of breaking up the ground.

The previous 30 years had seen a quite remarkable explosion in the number of princely gardens in the Netherlands – Maurits's at the Buitenhof, and Frederik-Hendrik's at Honselaarsdijk, Rijswijk and Huis ten Bosch. The main influence in their design had been Italian, at first through military architecture and city planning, and then inspiration from the architects such as Scamozzi and Palladio. The influence of France appeared in the decorations, with several spectacular *parterres de broderie*. However, there was an underlying tendency to plainness and utility in the Calvinist background. Hofwijk had no *parterres* – just some flower gardens – and drainage, planting and improvement frequently recur in theory and practice. A satisfactory balance between the sensual and the intellectual was due in large part to the Princes of Orange, chiefly William III's grandfather, Frederik-Hendrik.

1.7 *Opposite*: Mauritshuis, in The Hague, a plan of the garden (1668). The garden belonged to Count Johan-Maurits, and was made about 1645

2

British Gardens
After the Restoration

2.1 *Previous page*: St James's Park, from Knyff and Kip *Britannia Illustrata* (1707). The canal and avenues were installed, probably to Mollet's designs, in 1660

The Restoration of 1660

At the outset of the second half of the seventeenth century the fortunes of the English monarchy seemed desperately low. King Charles had been beheaded in 1649 and the young exiled prince, despite styling himself Charles II, was condemned to move himself and his impoverished court about at the mercy of other powers. At first he could count on at least two of them being friendly. In France, the ministers of Louis XIV extended a protective wing to his aunt, Queen Henrietta Maria, Charles's mother. Second, Willem II, Prince of Orange, had married Charles II's sister Mary in 1641, and could be relied upon to provide haven in the Netherlands. However after Willem died in 1650, Dutch hospitality wavered until one of the conditions of a peace between Oliver Cromwell's Protectorate and the Dutch States-General in 1654 was the exclusion of Charles from their borders. However, the tide turned, and in May 1660 Charles was restored to the English throne.

The reputation of Charles's dissolute court was quickly overlooked as he and his brother James, the Duke of York, became two of the most eligible bachelors in Europe. In October their mother, Henrietta Maria, followed their return to England to ensure suitable matches. She was horror-struck to discover that just the month before James had privately married Anne Hyde, the daughter of Edward Hyde, who, although Charles's trusted advisor and Lord Chancellor since 1658, was a commoner.

Anne had gone with her royalist family into exile in Breda in 1649 aged 12. Five years later she was made a maid of honour to James's sister, the Princess of Orange, in whose service she met James. In 1659 they contracted to marry. By the middle of 1660 it was clear that she was pregnant, and despite the reluctance of Charles, the embarrassment of her father, and the opposition of James's friends and servants, and above all his mother, James publicly announced the marriage in December. Although Anne produced many children for James, the only ones to survive were Mary, born in 1662, and Anne, born in 1665. As for Edward Hyde, he was made a baron late in 1660, and at the coronation in April 1661 he was created Earl of Clarendon. He remained Lord Chancellor till overwhelmed by his enemies in 1667.

Henrietta Maria's plans for Charles went better. Even before he returned to England the Portuguese ambassador was negotiating for a marriage with Catherine of Braganza, the 22-year-old elder sister of King Alfonso. The advantages to Portugal were the alliance against her powerful neighbour Spain and the English navy's protection from the Dutch fleet. The Portuguese promised Tangier, Bombay, freedoms for English merchants in Portugal and a vast settlement. The Spanish ambassador offered counter-inducements and stated, correctly, that the infanta was no beauty and incapable of bearing children. However, the negotiations were completed and the treaty signed in June 1661. The Earl of Sandwich, Commander of the Fleet, was sent to fetch Catherine.

St James's, Hampton Court and Greenwich

To emphasise the rebirth of the monarchy grandiose plans for improving the royal palaces that had survived the depredations of the Commonwealth were afoot. The palaces were all over 100 years old, and Charles, who had seen the latest styles of Europe, must have felt they were showing their age. The parks had been stripped of much of their timber, and the gardens were unfashionable, so clearly they needed some radical attention too.

The Office of Works could call on the services of two competent architects

– Hugh May and John Webb. However Charles was still short of money and so plans for his major project, the rebuilding of Greenwich Palace, were not even started until the summer of 1661. Similarly, James's plans for restyling his palace, the rather battered Richmond Palace, foundered in 1662. However, improvements to parks and gardens were cheaper and perhaps for this reason they actually went ahead.

In about 1640, Henrietta Maria had employed the well known André Mollet to reform the gardens of Wimbledon Manor for her. The old knot gardens and smaller orchards immediately behind the house were converted into two panels of *parterre de broderie* and two plainer grass ones, while the larger orchards beyond were made into a wilderness and a maze. Then in 1651 Mollet had written about his grandiose ideas concerning the planting of avenues to lengthen the axis of gardens.

Mollet had not lost his connections with England despite the Civil War. He was in England in 1658, and was presumably on hand at the Restoration. A canal was dug in St James's Park in September 1660, aligned on the private steps down from Whitehall Palace. Planting consisted of a semicircle of trees from which radiated walks along the canal's banks and other small walks to the side. Quite probably the St James's layout was to Mollet's design, and in June 1661 Mollet and his relative Gabriel were rewarded with the post of the King's Gardeners at St James's Palace.

Edmund Waller wrote this year to eulogise Charles II's reformation of 'this fair Park, from what it was before':

> For future shade, young trees upon the banks
> Of the new stream appear in even ranks:
> The Voice of ORPHEUS, or AMPHION's hand,
> In better order could not make then stand.
> May they increase as fast, and spread their boughs,
> As the high fame of their great owner grows!

Alongside further improvements at St James's, the Mollets were soon also at work at Whitehall and Hampton Court. These changes required an administrator who could organise them and keep the accounts. Hence, in December, Adrian May, a brother of Hugh May, was appointed 'supervisor of the French gardeners' employed at these places.

This last post was no mere sinecure, because in the winter of 1661/2 £1,466, a huge sum for that time, was being spent on planting and the making of a canal at Hampton Court. The design was a repeat of the St James's canal with flanking walks and tree semicircle. However it was on a vaster scale, and given a more definite purpose. A balcony which would be in the new queen's apartments when she arrived was gilded, and on this balcony the whole layout of canal and avenues was aligned. It was the St James's formula once again, but on such a vast scale that views down the canal disappeared into the far distance. The 758 limes planted were obtained from an importer and gained the approbation of John Evelyn: 'The *Park* formerly a flat, naked piece of Ground, now planted with sweete rows of *lime-trees*, and the Canale for water now neere perfected.' The same winter the underkeeper of Greenwich Palace had approval to form a flight of twelve grass steps 40 yds wide up the scarp of the hill behind the Queen's House at Greenwich. These were flanked by Scots pines brought from Scotland by the Duke of Albemarle.

It was to be nearly a year before Sandwich returned with Catherine of Braganza. At last, in May 1662, she arrived in Portsmouth, was married to

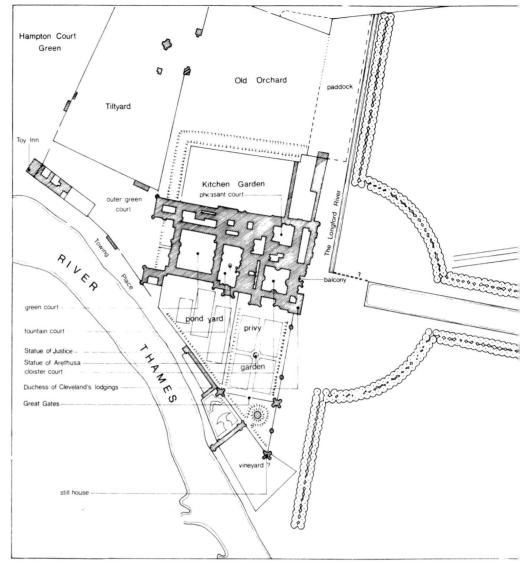

2.2 Hampton Court, reconstruction plan of the gardens and avenues in 1670. The canal and avenue of 1661/2 introduced a new scale of ornamental planning in Britain

Charles and escorted to Hampton Court where the completed scheme could be seen. Here was enacted a great celebration of Charles's birth and restoration. The couple stayed at Hampton Court till 23 August when the Court made a magnificent entry to Whitehall.

As far as Greenwich was concerned, Charles II expressed his wish, only a few days before Catherine landed, for André le Nôtre, by now famous for Vaux-le-Vicomte, to come and provide a much grander design. His request was passed to Louis XIV, who assented, despite Le Nôtre being fully engaged at Fontainebleau. Le Nôtre made plans and sent them across, though he himself did not visit England. Not surprisingly, the layout was reminiscent of Vaux-le-Vicomte. The focus of the Greenwich scheme was going to be a large *parterre* with fountains under the hill and adjacent to the Queen's House. It was to be surrounded on three sides by terracing and groves of elms, and beyond was to be a network of rides criss-crossing the park. The levelling for this *parterre* and the terraced walks on three sides was carried out to Le Nôtre's detailed specification, and was costly – nearly £2,000. By

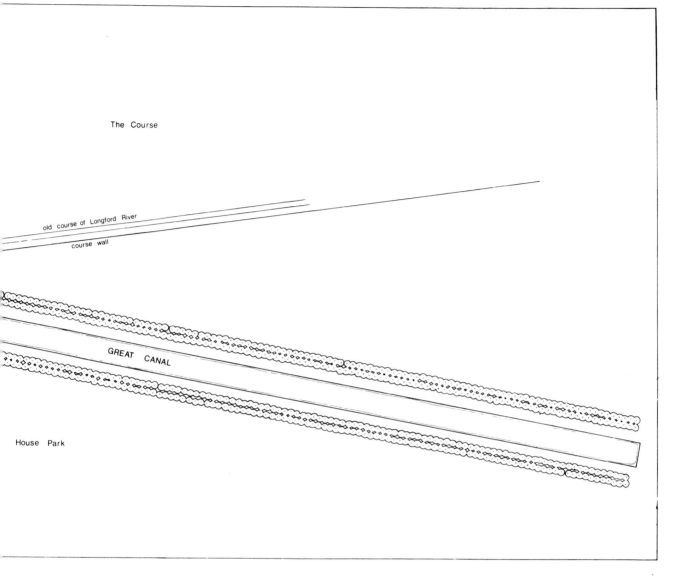

The Course

old course of Longford River

course wall

GREAT CANAL

House Park

January 1663/4 John Rose, who had once trained under Le Nôtre, was engaging men to carry out planting, probably of the 500 'greate Elme Trees for the Terrace Walks'. The previously-made twelve grass steps took the central vista up the hill to a new avenue that disappeared over its crest. This avenue formed the spine of a network of rides in the surrounding parkland, some parallel, some transverse, and some diagonal.

Charles pressed for Le Nôtre to provide further details and a design for a cascade down the hill. However, the levelled area remained unfilled by *parterres*, and it seems that during the middle years of the 1660s the enormous expense of the palace was beginning to throw the whole scheme into doubt. However this was not before 7,600 trees had been planted which, with the terracing, had already cost Charles £3,604 on the park alone.

While the infant Princess Mary grew up at the same time as those limes and elms at Hampton Court and Greenwich, she was not at first destined for glory as they were. She and Anne were brought up at the distinctly

2.3 Greenwich Park, 'Pepys's plan' (sometime 1675–80). This shows the platform and groves made to André le Nôtre's design in 1663/4. Boreman's Bower is at the top (south) of the plan

2.4 *Opposite*: Greenwich Park, sketch design for *parterre* earthworks by André le Nôtre (c. 1663)

old-fashioned Richmond Palace, where the gardens were galleried in the French style of around 1500. Despite James's decided Catholicism, his children were to be brought up as Protestants. Their governess was a safe Anglican, Lady Frances Villiers, whose two daughters Betty and Anne provided the two princesses with companionship. As they reached adolescence they gained a new friend, their religious instructor Henry Compton, who was the Bishop of London from December 1675. The next month he confirmed both Mary and Anne. When Mary was given away in 1677 to William, the Prince of Orange, it was Compton who married them.

A new era for garden design in Britain

It was to be a dozen years before Mary was to return to England as queen, during which time there was a remarkable period for country houses in England, not least in the gardens. Unfortunately Richmond Palace was further demolished soon after being granted to Lady Frances's husband, Sir

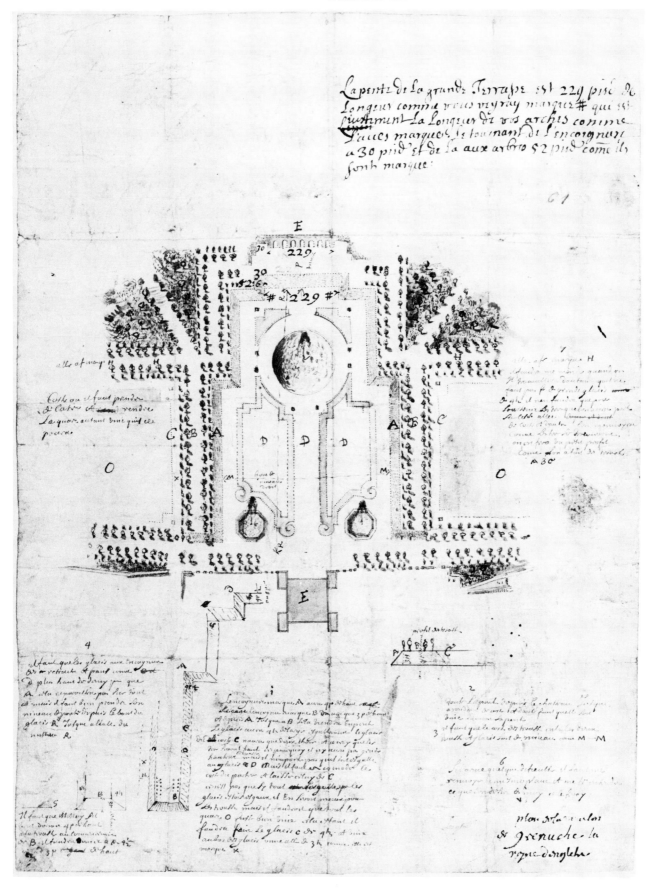

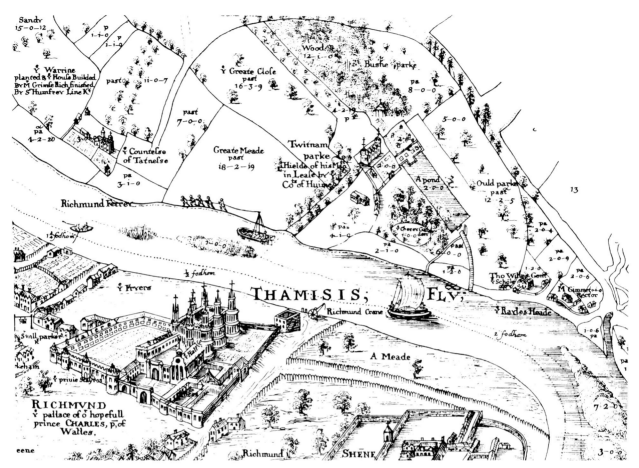

2.5 Richmond Palace, detail from map by Moses Glover 'Istelworth Hundred' (1635). The galleries around the Richmond garden can be seen. Across the river is Twickenham Park with its early avenue and semicircle

Edward Villiers, in 1680, but in general there were great improvements all over the country. The renewed foreign influences, especially from Italy and France, were galvanised into a coherent style, some aspects of which were peculiarly English.

The French and Dutch had traditions of highly-organised garden layouts consisting of *parterres* under the house, horticultural areas to the sides, and a wilderness and perhaps orchards beyond the *parterre*, all generally encompassed by a rectangle of walls or, in the Dutch case, rows of trees and canals. Small pavilions were not unusual at the corners. The French tradition combined with axial treatment; the approach would be extended behind the house as the long axis of the rectangle. At the far end of the garden the vista would be continued by another avenue. The junctions of the avenues to the rectangle were often by means of a half-moon of trees. The approach avenue would terminate in a half-moon outside the rectangle, while part of the far side of the rectangle would be pushed out into another half-moon. In variants more in the Italian style the wildernesses were omitted, and the *parterre* was surrounded by terraces from which the layout could be appreciated when promenading. At the far end of the garden, under a terrace, there could be a grotto.

The Netherlands was well suited to drawing-board designs, but in England it was often difficult to perfect the organisation of a layout because of existing buildings, roads, rivers, topography and all the other inherent irregularities of the English countryside. Nevertheless, attempts were made, some successful, as at Ham House in Surrey; other attempts were less successful, for example, at Ragley in Warwickshire, where the house was built from 1679 to 1683 to the designs of Robert Hooke, the mathematician. Although on sidelong ground, the Ragley garden was clearly copied as closely as possible from one of Mollet's designs in *Le Jardin de Plaisir*, even down to the rows of trees encircling the rectangle and the half-moon at the end of the avenue.

From the start, the more successful English designs were those that managed to reconcile the geometry of an organised plan with the natural terrain. The Great Garden at Wilton, in Wiltshire, which had been made from 1633 to 1635, was said by John Aubrey, the antiquarian, to have been one of the first places where an 'Italian' garden was made in England. In fact it had been designed by Isaac de Caus, a French-born naturalised Englishman. He laid it out to the side of the house where the valley floor was level and where the termination of the garden proper could coincide with the start of the rising ground. It comprised a vast walled enclosure extending from the south front and divided by a broad walk that passed various squares and plots of *parterres* and wildernesses and focused upon an elaborate grotto in the centre of the raised terrace. The eye was taken beyond the terrace, up the hill to a semicircular exedra cut into the hill, and up again to an equestrian statue of Marcus Aurelius on a wooden triumphal arch. The four *parterres* nearest the house are believed to be the earliest *parterres de broderie* in England, but it was the regular yet pragmatic planning of the whole that made Wilton such a forceful influence for the rest of the century.

2.6 Ragley, from Knyff and Kip *Britannia Illustrata* (1707). Compare to the ideal plan by André Mollet

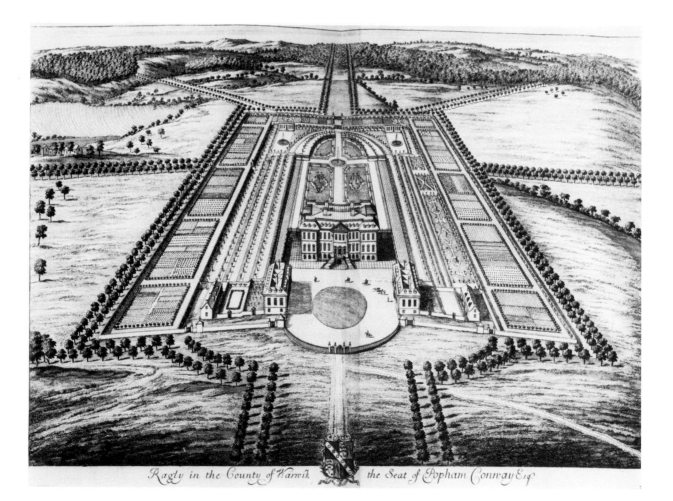

Ragly in the County of Warwik   *the Seat of Popham Conway Esq*

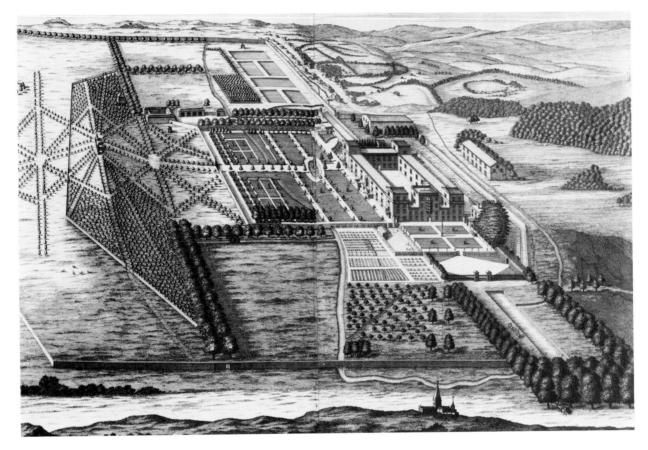

2.7 Wilton, plates 57–60 by H. Hulsbergh in *Vitruvius Britannicus*, Vol. III (1725). The garden of the 1630s was made to the side of the house, terminating at the foot of wooded rising ground. The formula was repeated by George London at Longleat

De Caus and Mollet were amongst the inventors of the *parterre de broderie* with floral motifs, the French style developed after 1610 and in the 1620s, and they understandably installed such *parterres* in their English designs. However, the English themselves were reluctant to follow. It was symptomatic that one French visitor who saw the Privy Garden at Hampton Court in 1663 described it as 'quite a handsome *parterre* made in grass in the English manner'. Indeed, the standard English *parterre* inserted in the new genre of organised, axial, gardens was of grass crossed with paths, and sometimes with statuary in the middle of the four quarters.

In Hertfordshire one could see Sir Arthur Capel's Hadham Hall, with an Italian garden made by 1639. Here one range of rooms was fronted by a balustraded terrace. Below was an unusually elaborate grass *parterre* with cross-walks and two concentric circular paths. On the inner circle were Italianate vase-like fountains, and in each of the four outer spandrels were statues. The side-walls enclosing this garden was punctuated by grand gateways after the style of Inigo Jones and terminating the wide central walk was a grotto. To its sides were stairs leading up to a terrace with end pavilions beyond which was the park.

John Evelyn too, back from an extensive sojourn on the Continent, had persuaded his brother in 1651/2 to let him make an Italian garden at the family 'villa' at Wotton House, Surrey. Evelyn filled in the moat to make a grass *parterre* flanked by low terraces as far as a steeply rising hill. This he shaped into an elaborate mount with avenues above. By 1653 either John or his cousin George had introduced one of the first pedimented temples (really a grotto under the mount) in an English garden.

One striking new development following the Restoration was the advancement of arboriculture. Of course, trees had always featured in old parks, but even so, a planned system of avenues was rare. During the Commonwealth there were great depredations of the parks, and by 1660 the prudence of replanting had become obvious, not least for the provision of ships' timbers. This induced John Evelyn and a committee of the Royal Society to meet and lecture, and in 1664 Evelyn's great *Sylva, or a discourse on Forest Trees,* was published. Whether or not it succeeded as a practical encouragement to plant oaks for shipbuilding, it was certainly the standard work for the numerous ornamental planters.

The effects of *Sylva* can best be seen by examining Cassiobury in Hertfordshire, laid out from 1669 for the Earl of Essex, the son of Sir Arthur Capel, and, according to Evelyn, 'that great Encourager of Planting'. Here was a most unusual forest garden. The house was being rebuilt at the same time by Hugh May, who had succeeded his brother Adrian as Supervisor of the Royal Gardeners in 1670. This makes it plausible that parts of Vaux or Versailles were in the mind of the designer of Cassiobury's garden. It was certainly an early example of an avenue system in which direction was turned by large circles. In the case of Cassiobury one large oval surrounded by 'treble rows of Spanish firr-trees' made a bowling green, whilst smaller ones were enlivened with fountains. Like Greenwich, Cassiobury stood apart from the conventional rectangular walled layouts, which only had avenues on the main axis through the house.

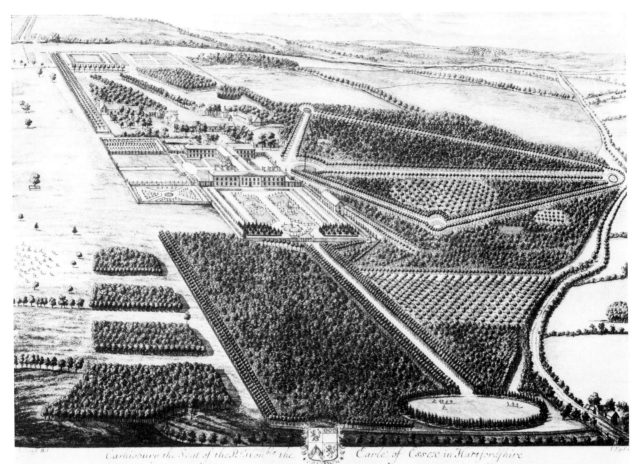

Cassiobury the Seat of the R.t Hon.ble the   Earle of Essex in Hartfordshire.

2.9 Cassiobury, from Kynff and Kip *Britannia Illustrata* (1707), showing the French-style forest garden with diagonal *allées*

The Brompton Park partnership

Essex's gardener was the remarkable Moses Cook who drew together his experience at Cassiobury into *The Manner of Raising, Ordering, and Improving Forest and Fruit Trees* (1676). Cook was one of the four founders of the Brompton Park Nursery in 1681. The senior partner was Roger Looker, Catherine of Braganza's gardener, and the others were John Field from Woburn Abbey and George London. As far as garden making was concerned, the two most active were Cook and London. The latter's origins are obscure, but it is known that he was an apprentice to John Rose, successor to Mollet at St James's in 1666. In 1675 London became the gardener to Henry Compton, then recently appointed the Bishop of London, and together they built up the collection of foreign rarities at Fulham Palace.

After the deaths of Looker in 1685 and Field in 1687, Cook sold his share to Henry Wise in 1689. Thereafter the immense nursery at Brompton Park grew in fame as 'London & Wise' and had almost achieved a monopoly before London's death in 1714. It was thus by mere chance that England's most important horticultural business achieved major influence in the same year that a Dutch king ascended the throne.

The purposes of Brompton Park were threefold: to provide plants of all descriptions; to regularise the use of correct names, particularly of fruit trees; and to undertake the design and construction of gardens. Thus the business was far more than a nursery and under George London played a leading part in horticulture. As a man of immense energy and highly respected character –

proved by his being sent by Bishop Compton as a personal escort to the Princess Anne on her escape from Whitehall to Nottingham (25 November to 1 December 1688) – London moved in the highest circles.

George London's domination in the field of garden design from 1681 and well into the next century, almost to the exclusion of anyone else, was extraordinary. Of course, there must have been other garden designers, but they hardly feature in the accounts, and right across the country for the whole of the Williamite period, the names of London and, after 1689, Wise occur in account after account. London visited and made suggestions for literally scores of gardens, and after about 1690 these were administered by Henry Wise.

Stephen Switzer, who trained in London's office in the 1690s, later

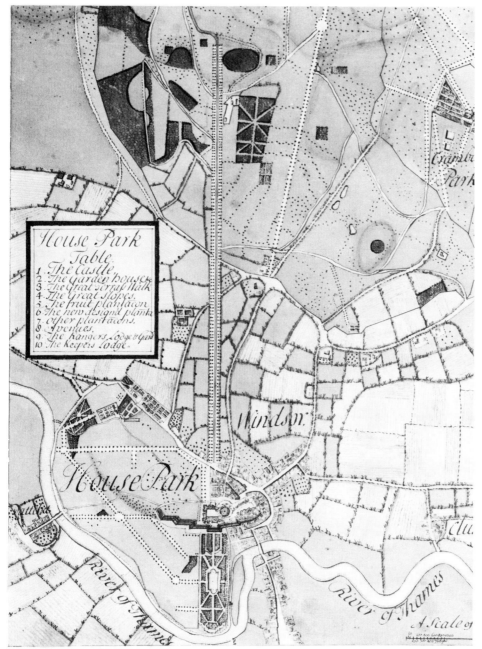

2.10 Windsor, detail of map from the office of Henry Wise 'An Accurate Plan of Windsor & Parks' (c. 1715). The 1683 avenue joining the castle to the Great Park can be seen, as well as Wise's Maestricht Garden

29

transposed much of London's theory and practice into his *The Nobleman, Gentleman, and Gardener's Recreation* (1715). In this he astonishes his readers by exclaiming that

> It will perhaps be hardly believed, in Time to come, that this one Person actually saw and gave Directions, once or twice a Year, in most of the Noblemens and Gentlemens Gardens in *England*. And since it was common for him to ride 50 or 60 Miles in a Day, he made his Northern Circuit in five or six Weeks, and sometimes less; and his Western in as little Time: As for the South and East, they were but three or four Days Work for him; most times twice a Year visiting all the Country-Seats, conversing with Gentlemen, and forwarding the Business of *Gard'ning* in such a degree as is almost impossible to describe.

2.11 Burghley House, map by J. Haynes 'An Accurate Survey of the House, Pleasure Ground & Park at Burghley in Northamptonshire' (1755)

By 1683 Cook and London were involved in major works at Windsor, Woburn Abbey in Bedfordshire, Burghley House in Northamptonshire, and Longleat in Wiltshire. Works at Windsor followed Charles II's abandonment of hopes of completing Greenwich. The situation of the castle left few

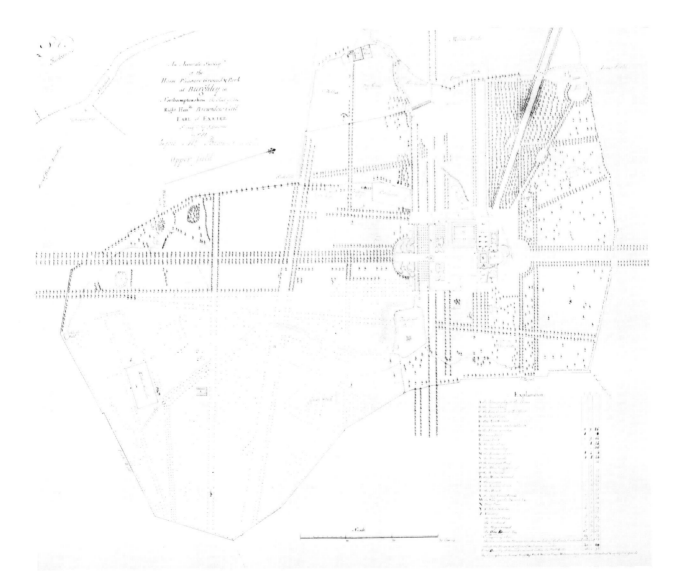

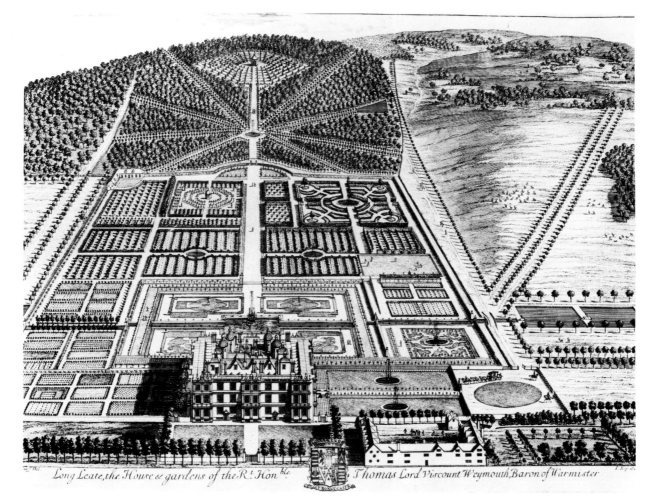

Long Leate, the House & gardens of the Rt. Honble ___ Thomas Lord Viscount Weymouth, Baron of Warmister

2.12 Longleat, from Knyff and Kip *Britannia Illustrata* (1707). This garden was made by the Brompton Park partnership in the mid-1680s

opportunities for a conventional garden layout. In 1680 is was decided to concentrate upon two features. The first was a wilderness on the floodlands below the castle to the north, called the 'Maestricht garden' after a memorable mock siege of that place enacted on these meadows in 1674. The second was an avenue to the south leading to the Great Park, which was delayed by negotiations for the land but which came to fruition in 1683. It was 240 ft wide, and consisted of 1,864 elms in four rows of 3 miles. The full extent of Cook's and London's contribution is unclear, but they were paid for digging a ditch and bank on either side of the avenue and planting whitethorn quicksets.

However, larger schemes for Cook and London were afoot elsewhere. In March 1683 'Mr Cook and Mr London's opinion about Burghley Garden' was sought, leading to the great formal undertakings shown on a survey made in 1753. A great rectangular garden south of the house was made consisting of a gigantic parterre containing a complex of a bason of water, a bowling green, grove and wilderness, two canals set transversely across the axis and divided by an octagonal goldfish pond, an orchard and vineyard before a semicircle termination. The old Tudor hunting park was transformed with grids of avenues, the main ones carrying the approach to the house and continuing this axis beyond the gardens.

The four partners also began a new garden at Longleat for Lord Weymouth in 1683, taking it in turns to spend a month on supervising the

2.13 Chatsworth, bird's-eye-view from the south-east (sometime 1707–11). The cascade was made by the Frenchman, Grillet

work. Here, to the side of the house, was another huge rectangle within which were organised *parterres*, waterworks, orchards and wildernesses. Beyond the half-moon termination the axis led up the hill to what was called the hexagon, the *point de vue* of the axial thrust up the hill. The cost of this enormous enterprise was about £30,000.

The gardens at Longleat provide a unique insight into London's contractual methods. After the major removal of earth from October 1683, each compartment was featured on a separate plan that had been extracted from the grand design. As soon as each compartment was finished and had received London's approval, the plan was signed and inscribed as such and payment authorised. For example, the plan 'to level green & make slope banks', effected by a James Cook at the Bowling Green, was passed for payment of £21 with London's words 'This is finished'.

Burghley and Longleat are in the mould of the classic French or Dutch garden of the time. Burghley was perhaps more reminiscent of the Mollet formula, and Longleat of De Caus's Wilton. Although the French ideal of setting the house on the axis could have been achieved at Longleat, London eyed the hill and saw the advantage of pushing the garden out to one side. A difference from Wilton was the glad acceptance of the river crossing the layout. As at Burghley, the axial thrust was tempered by the transverse placement of the long canal.

Magnificent as these places were, Chatsworth was a high-point of perfection in the geometry of the large country house *parterre*, the cut-work of such sophistication that it can be identified as by London and no other. He signed for the West Parterre fronting the Bowling Green in August 1688. It measured 245 by 187 ft and cost £120. Then, in June 1694, he signed for the Great Parterre, the show piece of Talman's south front, measuring 473 by 227 ft, and the contract states explicitly how each quarter should be laid out, 'with borders of good Earth fit to receave such a Collection of Hardy Ever-greens and flowering trees, Shrubs and flowers', with a 'division for Sparr of near 4 feet broad' round the borders. There was to be 'Cutt worke in grasses, with Centres for two Statues and four Trees in cases, the Cutts in grasses are to be covered with ye brightest Sand'. Here was John Nost's Sea Horse and Neptune fountain, in Switzer's words 'that stupendous Perform-ance at Chatsworth'. There was water everywhere, including Grillet's cascade and some fine *repoussé* ironwork by the Frenchman, Jean Tijou.

One particularly significant professional association needs to be stressed at this juncture: that at Burghley, and at Chatsworth, London was working alongside the architect William Talman, and it is likely that from this time London was on call at every building by Talman requiring garden works. Designs of the 1680s for which this association is probable include Bretby in Derbyshire and Dawley in Middlesex.

The house and garden at Bretby were improved in stages from 1669 and

2.14 Bretby, from Knyff and Kip *Britannia Illustrata* (1707). The *parterres de broderie* and the waterworks were remarkable

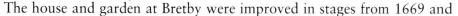

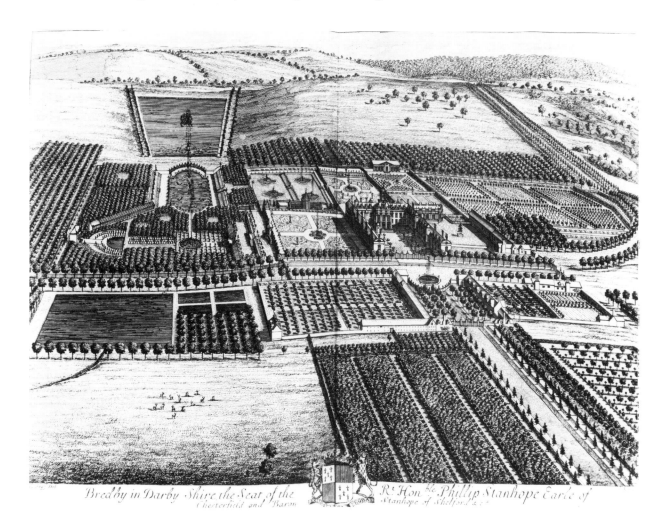

Bredby in Darby Shire the Seat of the R.ᵗ Hon.ᵇˡᵉ Phillip Stanhope Earle of
Chesterfield and Baron Stanhope of Shelford &.ᶜ

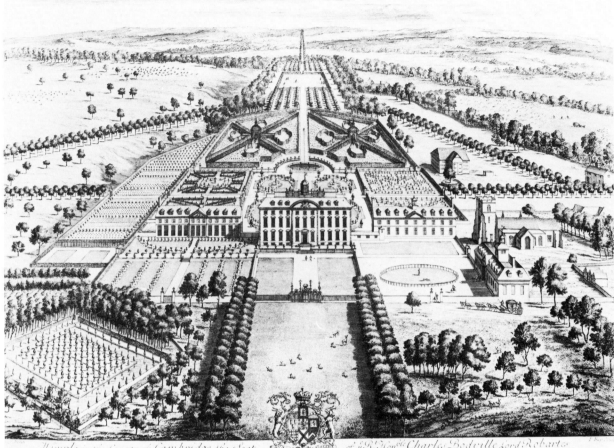

Wimple in the County of Cambridge the Seat of ye Rt Honble Charles Bodville Lord Robartes Baron of Truro Viscount Bodmyn and Earl of Radnor &c & Custos Rotulorum of ye County of Cornwall

2.15 Wimpole, from Knyff and Kip *Britannia Illustrata* (1707). The forecourt gates may never have been erected

into the age of William III. The Mollet-style *parterres* from the beginning of this period are in perfect accord with the house that must have been refashioned by a French architect for the Earl of Chesterfield. When viewed by the topographical artist Leonard Knyff, however, London and Talman had intervened, with Grillet assisting with the hydraulics. No garden could exceed Bretby for the display and manipulation of water. It was a water garden *par excellence* and came alive with the flashing of fountains, no less than seven on the upper level around the house and six in the valley, with a vast one flinging up a jet as high as Chatsworth's more celebrated Sea Horse and Neptune Fountain.

Lord Ossulstone's Dawley boasted six big squares and a walk terminated by a glorious ironwork gate on Tijou's style. Here the quality of the *parterre* work was outstanding, especially the ten groups of complicated patterns in front of the greenhouse.

The partnership of London and Talman was remarkably complementary. Both fleshed out the architectronic framework in their own ways: London with paths, *parterres*, basons and planting, and Talman with garden structures and the products of his team of sculptors and ironworkers. By the 1690s Talman emerges as a master designer of garden buildings, not the least greenhouses. At Chatsworth, Dawley, and probably Wimpole, Talman provided exquisitely small-scale architectural essays that partner perfectly London's orangery gardens.

3

The Gardens of the
Dutch Court of William III

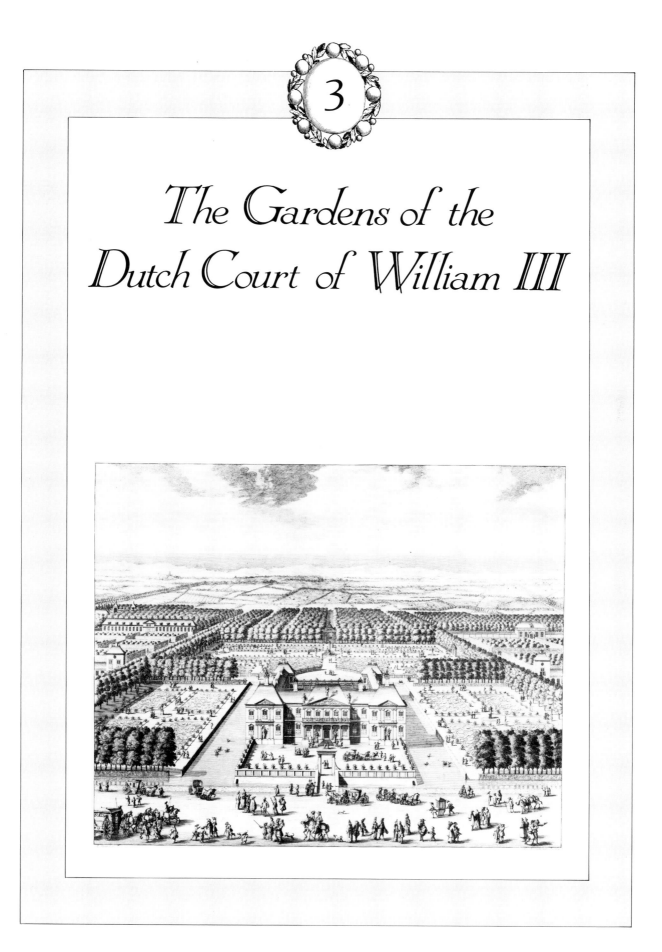

3.1 *Previous page*:
Honselaarsdijk, by Daniel
Stoopendaal 'Maison
Royale de Honslardyk avec
ses Jardins' (c. 1705).
Parterres had replaced the
bosquets behind the house
by 1680. The orangery of
that date can be seen top
left

William and his circle

In November 1650 Mary Stuart, eldest daughter of Charles I, gave birth to a son in The Hague. Rejoicing mingled with sorrow, because eight days beforehand her husband, Willem II, Prince of Orange, had died of smallpox. The boy, also William, spent much of his childhood in the large, rambling, complex of buildings in the centre of The Hague, the Binnenhof Palace, which served as the stadholder's official residence, as well as being the headquarters of the States-General.

However, William was also heir to the considerable possessions of the Nassau Demesne. Hence William also resided at times in the palace of Honselaarsdijk, near The Hague, built by his grandfather Frederik-Hendrik, and there were other family properties at his disposal. There was Rijswijk, Dieren near the expansive and barren heaths and forests of the Veluwe in the province of Gelderland, where hunting was excellent, the castles of Breda and Buren, and a palace in Brussels. The Huis ten Bosch in the woods near The Hague continued to be lived in by William's grandmother, Amalia, till her death in 1675 when it was loaned to an aunt, Albertine Agnes.

The offices of stadholder and captain-general of the army were traditionally given by the States-General to members of the House of Orange, the last one having been Willem II. However the freedom-loving provincial rulers had a deeply ingrained fear of too much power in the hands of one man, and when he reached maturity the young prince William was not automatically given these two offices previously held by his father and grandfather.

However, when in 1672 the republic suffered invasion by the armies of Louis XIV, bent on humbling the Dutch, the States-General, normally the political opponents of the House of Orange, had to bow to the popular wish that William should be elected stadholder and captain-general. Under William's direction the inexperienced Dutch army was welded into one of the most effective fighting forces in Europe. Late in 1672 he began to take the offensive against the superior French forces, and by the end of 1673 almost all French troops had quit Dutch soil. William was hailed as 'the Redeemer of the Fatherland'.

When not on a campaign or busy with affairs of state William relaxed at the hunt with his friends. Despite his small and weak frame, William came into his own in the field, as a man of action, huntsman and military campaigner. Sir William Temple, England's ambassador to the Dutch Republic from 1668 to 1678, said that William 'thinks himself the better in health and humour the less he is at rest'. William showed surprisingly little concern for his own health and safety; on one occasion only the sharp shooting of his cousin Ouwerkerk saved his life.

William never enjoyed Court life very much; he found its formality choking. Even when he later became King of England, William still tried during his annual visit to the Netherlands to get away from Court life even though his main purpose in going there was the Nine Years' War. One commentator, Edward Southwell, the son of Sir Robert Southwell, Secretary of State for Ireland, remarked:

> His Majesty went this morning to Loo. He never stays Longer than 3 or 4 days at the Hague either going or coming; for he is Soe crowded with People, and pester'd with Applications for employments, that it tires him quite out.

The small circle of friends with whom William spent most of his time included his three cousins descended illegitimately from his grandfather Prince Frederik-Hendrik or his great uncle Prince Maurits – Count Willem Adriaan van Nassau-Odijk, Hendrik van Nassau, Lord of Ouwerkerk, and Willem Hendrik van Nassau, Lord of Zuylestein. Zuylestein's father was William's governor, and William's more distant cousin, Count Johan-Maurits van Nassau-Siegen, the one-time Governor of Brazil, was his mentor in matters of statecraft and architecture. However, William's closest friend and advisor was his former page, Hans Willem Bentinck.

William's early garden improvements

Besides prowess in fighting and hunting, William showed early that he had a great interest in paintings, sculpture, architecture and gardening. Prince Frederik-Hendrik and Count Johan-Maurits had used Jacob van Campen and then Pieter Post as architects, and from 1645 Post was officially Architect to the Stadholder. In the same year Post named his youngest son Maurits after his godfather, Count Johan-Maurits, and the young lad in due course became an architect too. Maurits Post worked for his godfather and was appointed William's architect in 1670 after Pieter died.

One of William's early gardening ventures was the modernisation of the garden at Honselaarsdijk. The gardener was Jan van der Groen, famous for his book *Den Nederlandtsen Hovenier* (1669). Probably at this time the circular walks dating from the time of Frederik-Hendrik were replaced with one large *parterre* garden adorned with statues and fountains, and a vista was established beyond the *parterre*, through the orchard, which led the eye to the dunes in the distance. In June 1669 Cosimo III de Medici, Grand Duke of Tuscany, saw some work in progress:

> The morning of the 21st . . . 6 miles away you can see a villa of the Prince of Orange called Onselerdic which is very gallant because of the multiplicity of *bosquets*, statues and delicious fountains, adjoining to a park which is not big but very interesting, they are putting everything into a better state.

Another Italian visitor saw Honselaarsdijk in 1677:

> The garden is divided and encircled by some canals of healthy water and terminating in a delicious *bosquet*, the trees of which are planted regularly forming many *allées* and very desirable prospects. Here in a separate enclosure are rare Indian birds and some waterfowl; nor is there lacking in the midst of the *bosquet* a number of pleasing well laid out canals. All the park is full of deer and game and is enclosed by a strong palisade.

The menagerie mentioned also had rare animals, such as a spotted Indian cat and an elk, and must have housed presents from Charles II – some exotic birds in 1671, and a lion and a tiger in 1674.

In 1674 William was on the crest of a wave following his military success, and embarked on the first building and gardening project that was substantially his own. He bought the estate of Soestdijk, in the Province of Utrecht, situated in a good hunting country that was not as far removed from The Hague as was Dieren. It was not an entirely new building, as it had been the country house of a mayor of Amsterdam. The house stood near the

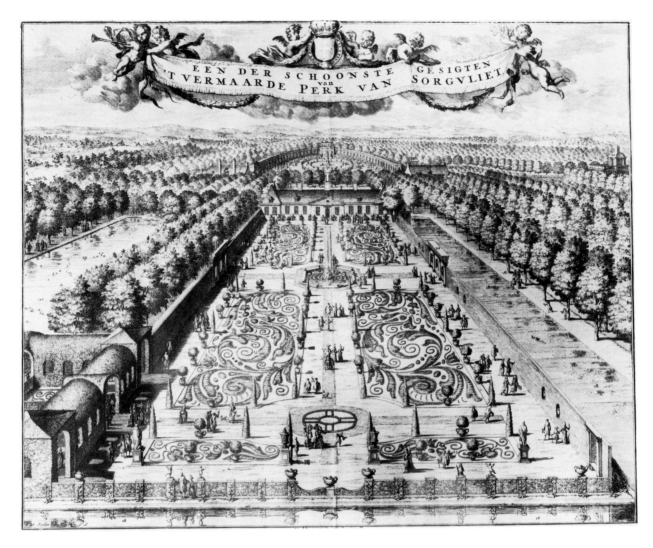

EEN DER SCHOONSTE GESIGTEN
'T VERMAARDE *van* PERK VAN SORGVLIET

3.2 Zorgvliet, the *parterre* from the pavilion, by Johannes van den Aveele (c. 1690). The orangery was beyond the house

centre of a moated rectangle, with a forecourt on one side and a small parterre to the back.

Maurits Post was commissioned to enlarge and convert it into a hunting lodge. Building works lasted from 1674 till 1678 and a new gardener, Christiaan van Staden, was appointed in 1676. Contrary to custom, the gardens were not axially aligned on the front and back of the house; instead the main new sections of the garden were laid out to each side. The famous bird's-eye-view drawings by Stoopendaal include a view of the gardens showing two large enclosures as wide as the older rectangle was long, reached by bridges across the old canals. These enclosures were filled with *parterres de broderie* flanked by orchards. Each of the four *parterres* had huge statues at their centres. In the enclosure to the right of the house there were also two fountains. The orchards consisted of dwarf fruit trees neatly planted in rows. The whole of this layout was enclosed by avenues of trees and canals, and surrounded by deerparks and vegetable gardens.

At exactly the same time Bentinck acquired Zorgvliet from the executors of Jacob Cats. Whereas the house was a simple Dutch classicist structure built about 1645, Cats's garden was full of mannerist ornament and symbolism and was hopelessly outdated by the time Bentinck obtained it. It must be said that Cats's garden was not very coherent in layout, or, being more generous, it was pleasingly confusing.

Count Johan-Maurits wrote down some 'Considerations' for the young Bentinck in December 1674. He suggested that a wild piece of countryside, 'a high and desolate pasture', covered with dunes and scrub should be included in the garden. This wild area also contained a 'lively stream' which, as Count Johan-Maurits pointed out, was rare in Holland. This should not be straightened but kept sinuous, as 'straight lines are not always pleasant'. The incorporation of naturalistic features in a geometric plan was very unusual, though Sir William Temple, who knew Bentinck well, also seems to have incorporated the natural course of a stream into his gardens at Moor Park in Surrey in the 1680s.

Bentinck left the house and the broad garden layout as they were, and mainly occupied himself with adapting or reconstructing *parterres* and structures. William visited Bentinck regularly at Zorgvliet and tradition would have it that, to surprise William, every time he came one of Cats's bucolic features was replaced by some novelty. Surprisingly, perhaps, Bentinck maintained the two mounts dating from Cats's time. One was a tetragonal pyramid, with a single tree at the summit, and was called Parnassus; from the other it was possible to see the estate, the town of The Hague in one direction and the sea to the west. Nor does Bentinck seem to have made any real effort to give the disorderly garden a more coherent structure. Perhaps Bentinck's aim, too, was a green refuge from the princely Court of The Hague.

One area to be drastically changed and modernised in its details was the *parterre* directly in front of the house. The whole area was sunk, and six *parterres de broderie* laid out. In the middle was a fountain. The *parterres* were surrounded by arbours with arches, pavilions and windows, and on the

3.3 Zorgvliet, general view by J. van den Aveele (c. 1690). The irregular brook included in the layout is bottom left. The 'Parnassus' mount, pavilion, house and orangery are top left

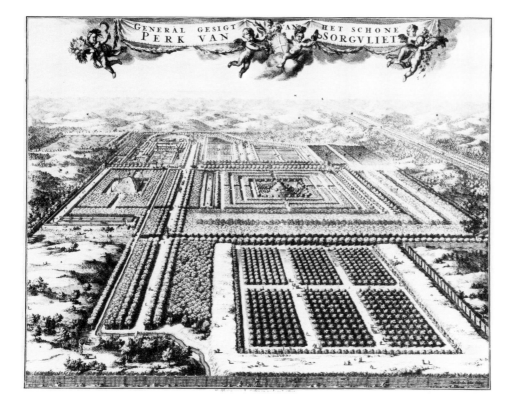

surrounding terraces were rows of trees. Along the far side of this *parterre* was a canal, and beyond that a small grotto with the Neptune on top. This was replaced by Bentinck with a tall, elegant grotto cum cascade which closed the axial view from the house over the parterres.

About 1676 an impressive semicircular orangery with a central pleasure house was built on the other side of the house. Its coved ceiling was higher than the roof of the old mansion. It was quite possibly inspired by Jacob van Campen's semicircular Palladian gallery, designed for Count Johan-Maurits's Springenberg at Cleves. The orangery was for its day very modern and advanced, incorporating the latest techniques of cultivating exotic plants. Bentinck's collection was one of the best in the Netherlands and contained many plants imported from the Cape of Good Hope and the East Indies, the first of their kind in northern Europe.

In 1698 a visitor, Thomas Bowrey, noticed chiefly:

> The Gardens Consists of Many fine Rows of Sycamores, Ewes and other Trees cut very handsomely, good Grass walks and some sandy walks, a fine Green house in the forms of a Half Amphitheater and Hansomly built, before which is very fine Ewe Trees and Hedges, with fine Orang and Bay Trees &ca. finely sett out. There is also a Groto sett Curiously with Shells, Rock Corall and Lookinglasses, and in it a Fountain. There is another Shell House with water Springing out of the Floor.

Another garden built up in stages and, like Zorgvliet, looking as if that was the case, was Zuylestein, rebuilt by Frederik-Hendrik in the early 1630s and given to his illegitimate son Frederik van Nassau. Frederik, William's governor, was killed in action against the French in 1672. William seems to have helped the son, Willem Hendrik, from the coffers of the Nassau Demesne to improve the property. The garden around the castle was enclosed partly by wall and partly by canals. Smaller canals ran through the kitchen garden areas. There was a fine *parterre à l'Angloise* by the castle, but it was not properly aligned on it, and the *parterre de broderie*, instead of being in front as the garden writers advised, was placed beyond it.

Mary and Honselaarsdijk

On 4 November 1677 William married his cousin, Mary Stuart, daughter of James, Duke of York, and a few weeks later they travelled to the Netherlands. Mary's household of 40 English people, including the Villiers sisters, soon settled happily into Honselaarsdijk, and mingled easily with William's friends. In fact Anne Villiers, one of the ladies-in-waiting, was soon married to Bentinck, and in 1681 Jane Wroth, another lady-in-waiting, married Zuylestein. Unfortunately William himself had a long affair with Betty Villiers starting in 1679, but this did not seriously affect the harmony at Court.

This Dutch Court was small and close-knit, a tight circle of servants and friends. It was, at the same time, homely, relaxed and orderly, very different from the disorganised and sleazy Court at Whitehall or the rigidly formal one at Versailles. William and Mary's shared pleasures were of a domestic family kind; card games and tea or supper parties with the Bentinck's. When they liked to escape from Court life in The Hague they went to Soestdijk or Dieren where William could hunt. Other close friends who could be visited from there were Baron Jan van Arnhem, Lord of Rosendael, and his wife.

Mary quickly fell in love with the Dutch countryside. She liked airy, well-proportioned Dutch houses, kept spick and span. Mary did not share William's passion for hunting, but she did share her husband's interest in domestic architecture, interior decoration and gardens. Designing houses, their interiors and gardens, was a relaxation for both of them.

A traditionally strong feature of Dutch gardening was the richness in flowers and plants. Perhaps Bishop Compton's enthusiasm for plants had been communicated to Mary; certainly she keenly adopted the Dutch passion for them, showing a personal interest in flowers and exotic plants. A special flower garden was made at Honselaarsdijk beyond the left-hand stables. The strong tradition of flower growing, which Jan van der Groen must have been part of whilst he was at Honselaarsdijk from 1665 till 1670, was continued by Charles du Buisson from 1675 till 1686, and then by Hendrik Quellenburg who was taken to Hampton Court in 1689. After that there was Arent Hoochlaar, Lawrens Bertram and Jan Quartier, who was instructed to dispatch a great quantity of plants and bulbs to the 'Great Garden' at Hampton Court in September 1693.

Instructions dated November 1678 to Du Buisson, who was in charge of 'all the gardens of the house at Honselaarsdijk', required him 'if possible to have flowers in all seasons in order to make two or three bouquets for the service of her Highness every week'. A record of such bouquets, bound in ribbon, was made in a flower painting which was one of a series commissioned by William, and no doubt a good deal of care went into arranging them. This must have been one of the earliest expressions of the art of flower arranging. Mary, after she had become Queen of England, took this tradition with her and had fresh bouquets of flowers from the Auricula Quarter at Hampton Court placed in her apartments.

Maurits Post, William's architect, died young in 1677, and his place was taken by Johan van Swieten, who built the long orangery at Honselaarsdijk in 1680, which cost 30,000 guilders. The orangery garden located between the orangery and the stables was divided by broad *allées* in six square blocks

3.4 Honselaarsdijk, 't' Koningins Speelhuys met de Prielen' by Karl Allard (c. 1690). This was Mary's place of leisure where she played at cards and drank tea

41

which were in turn enclosed by hedges. In the summer orangery plants were placed there in rows. Exotic plants were distributed over the balustrade around the court, on several *parterres* on both sides of the house and possibly also in the central *parterre* behind the house.

Meanwhile Dieren needed some improvements. It was described as 'an old and ill-kept house surrounded by a dry and over-grown moat'. Some work may have started in 1677, but the accounts of the Nassau Demesne indicate that the large sums were spent on Dieren from 1679. William had a new wing added onto the old castle, and amongst the garden improvements was an asymmetrical curvilinear water-maze. This was highly unusual in a time when everything had to be symmetrical, and not dissimilar in general layout to the labyrinth at Versailles.

Edward Southwell said of Dieren in his journal of 1696:

> The House is small and very old, but the gardens are very neat and pretty. There is very good fruit in them; and I Saw Noe where Gravell-walks but here. The bouling Green, Arbour of Venus round a great Pond, the Grotto & cupid drowning in a fountain are all very entertaining. There are alsoe Severall Pretty Inventions for wetting Gentlemen & Ladys. The River Yssel runs close by the Garden, . . . All the Country here about is very pleasant. There are fine woods & Green Feilds, . . . The King is very fond of this Seat, & talks of building an apartment on the Garden side for himselfe. Mongr. Luxembourg was here in the great Warr of 1673 and caused all the avenues to the House to be cut downe, which was thought a poor piece of Revenge but they are Since restor'd & finely grown up.

Southwell continues, mentioning that 'His Majesty is always very easy and in good humour at these Places'.

Emulating France – Clingendaal and Huis ten Bosch

William's Court was not against French culture despite the bitter political antagonism between the Dutch and Louis XIV which plagued the last part of the seventeenth century. A low point of national self-esteem had been in 1672, when many Dutch nobles had seen their ancestral seats burnt by the French, but now a new sense of confidence and pride sprang from having driven the French out. There was also a recovery economically. The patricians and the nobles of William's Court started to rebuild their houses and castles, often dating from the Middle Ages, in a more fashionable, richer style, and very often to surround them with elaborate gardens.

With the death of Maurits Post in 1677, and of Count Johan-Maurits himself in 1679, William's court had lost its former arbiters of architectural taste. The Dutch classicist style, the style that had come to symbolise the young republic's new identity, remained the standard in architecture and gardening, but at the same time an admiration for the achievements of the French in garden art must have been dawning. Several Dutchmen by this time knew the gardens of France well – such as Christiaan Huygens, one of Sir Constantijn Huygens's sons, and William's cousin Odijk who had been an ambassador to Versailles in 1678 – and these men were keen to set new standards in garden design.

Christiaan Huygens was a scientist who spent many years at the Academie des Sciences in Paris till forced to leave during a worsening political situation in 1683. He wrote frequently to his family, including his brother-in-law

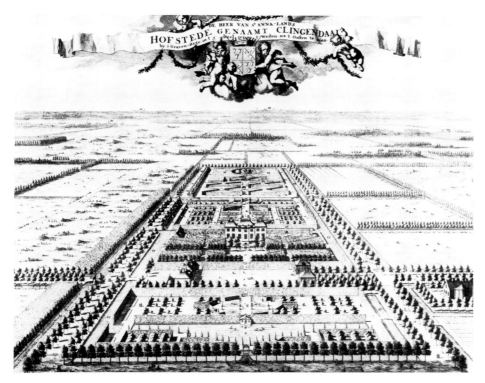

3.5 Clingendaal, bird's-
eye-view from the west by
Leonard Schenk (1680)

Philips Doublet, about Paris fashions and arts, sending descriptions, drawings and prints. Doublet was from an immensely wealthy family from The Hague which had held the lucrative post of Collector General of the Union. In 1680 Doublet inherited the estate of Clingendaal, and set himself the task of reshaping the house and gardens in an improved style.

Clingendaal's main axis was parallel to the dunes, the whole estate was laid out as a ribbon about five times as long as it was wide, between the rising dunes and the flat meadows of the countryside. The narrowness of the estate was a major problem in introducing a grand design. The approach too was awkward – from the side and at one end. It was given a conventional treatment of a wide avenue flanked by canals and a forecourt with flanking service buildings, here the gardener's lodge and the coach house. However the long low building to be seen through the arch on the far side of the spacious forcecourt was merely the stables and bathhouse. Once in the forecourt, the house was revealed to the right beyond another forecourt flanked by *bosquets* framing the house. This change in direction was counterbalanced to some extent by a pleasure house to the left, beyond a *broderie* garden with a few small statues.

The distance between house and pleasure house was taken as half the length of an inner layout within the estate. The house was placed in a cross-canal, which was not only beautiful in that it gave reflections of the house in the water, but structural in that it divided the inner layout into the forecourts on the one side and the main *parterres* on the other. The only access to the latter was via a 10 ft wide corridor through the house. The inner layout was enclosed at each end by a pool. The canal at the pleasure house was widened by a half-square with an apse, and the broad canal beyond the *parterres* had a semicircle of land projecting into it. This was the classical formula of semicircles on the axis at each end of a layout, but here introduced in a somewhat contrived manner.

The earlier gardens and orangery with a circular pond were incorporated into the *parterres* but under the house there was a small but highly finished new *parterre de broderie* completely in box. Beyond the main *parterres*, and at first sight outside the garden proper, were tall *bosquets*. These were in fact easily reached via gates at the sides, and their numerous axial and diagonal paths provided opportunities for wandering at leisure away from the pressures of Court. The furthermost part of the *bosquets* was in fact the more complex, more like a labyrinth.

Clingendaal was a very individual solution to the adversity of the site. The character was a little whimsical, but adhered to the French principle of development along a central axis. At the same time the several cross-canals, cross-hedges and cross-axes formed a typically Dutch succession of compartments or rooms and gave many sideways views of the Dutch countryside, creating much diversity. Doublet had created one of the most remarkable Dutch gardens of the period. He had already finished this work by 1687, when the Swedish garden architect, Nicodemus Tessin, wrote: 'This is the best to be found in gardens around The Hague.' His account of the garden corresponds closely to the series of engravings that date from about 1690.

Tessin also remarked that Doublet directed William III's alterations to the gardens of Huis ten Bosch:

3.6 Huis ten Bosch, general view (c. 1690), showing the *parterre* behind the house like that at Chantilly

In the garden everything was made new, under the direction of the Lord of Sint Annaland (Philips Doublet), the large parterres were made after the pieces of the Orangery at Chantilly, but here they were embroidered;

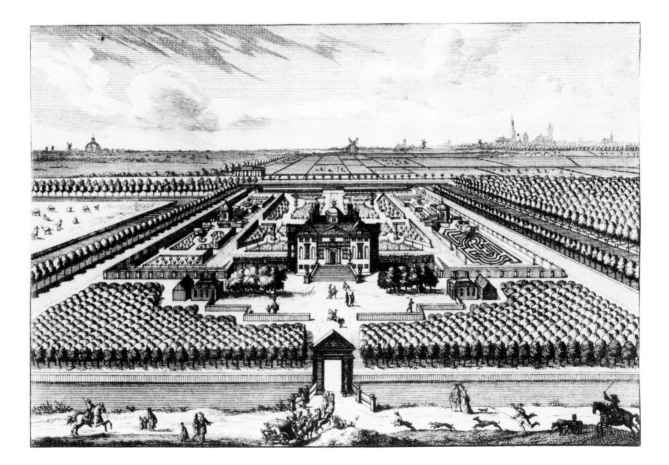

alongside the green pavilions there were a number of tall lattice pieces, heavily overgrown and standing before the walls . . .

William had bought back the lease on Huis ten Bosch from his aunt Albertine Agnes in 1685/6. The main divisions of the walled and moated area were not altered, and the two octagonal pavilions were maintained and incorporated in the new design. However the Pieter Post design of the four square *broderies* from the time of William's grandparents was removed; the new layout, as Tessin remarked, was similar to the Parterre de l'Orangerie at Chantilly. In the central square was an octagonal pool surrounded by flower beds containing statuary, and the outer part was divided into four sides by diagonals at the corners. Also the old kitchen gardens to the side were planted as a maze.

The hunting seat at Het Loo

William's main requirement in the early 1680s was for a larger hunting seat in the Veluwe than Dieren provided. He purchased an old castle with a good supply of running water called Het Loo in 1684, and wanted a new, comparatively small, seat with gardens on the estate. Although Van Swieten remained the official architect until 1689, William had in the meantime found another with more verve. This was Jacob Roman, a former sculptor who took up architecture only in 1680. He was first paid by William for 'the making of all the arbours and other works at Honselaarsdijk' and for 'an inspection tour of the manor of Dieren' in 1684. Roman was probably responsible for the trellis pavilion on the far side of the great *parterre* at Honselaarsdijk.

When in 1685 Louis XIV revoked the Edict of Nantes, which had extended religious tolerance to the Huguenots, several hundred thousand of them sought to leave France. They included many of France's most skilled artisans and artists, and one in particular, Daniel Marot, was eagerly employed by William. Marot was still only 24, but skilled in engraving and designing decorative patterns for interiors, ceramics and *parterres*.

William also had a new 'Intendant of His Highness's Country Houses, Plantations and Gardens' from August 1685. This was Daniel Desmarets, originally a pastor of the Protestant Walloon church from the south Netherlands, who moved to that denomination's church in The Hague in 1662. By the mid-1670s he was displaying a strong interest in exotic plants, and was acting as intermediary for William in building up the prince's collection. Desmarets was persuaded to join William's household at Honselaarsdijk in 1684, and before long he was indispensable both in administering the changes at Het Loo and in building up William's collections of exotics still further. As far as the plantations and gardens were concerned, Desmarets seems to have taken instructions from Bentinck who was made 'Forester of the Stadholder' in 1681.

Mary laid the foundation stone in May 1685 for a rather modest new mansion at Het Loo, consisting of a main block linked by two quadrant colonnades in the Palladian style. The colonnades were linked to two L-shaped service wings which contained kitchens, office, orangery and stables and enclosed a forecourt. The house was part of the formal layout aligned on a main north-south axis which was almost square in overall plan, measuring 225 by 250 m.

One half of this rectangle contained the house, the service wings, the

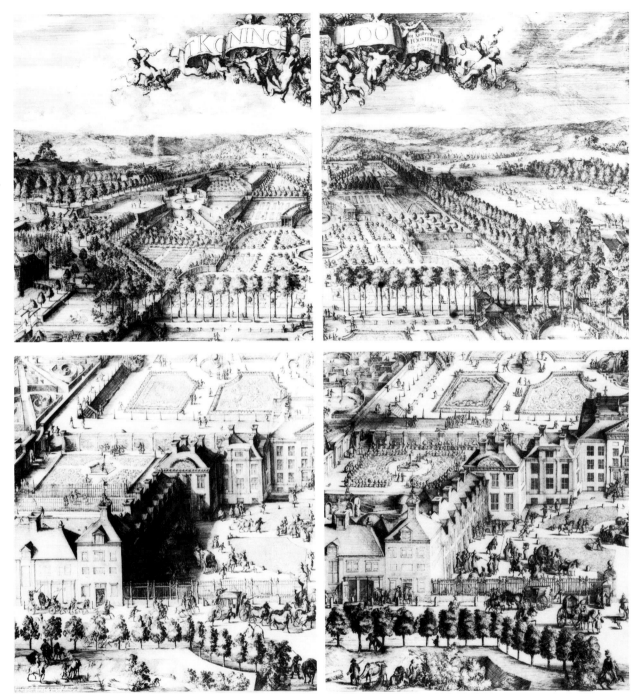

3.7 Het Loo, general view by Romeyn de Hooghe (c. 1700). One of several panoramas of the most celebrated gardens in the Netherlands. The further half of the garden was added in the early 1690s

forecourt and two private gardens on the east and west side of the house. The other half consisted of a large sunken garden, enclosed on three sides by terraces and bordered on the north side by a tree-lined avenue that lead in a westerly direction to the old castle. This sunken garden and the two private gardens were enclosed by brick walls, 3.5 m high, that kept out wind and sand, wild animals, and all the roughness and disorder of nature. The sunken garden was broader than it was long, as at Honselaarsdijk, and had a rather dominant cross-axis as at Huis ten Bosch.

Mary's apartment overlooked her private garden – to the east of the house, it was called 'the Princess's Garden' – which contained flower *parterres* with a magnificent arbour over the paths. Mary was able further to indulge her interest in plants and flowers in this garden, and it gained a large collection of exotic plants in pots and tubs. During the winter they were housed in the neighbouring orangery in the eastern service wing. William's apartment on the west of the house overlooked 'the Prince's Garden' which had *parterres*. His bowling green was an unusual feature in the Netherlands; presumably this is partly why an Englishman, Ralph Mose, was employed to look after the fine turf at Het Loo.

The privacy of these apartments and gardens typified the lifestyle which William and Mary sought in the Netherlands. In contrast to these two gardens, the sunken garden behind the house was a more public space. It was seen as an extension of the public spaces inside the house, as attested by its name, the 'Buytensael', or outdoor hall. A gilded wrought-iron gate that marked the exact midpoint of the square which formed the layout was the main entrance into the garden from the house. It gave access to the terrace that ran round three sides of the Lower Garden. Immediately in front was a semicircular flight of steps leading down into it. On either side stood two large sandstone sculptures symbolising the river gods of the Rhine and Ijssel, thereby indicating the geographical situation of Het Loo.

The garden had eight square *parterres*: the inner four were highly intricate *parterres de broderie*, while the outer four were grass *parterres* or *parterres à l'Angloise*, whose simpler designs provided a setting for stone and marble statues. The borders of all the *parterres* were filled with plants, flowers and juniper pyramids. One of the advantages of the site was that, exceptionally in the sandy Veluwe, there was a supply of water suitable for fountains, and the gardens of Het Loo were in fact especially renowned for the diversity of water in fountains, *jets d'eau*, cascades and rills. The main axis through the sunken garden was edged with small canals which broadened at regular intervals to receive jets of water which, with the white marble and gilded lead statues, formed the vertical elements in an otherwise flat garden.

Outside the square layout of the house and gardens was a park of over 100 ha containing a wilderness, *bosquets* with paths in a star pattern, fountains, ornamental ponds, fishponds, kitchen gardens, a falcon house, dogkennels, a menagerie, an aviary and other features. Outside the park was the large wild area of heather and scrub of the Veluwe, making a strong contrast between the cultivated gardens and park and the wilderness of the surrounding countryside. In this rough, wild environment the geometrically laid-out gardens and park were a most remarkable sight: Nature subjected to science.

The earliest known travel description of Het Loo was that of Nicodemus Tessin in spring 1687. He was full of praise for the beautiful lawns and the numerous fountains. The large garden behind the house had just been set out when Tessin visited, and the house itself was only just finished. Also the Prince's and Princess's Gardens were in the process of being laid out. Tessin mentions a stately drive with four rows of trees; it sounds as if they were planted large.

Het Loo was not a canal garden, but its enclosed, rectangular layout maintained the Dutch classical garden tradition established earlier in the seventeenth century. The impression of the whole is of a unified structure and small scale. Only in Marot's decorations of the embroidery parterres do we feel the spirit of the French Baroque.

3.8 *Overleaf*: Zeist, 'Veue de la maison de Zeyst avec ses jardins' by Daniel Stoopendaal (c. 1700). French decoration and an extended axis within a sophisticated Dutch canal garden

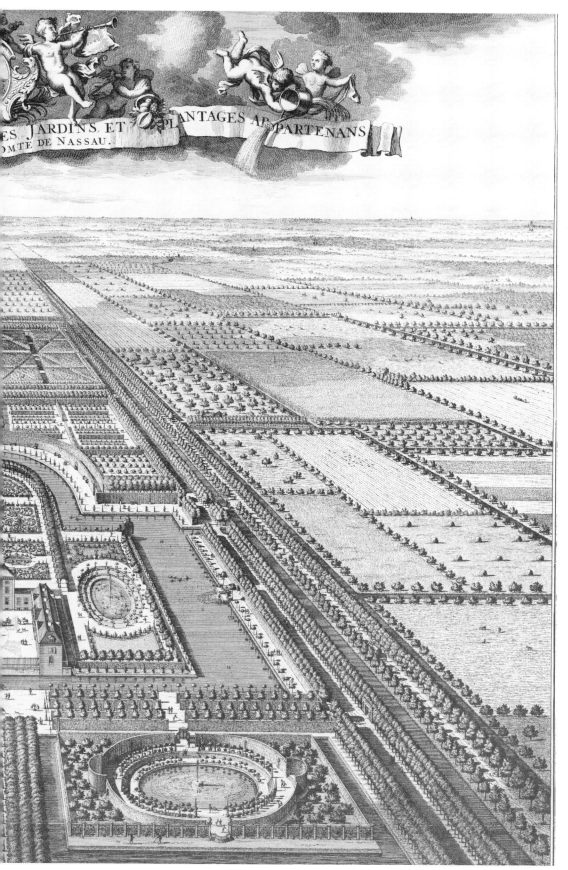

ES JARDINS, ET PLANTAGES APPARTENANS
OMTE DE NASSAU.

Zeist, Heemstede and Rosendael

Odijk's own garden at Zeist, near Utrecht, made at very much the same time as Het Loo, was no half-hearted attempt at axial treatment – it had an extended main axis that in total was 5 km long. Odijk commissioned Jacob Roman to design the house and probably the outline of the large garden, which at about 23 ha was one of the largest in the Netherlands. Daniel Marot was asked to decorate the interiors of the house and the gardens. Odijk himself may have been partly responsible too. In the summer of 1686 Princess Mary asked him to go to Het Loo to see the progress of the work there, suggesting a more than casual interest by Odijk in design.

The house at Zeist stood on a island surrounded by broad canals. In front was the forecourt, to the rear a massive *parterre de broderie* extended well beyond the rectangle of the island. It was finished by a semicircle and enclosed by a hippodrome-shaped open-sided arbour. To the left-hand side was a *parterre à l'Angloise* and another rare bowling green, perhaps intended as private gardens as at Het Loo, and on the right-hand side was a sunken pool with a large *jet d'eau* and plants set out around the banks.

This island was just the immediate garden. The approach was by a triple

3.9 Zeist, 'Carte du Camp d'Utrecht' by C. van Baarsel. The wider estate planning can be seen

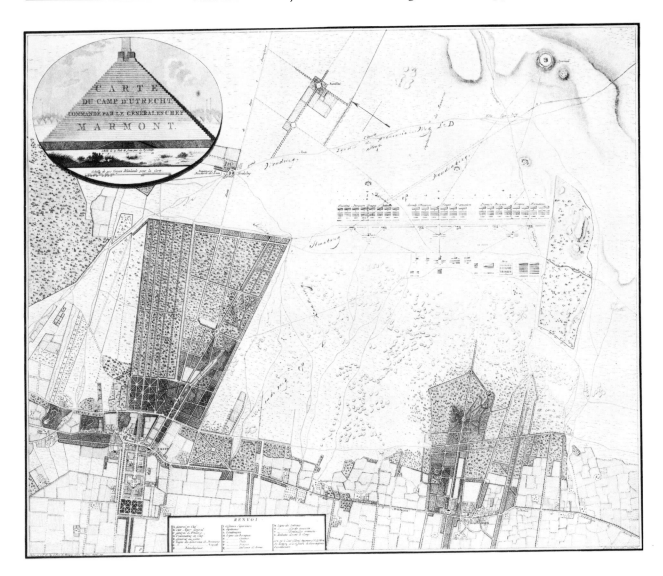

avenue of beech, to the right of which on another island was an orangery garden like that at Zorgvliet, but completely circular, and to the left on a third island was a *bosquet*. On the outside of the canal of the main island were high-clipped hedges sheltering a walk with splendid and ever-changing views inwards across the island. The strong axis provided by the approach avenue was continued at the rear of the house from this walk by another triple avenue. The hedges concealed large kitchen gardens to either side of the avenue and, beyond, more *bosquets*.

The bird's-eye-view of Zeist by Stoopendaal only shows the area directly bordering and beyond the house. The most remarkable feature of this estate was the long axis which is continued to either side for several kilometres as an avenue. Much of the estate, not seen on the view, was groves of firs and deciduous trees planted with radiating rides like stars – *sterrenbossen*.

At Zeist there is no mistaking the rigid rectangular framework of the Dutch classical canal garden. The semicircular end of the *parterre* island also had Dutch precedents: for example, the arbour ending the garden of Rijswijk. However, at Zeist these elements are more developed: the broad moat around the castle was treated as a mirror frame, and the semicircular end was no mere appendage – it was part of the magnificence of the *parterre*. Above all, the unification of all parts of the estate around the main axis was a wonder of organisation. Zeist was a successful blend of Dutch and French features. Although many features paralleled those at Het Loo, the quality of the overall layout made William's palace look pedestrian by comparison.

Another layout of the same time was the nearby Heemstede. Diederick van Velthuysen, a wealthy and fervent supporter of William III, bought the house and estate in 1680. The property was long and comparatively narrow with an east-west orientation. Van Velthuysen most probably commissioned Marot to modernise the interior of the house and to lay out the garden.

Situated in the flat Dutch polderland, Heemstede's layout was a highly sophisticated repetition of the straight lines of the surrounding country. As shown in Stoopendaal's bird's-eye-view, made around 1700, there were four sets of parallel double avenues along the length of the estate, two brushing past the sides of the forecourt, and the other two at the edges of the property. A cross-avenue passed the face of the forecourt. Heemstede was near a river, the Vaartsche Rijn, alongside which was the main highway, but with the entrance facing away from it. There was no grand avenue approach; the most that could be done was to take the drive along a perimeter avenue before turning into the cross-avenue.

These avenues also divided the garden in sections. In the central space the forecourt was succeeded by the moat, itself surrounded by rows of trees, and behind the house was a very splendid *parterre de broderie* with a central pool with *jet d'eau*, obelisks at the corners and, a contemporary reported, 'statuary adorns the garden, the statues of four princes of Orange, who liberated the country of the violence and tyranny of Spain'. On the west side of the *parterre* garden, on the main axis, was a huge 'fountain gate' down which water cascaded in steps. This gate gave access to a semicircular orangery garden similar to the orangery garden at Zorgvliet. The orangery trees and plants were placed around a masonry bason surrounded by terraces. The concave east-facing walls would have trapped the morning sun and provided protection against the winds. At the centre of the curved wall, on the end of the main axis, was a gazebo overlooking the highway and river.

The Dutch tendency to combine the ornamental with the useful is exemplified at Heemstede by the orchards and kitchen gardens, treated ornamentally, not far from the sides of the house and *parterre* and between

3.10 *Overleaf*: Heemstede, 'Plan ou veue de Heemstede' by Daniel Stoopendaal (c. 1690)

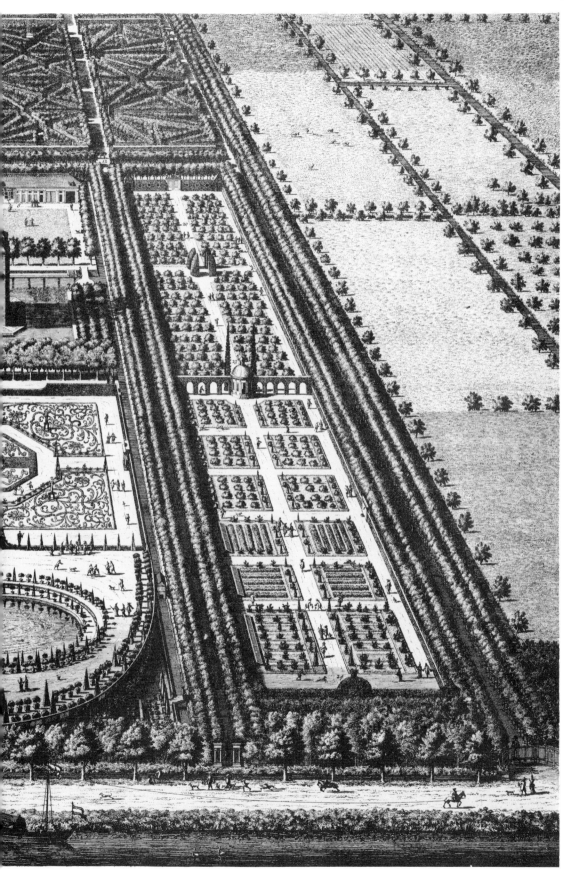

the outer pairs of avenues. These areas were reached by bridges over small canals. The northern area had the orangery within an orchard of dwarf apple trees, and the southern area had another orchard alongside the house and the kitchen garden alongside the orangery garden.

East of the cross-avenue was an area of *bosquets* with path systems in the shape of stars. These were planted with dense clipped hedges of hornbeam and elm, with coppice in the interstices. Amongst the *bosquets* was a roundel, a place where twelve paths came together, and where statues were placed. There were fishponds with trained hedges around them, and a section for game with pheasants, deer, peacocks, and East Indian ducks. There was diversity in the planting of the whole estate. The avenues were planted with elms, beeches and limes, while fir trees were in places planted along the paths in the wilderness.

Heemstede must have been quite a sight with its avenues and *bosquets* standing out from the flat polderland fields. In many ways it was one of the most successful examples of late-seventeenth-century Dutch formal gardens, though leaving the trees around the moat was incomprehensible as they would have cut off the view of the *parterres* from the house, and the orangery was oddly placed at some distance from the splendid orangery garden.

With their emphasis on parallel axes, still water and rectangular enclosed shapes, Zeist and Heemstede were the sort of layouts that exerted an influence in Germany, and to some extent in England. An entirely different sort of site from these places was found at Rosendael, in Gelderland. Here Baron Jan van Arnhem had a valley and plenty of running water.

The irregularity of the valley meant that a regular design would have to incorporate changes of direction. Van Arnhem placed some Marot-style *parterres* on the side of the hill rising from the moat of the castle, but he appreciated the old castle too. He maintained the two early-seventeenth-century mannerist gables of the castle and he used the huge and ancient round tower as a pivot to turn the whole layout round a quarter circle, so that a series of delightful ponds which curved down the valley could be embraced in the formal layout. The scheme was thus planned to respond to the natural qualities of the site.

However, the garden was most striking because of the important place given to running water; the water of many brooks upstream were conducted to the top of the hill above the *parterres* which provided a remarkable display of cascades and fountains. Water cascaded down the axis between the *parterres*. Halfway down were arches under a terrace, and in front of them water spouted from eight urns making arches of water under which one could walk towards the grotto. The grotto, lined with shells, coral, mother of pearl and mirror glass, could not, however, be entered because a powerful water cascade impeded this. Another cascade took the water down from the grotto to the moat underneath arches of water from *jets d'eau*. In addition the *parterres* contained four fountains. The sound of falling water was everywhere. Edward Southwell saw Rosendael in 1696:

> But whatever is wanting in the House is fully made up in the garden. The terraces are noble, the Parterres very fine, and there is a great plenty of water, which supplies the fountains all day long.

Van Arnhem was a trusted ally of William and his representative in the province of Gelderland. Rosendael was not far from Dieren, and informal visits cemented the friendship. A tangible commemoration of William's

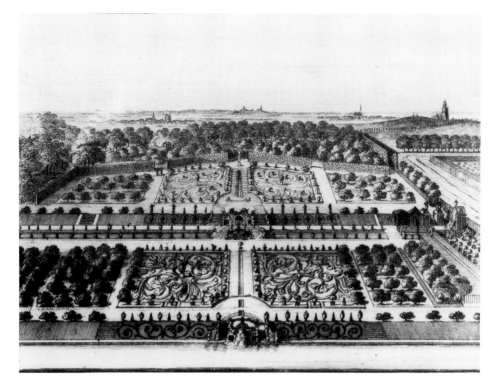

3.11 Rosendael, 'der terrassenaanleg', by Pieter Schenk in *Paradisus Oculorum* (1702)

hunting exploits was the 'Grotto of the Deerheads' adorned with the antlers of deer killed by him. Before she left for England to be crowned queen, Mary commissioned a large collection of China and Delft ware for Johanna van Arnhem. A cabinet was built near the Grotto of the Deerheads to house it, called the 'Queen's Cabinet'. In this there were a gilded statue of Mary, small fountains, and fine murals and a painted ceiling depicting Rosendael with its gardens, exotic birds, and negro pages serving fruit in China plate.

William and his circle had hunting gazebos all over the Veluwe. Here at Rosendael there was a small domed octagonal one in the park called 'the King's little house'. It was richly built to designs by Marot, crowned with a lantern and adorned with the king's coat of arms in marble. A contemporary description says that it was 'founded by the favour of the King'. It had mirrors on all walls, and there was a statue of William in front of the fireplace, a kitchen and a staircase leading to a roof terrace from which one could enjoy the view. Underneath was a wine cellar.

Het Loo, *residence of the King of Great Britain*

Having returned to Britain for her coronation, Mary never again set foot in the Netherlands. This was obviously a source of regret: '. . . to see again a country which is so dear to me and people with whom I have lived so long, so happily and with such contentment.'

William was too occupied in the winter of 1689/90 with Irish and Scottish affairs to be able to leave Britain, but, as the stadholder, needed an envoy in the Netherlands. Bentinck, now Earl of Portland, was sent, but William wrote (in French):

I ask that, amongst all your important tasks, you do not forget Loo, nor to

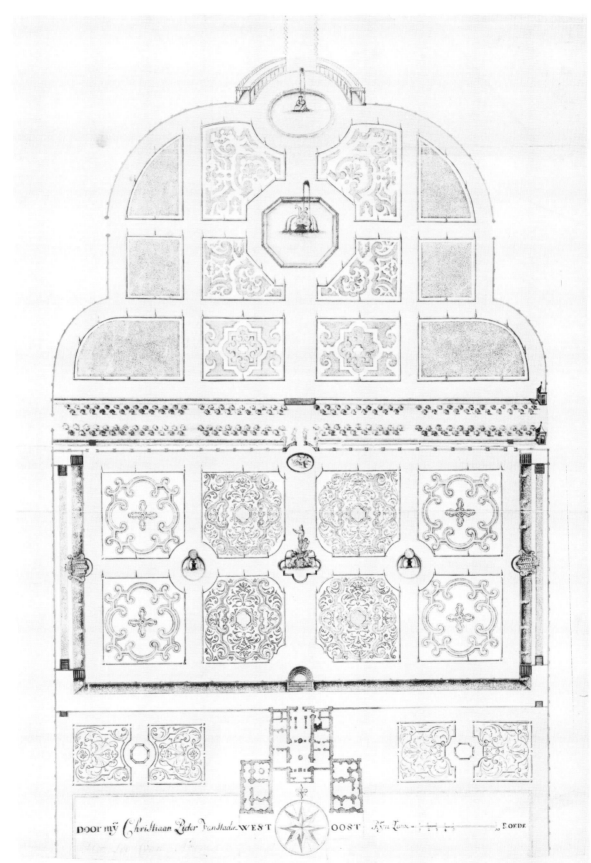

go there and sort out what remains to be done; you know how that place is close to my heart.

3.12 *Opposite*: Het Loo, plan by Christiaan van Staden (c. 1700). The completed gardens within the wall

Before Portland returned in the spring he did indeed go, and to Dieren too. Het Loo he found in 'very good order and very neat', but at Dieren 'I discovered that I was much needed in view of the damage to the new dyke and to the little maze.' The fault lay with a drunken gardener who was sacked on the spot.

William was able to leave Britain in 1691, travelling to The Hague in order to chair a conference of European powers united in their struggle against Louis XIV in the Nine Years' War. The entourage of the king had increased to such an extent that accommodation at Het Loo was insufficient. The plan to enlarge Het Loo was born; the archives of the Nassau Demesne recorded for this year: 'When the Prince thereafter occupied the throne of Great Britain, he decided to make the Princely seat into a Royal seat, thereafter the buildings, groves, plantations and fountains multiplied or enlarged.' Mary meanwhile remained behind at Kensington and Hampton Court, and did so every succeeding year while William went to oversee the Dutch conduct of the war.

A second stage in the development of Het Loo thus took place from 1692 to 1694. In order to enlarge the house the curved colonnades between house and wings were replaced by four abutting pavilions. Constantijn Huygens junior noted in his journal in April 1692: 'The King said that the new building on the side of the main house would give comfort but no increase in beauty.' Meanwhile further *parterres* designed by Marot were made in a new, or Upper, garden, thus greatly extending the north-south axis. Beyond the Upper Garden an avenue of trees cut through the park to an obelisk in the distance. Other new features outside the garden wall were a *bosquet* to the left and a fountain at the reservoir with water channels made in the shape of the cypher 'WM' (for William and Mary).

The avenue across the top of the Lower Garden was now within the garden area, and between the lower and upper parts, thus dividing it into two distinct sections. At the north end of the Lower Garden a new oval fountain basin was added in the main axis in the middle of which was a statue of Hercules strangling two water-spouting snakes. Beyond this new fountain two quadrant balustrades indicated the beginning of the new garden. The Upper Garden was bounded by curving walls, and terminated at its northern end in the two quadrant colonnades removed from the house. A good view over the gardens was to be had from the colonnade roofs. Being semicircular, the colonnades also provided a backdrop for the new King's Fountain, the main jet of which rose nearly 14 m into the air.

One effect of the extension of the garden was that the once dominant east-west cross-axis through the old, or Lower, garden now became subsidiary. Together with the extension of the north-south axis, the extension also gave the garden as a whole a feel much more like Zeist than Honselaarsdijk. However, because it was also enclosed, except for the main axis, there was not really a connection with the surrounding landscape. Probably William himself was not fully converted to the Zeist model; he insisted that the avenue of trees leading to the old castle was maintained, though with the lower branches stripped up, which left the garden clearly in two parts.

The entire plan was completed about 1700. Het Loo had become a major palace with maintenance requirements to match: the salary list for Het Loo gardens in 1695 mentioned three departments, each with its own head: a

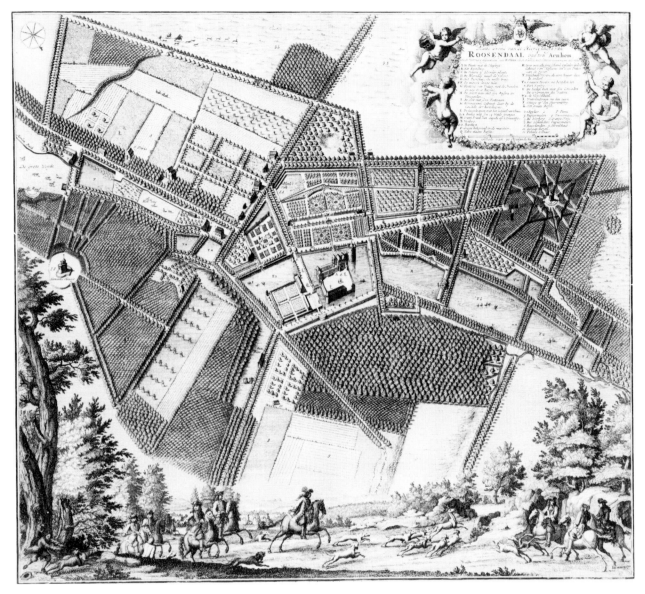

3.13 Rosendael, 'platte grond' by Jan Smit (c. 1700). The owner's passion for hunting is reflected in the hunting scene below

head gardener with twelve gardeners, a head gardener of the lawns and gravel paths, and a head fountaineer with eight helpers. The gardens became widely known and were visited, described and depicted extensively.

Each autumn William spent several weeks hunting at the Veluwe, staying at Het Loo or Dieren, recuperating after the summer's campaign and hunting with great intensity. Even after the Peace of Rijswijk in 1697, which brought the end of the Nine Years' War, he continued to visit Het Loo each summer in spite of there being no pressing reason to leave England. It seems likely that William's hesitation in improving his English palaces, which lasted till August 1699, may well be attributed to his sojourns in the Veluwe.

In these later years William stayed again with the Van Arnhems at Rosendael. Baron Jan van Arnhem tried to make the king as comfortable as possible. In a letter of April 1698 Van Arnhem tells the king that he is building a stable for 16 of the king's horses: '. . . to give more comfort to Your Majesty's horses, when we have the mercy to see Your Majesty at Rosendaal.' William's love for the Veluwe is testified by the letters he wrote, among others, to Van Arnhem from Kensington in March 1699: 'I can not tell you enough how I long for the Veluwe, hoping that I will see you and the Lady of Rosendaal soon there, your good friend William.'

De Voorst and Middachten

In 1688 Arnold-Joost van Keppel had landed in England with William as one of his pages. In 1691 William's attention had been drawn to him when Keppel broke his leg in a hunting accident. His cheerful countenance and amusing conversation made him popular with the king. By 1696 it was clear that Keppel had supplanted Portland as William's constant companion, and he was elevated into the English peerage as Earl of Albemarle in January 1696/7. Portland became increasingly resentful, and he and Keppel often quarrelled and once almost came to blows.

The formerly poor country squire was given considerable sums of money which enabled him to live up to the standards required by his exalted station. It is known that in 1692 Keppel had large sums of money transferred to the

3.14 De Voorst, 'Vue et Perspective de Voorst' by Daniel Marot (c. 1700). There are several similarities both with Het Loo and Zeist

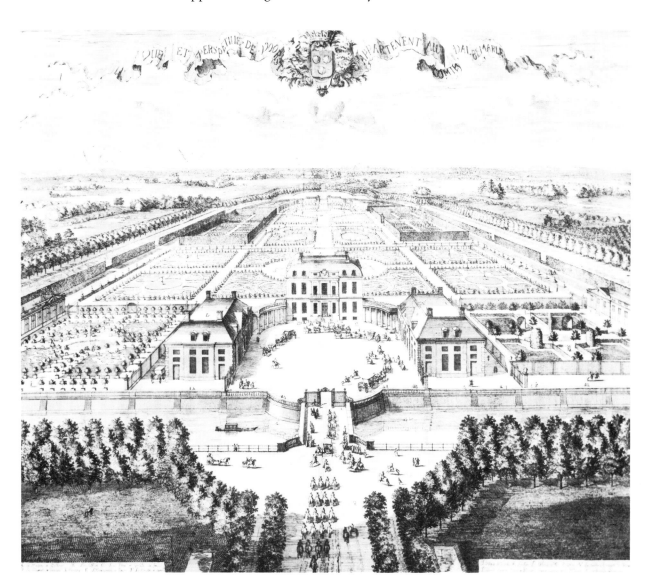

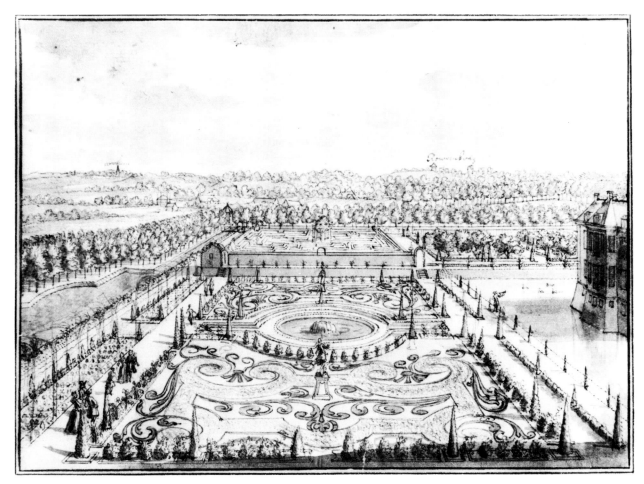

3.15 Middachten, sketch of the *parterre* and maze behind the castle (c. 1700)

Netherlands and, in July 1698, William purchased Twickenham Park, in Middlesex, and made a present of it to Albemarle who had no country seat in England. Tradition has it, though, that earlier, in 1697, William had ordered a new house at De Voorst, near Zutphen, to be built at his own expense and afterwards gave it to Albemarle. This might explain a model of the house by an English cabinet maker, perhaps to the designs of William Talman, who at that time was the comptroller of the king's English Office of Works.

However, it seems likely that the final design and execution of the project for the new house and gardens involved both Jacob Roman as the architect and Daniel Marot as the designer of the interiors and the *parterres*. They had worked together at Zeist, Het Loo and other houses and gardens of William and his circle, and so their cooperation could have continued at De Voorst. William used the place as a *pied-à-terre* during his hunting trips on the Veluwe, and in the house was an apartment permanently at his disposal. Indeed, the house looked much like the early Het Loo, having the same quarter-circle colonnades linking house to service wings.

The general outline of the gardens, 290 by 430 m, was similar to the expanded layout of Het Loo: both had enclosed gardens below each wing, a terraced sunken garden directly behind the house with eight *parterres*, a fountain in the centre, and a further garden with semicircular arboured termination. The gardens were much the same size as Zeist. In fact, the enclosing canal and the shape of the further garden were very reminiscent of Zeist too. De Voorst was one of the most illustrious and important stately buildings in the United Provinces, and it must surely be due to Marot that a grandiose unit was created of drive, forecourt, house and gardens.

In 1697 Albemarle got permission from the town of Zutphen to extract water from the River Berkel to make the fountains function in the garden. William's physician, Walter Harris, visited (probably in the winter of 1697/8), remarking on the waterworks but also that the house and garden were not yet finished:

> Once I rid from Dieren to Zutphen, over the Issell, in order to see a most noble and Magnificent House of the Right Honourable the Earl of Albemarle, that his Lordship has lately built about half a League from Zutphen, and from which city there is a very spacious Avenue or access made to the House, between a double Row of Trees; his Lordship possessing a considerable Estate in that Province. This House has Noble Gardens adjoining it, and made after the greatest Models with Terras Walks, Fountains, Cascades, Canals, etc. They were not finished no more than the house, when I went to see them after the last campaign.

Engravings by Pieter Schenk and Jean Marot show the finished result.

About the same time that De Voorst was underway the reconstruction of Middachten was nearing completion. This medieval Gelderland castle, with its moat and surrounding gardens, was not far from Dieren, being similarly close to the River Ijssel and on the outskirts of the Veluwe. Middachten was heavily damaged by the French during their retreat in 1673. Godard van Reede, Lord of Ginkel, came into possession when his wife inherited it. Ginkel had been trained for a military career which took him to Ireland in 1690. He completed the defeat of the supporterts of James II for which he was made Earl of Athlone by William in 1691/2.

Between 1695 and 1698 Athlone completely renovated the castle and laid out an impressive garden. The architect Stephen Vennecool transformed the almost square medieval building into a building of classical proportions. The old moat was formalised and with the renovated castle it was turned into the central feature of the new rectangular layout of the formal gardens surrounding it. That the gardens were not finished in 1696 is apparent from Southwell's comment: 'The Gardens will be very good, my Lord makes very large Plantations; and for 2 or 3 Miles about, the very high Roads & crops roads are planted in double Rows with all the Regularity imaginable.'

The 'very good gardens' consisted of a *parterre de broderie* on the main axis behind the castle, flanked by hedged mazes, while to both sides of the house and forecourt orchards were laid out. The plantations surrounding were perhaps more striking, even though they followed closely the early Honselaarsdijk formula, publicised by André Mollet nearly 50 years before. The rectangle was enclosed by a canal which was widened into a projecting half-octagon and apse at the end of the garden. The drive in front of the castle ended in a half-circle of trees as at Honselaarsdijk and Het Loo, while the whole rectangle with canal was enclosed by four lines of trees which, beyond the half-octagon, gave way to an avenue allowing an uninterrupted view to the River Ijssel along the central axis. This restrained and somewhat conservative layout was quite grand, but otherwise a representative example of the combination of French ideas and Dutch tradition in the days of William and Mary.

4

The British Gardens of William and Mary

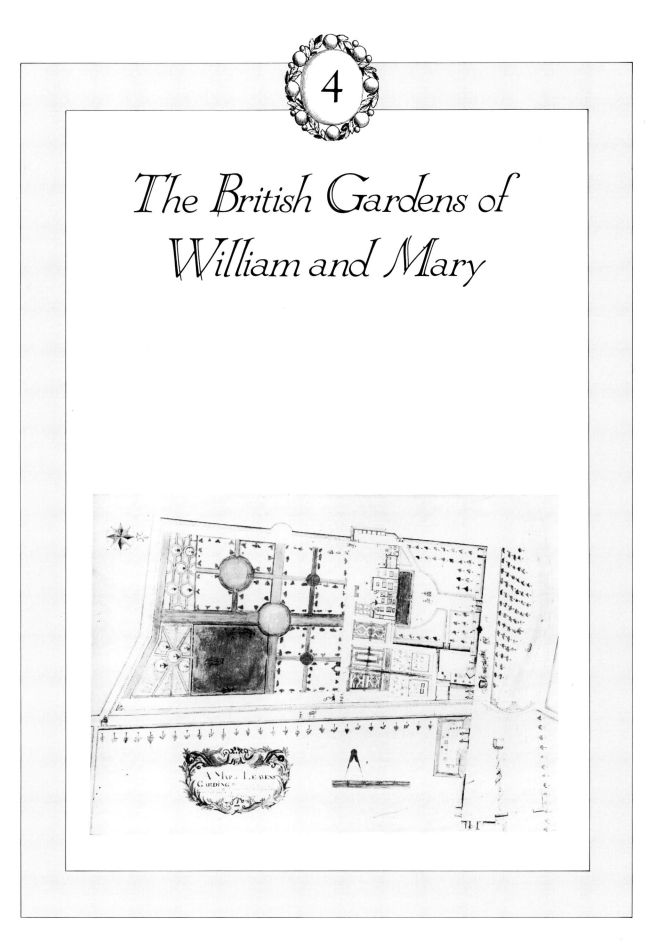

4.1 *Previous page*: Levens, in Westmorland, 'A Map of Leavens Garding' by R. Shiping (c. 1720). This garden was made under the direction of Guillaume Beaumont

The Royal Gardens administration

In February 1688/9 the crown of England and Ireland was offered to William and Mary, as joint monarchs, in place of James II. The various offices of the Crown were distributed from early April 1689, amongst which was that of Superintendent of the Royal Gardens. This went to Hans Willem Bentinck, still the closest of William's few personal friends and whom he created Earl of Portland in June.

Portland had, of course, already superintended William's gardens in the Netherlands, in his appointment as Forester of the Stadholder, and, not surprisingly, brought over those he knew and trusted. Hendrik Quellenburg was brought across from Honselaarsdijk to be a head gardener at Hampton Court, and it is noticeable that the other two – Samuel van Staden and Caspar Gamperle – had Dutch names, as did Henrich Timmerman of Kensington Gardens. Some of Mary's skilled horticulturalists were clearly Dutch too, Hendrik Floris, Herman Jansen Valck and Cornelius van Vliet helping her to set up her collection of exotics in England.

Portland had the tact to select the Englishman, George London, to be his deputy, at a salary of £200 per annum. Portland also appointed a comptroller and an accountant. The former post at £140 per annum went to William Talman, who had also recently been favoured with the appointment of Comptroller of the Office of Works, which, under the surveyorship of Sir Christopher Wren, was responsible for royal buildings. The accountant was a Dutchman, Caspar Frederik Henning, at £100 per annum.

This organisation was expected to bid to the Lords of the Treasury for warrants to pay its costs and to pay for whatever gardeners, contractors and labourers were required. Meanwhile the Office of Works was responsible for garden buildings, and it helped that Talman was the comptroller for both organisations, and that he and London were close friends.

There was also some overlap between the responsibilities of the Royal Gardens and the Office of Woods and Forests. In October 1699 there was a dispute with the Surveyor of Woods, Philip Ryley, who would normally have been responsible for works and maintenance in the parks. Henry Wise had been planting horse chestnuts and limes in the Great Avenue in Bushy Park, and was railing them in under the direction of George London. Ryley insisted that this was his responsibility, took the issue to the Treasury and won his point.

James II's displaced gardens administration centred around Colonel James Grahme who effectively became Supervisor of the Royal Gardeners in succession to Hugh May in 1683/4. The royal gardener at St James's had changed too. John Rose had been succeeded by Captain Leonard Gurle in 1677, and in 1685 Gurle was succeeded by Antonio Verrio, the painter. Guillaume Beaumont, a Frenchman, with a nursery at Bagshot, in Surrey, seems also to have acted as a royal gardener under Grahme. Beaumont started some new gardens at Hampton Court, probably the wilderness made out of the Old Orchard. This was a geometric layout of paths flanked by high clipped hedges, probably of hornbeam. A pine tree was planted in the central 'room', whilst the interstices between hedges were filled with elms. One of the woodland compartments was planted as a maze and one of the *allées* was widened out for a 'Troy Town' – a form of maze cut into turf. Both features were ancient forms, and their installation in a new wilderness may have been an attempt to reflect a sense of the history of the palace. All this Beaumont now had to abandon to George London.

As for Grahme, he thought it wise to spend more time at his home at

1. Honselaarsdijk, by Balthazar Florentius a' Berckerode (c. 1640). This shows Honselaarsdijk largely as made in the 1620s, though with the addition in 1633 of André Mollet's *parterres* to each side of the mansion

2. Huis ten Bosch, view over the *parterre*, by Jan van der Heyden. This is the *parterre* made about 1645 and which was replaced in 1685

3. Soestdijk, bird's-eye-view by Daniel Stoopendaal (c. 1680). One of William's early improvements

4. Honselaarsdijk, early-eighteenth-century view of the mansion from the *parterre* by J. van Haastert

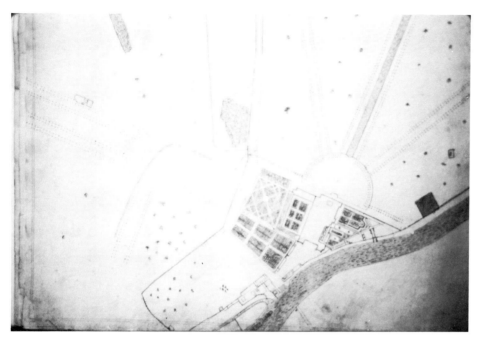

4.2 Hampton Court, a plan of the gardens and park, with an unexecuted Trianon-style retreat across the Thames by William Talman (c. 1698). (South is to the right)

Levens, in Westmorland, and decided to commence a new garden there. It must have been some compensation for Beaumont to be asked to design it, and that by 1694 another of Beaumont's patrons was Lord Weymouth at Longleat.

Hampton Court

William and Mary were keen to create a sumptuous and modern palace out of the old one at Hampton Court. As Daniel Defoe put it: 'King William fix'd upon *Hampton-Court*; and it was in his Reign that *Hampton-Court* put on new Cloaths and being dress'd gay and glorious, made the Figure we now see it in.' The Surveyor of Works, Sir Christopher Wren, immediately began drawing up ambitious schemes for almost the complete reconstruction of the palace.

The unsatisfactory approach from the west was to be replaced by one from the north, crossing Bushy Park and aligned on the Great Hall. The Great Avenue of 1,050 limes across Bushy Park was thus planted. It had quadruple rows on each side, unheard of previously, and at the south end it widened out to embrace the intended forecourt width. There was also an intention to have a bason about two-thirds of the way along the approach. Similar basons were made at Woburn Abbey and Wanstead, both designed by George London. They appear to have been placed for the reflection of the façade on the water surface, and as incidents on otherwise very lengthy approaches down avenues.

Wren's scheme for reorientating the palace had to be abandoned, and the bason was shelved for ten years. At least, though, Wren's new east front did proceed. This was designed around the axis already formed by the Long Water and its avenue. It seems that 2,176 more limes were planted in diagonal- and cross-avenues in the House Park. The Kingston Avenue radiated from the centre of the central room in the new east front, Queen

Mary's study, and was aligned on the tower of Kingston Church (which was not quite 30 degrees from the centre line of the canal). Ditton Avenue was planted at the same angle to the south. A cross-avenue ran past the end of the Long Water and joined the Ditton Avenue at a circle of trees and the Kingston Avenue at an untidy arrangement which had to maintain the vista to the church.

A *parterre* to set off Wren's new block was required, and its size was predetermined by the semicircle of limes. Quite simply, the Great Parterre, or Fountain Garden as it became, was to be quite enormous, one of the biggest *parterres* anywhere. Wren probably preferred a fairly simple grass and gravel layout. However, there is a sketch by Daniel Marot, dated August 1689, from the roof of the former palace showing an intended *parterre à l'Angloise* – a lawn out of which was cut geometric patterns filled with coloured gravels.

The sketch also shows a broad central path aligned on the canal and two semicircular paths, one close to the limes and the other at about half the radius of the outer. At the intersection of the inner semicircular path, on the central path, a large oval bason was indicated which was intended for a

4.3 Hampton Court, design for the *parterre* by Daniel Marot (1689). This design was implemented except that *broderie* was put in the central portion

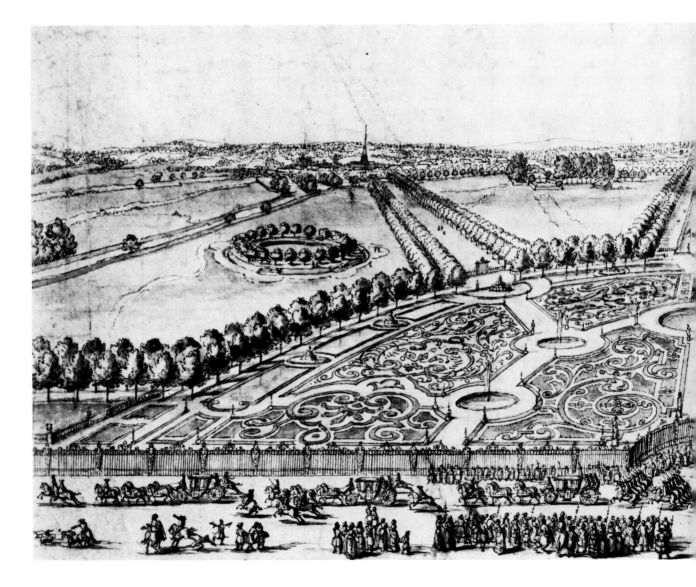

Great Fountain. The area outside the inner semicircular path was broken by four radial paths, and at the intersections and at other places along the outer path there were further pools, making 13 in all.

With this number of fountains, and with pipes being laid throughout the horticultural parts of the gardens, the waterworks had to be ambitious. The Longford river was repaired, and 3,123 yards of elm pipe were laid from the Conduit House in Bushy Park to the *parterre*, where a network of lead pipes supplied the fountains. However, the extensive revisions that this system was to undergo in 1700, and the final abandonment in 1708 of all but the Great Fountain, suggests that the reservoir capacity, the head (only 13 ft) and the length and diameter of the pipes never gave a satisfactorily powerful jet at the fountains.

The semicircle of limes was included within the *parterre* garden. Further paths were made under the limes so that the *parterre* could be observed from the shade. It was planned that the whole garden should be encircled by ironwork railings with twelve ornamental panels and with elaborate gates at the diagonal avenues, all by Jean Tijou, the Frenchman renowned for his work at Chatsworth. There were also railings down the western side of the

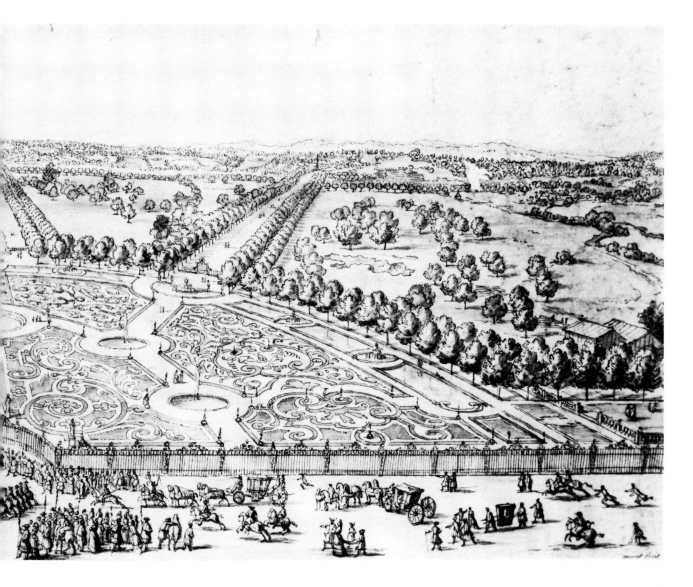

parterre, i.e. between it and the gates on the east front of the palace. The space between was available for drawing up carriages, and remained contiguous with the park. Presumably, though, it was well kept, perhaps even gravelled to allow the carriages to use it.

The whole Great Parterre project was clearly thought of, and probably executed, in 1689 and 1690, though the panels remained in Tijou's workshop. Within the inner path there was a *parterre de broderie*. Clipped evergreens were planted alongside paths. There were about 304 yews clipped to obelisks and 24 silver hollies clipped to globes.

The Privy Garden, which was below the other front of the Wren block, also underwent a major change in 1690/1. The old centreline of the garden was retained, and even provided the centreline of the new south front, but the side terraces were widened and heightened, and the *parterre* was replaced. The old Banquetting House in the Mount Garden was taken down in October 1690 and the mount levelled within the area of the garden soon after. The two towers at the corners of the Privy Garden were demolished in November. The bricklayer made foundations and built up two new terrace

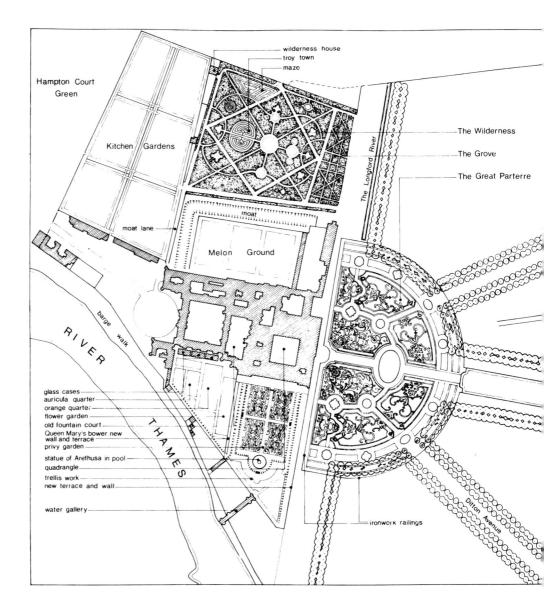

walls to widen the garden. To the west the new wall ran through the nearest garden in the Pond Yard, thus removing a path around the back of this garden and part of the garden itself. This new terrace was graced by an arbour of wych elm, known as Queen Mary's Bower, perhaps to block the unsuitable view westwards. To the east the new terrace gave a good view over the Great Parterre.

The grass quarters of the *parterre* were replaced by *gazon coupé* – a form of cut-work, making a pattern of bands of sand within the turf and dispensing with flower beds and the like. The southern wall of the Privy Garden was demolished, and substituted by trellis, presumably intended to be temporary until the Privy Garden could be extended over the Mount Garden and Water Gallery. The line of the trellis was broken by a circular pool in the middle of which the statue of Arethusa was re-erected on a new white marble base by the sculptor, Edward Pierce, which turned it into a fountain.

The central portion of the lower storey of the new south front was given large glass doors and windows, and was used as an orangery, from which

4.4 Hampton Court, a reconstruction of the layout of gardens and avenues in 1696

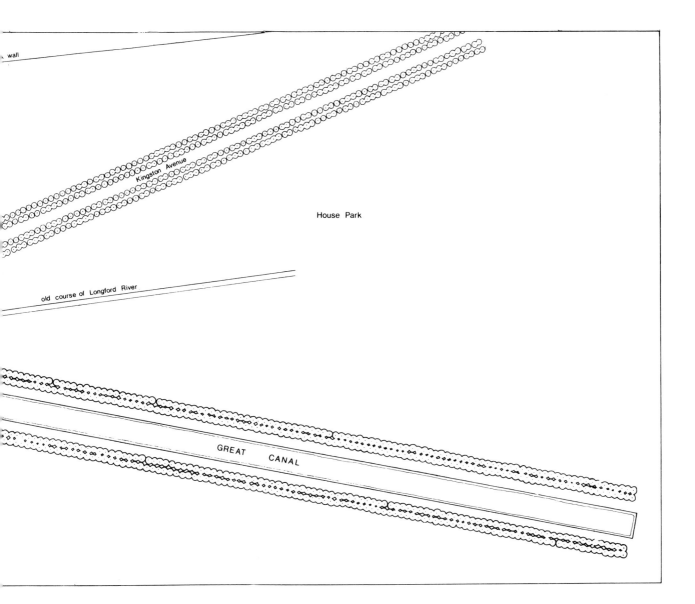

wall

Kingston Avenue

House Park

old course of Longford River

GREAT CANAL

69

bays, orange trees and lemon trees would be wheeled out onto the platform between the palace and the Privy Garden. The orange trees were taken from William and Mary's collection in Holland, and were transported over by Herman Jansen Valck.

The old Pond Yard became Queen Mary's preserve. In it she assembled in just a few years a quite remarkable collection of botanical specimens. Its core was the collection from the East Indies, Ceylon, the Cape of Good Hope and other parts of the globe made by Gaspar Fagel, the Grand Pensionary of Holland. He had died in 1688, and his collection was purchased by William and Mary, and was installed at Hampton Court by early 1690. Not content with this, Mary sent collectors to the Canaries and to Virginia. In order to house these tender exotics Mary had three 'glass cases', or 'stoves', built by Hendrik Floris to the latest Dutch specification. The collection continued to grow under the superintendence of Dr Leonard Plukenet, the botanist.

Mary's interest in flowers required that, as at Honselaarsdijk, she always had cut flowers in her apartments. One of George London's duties from April 1689 was to supply cut flowers to the royal apartments in Whitehall Palace. Presumably this also extended to Hampton Court. Two of the three garden enclosures in what became known as the Glass Case Garden were devoted to flowers. One was called 'The Auricula Quarter'. Both this quarter and the 'flower garden' had small fountains for watering plants, supplied from the main system within the Fountain Garden.

The king's Privy Orchard, made by Henry VIII, had been converted into the Kitchen Garden in Stuart times, and now was changed again to a huge Melon Ground. It was divided into three rows of hotbeds, ideal for fast growing tender crops like melons, cucumbers and pumpkins. In 1693/4 the Melon Ground was also being used to germinate seeds from the Cape of Good Hope, from the East Indies and from Barbados. The nearby Tiltyard was divided into six quarters by walls and became the new kitchen gardens.

The west front of the palace was altered by the final filling of the moat in 1690, and by the laying out of a circle in gravel in front of the gatehouse. Having abandoned the northern approach, there was unfortunately nothing that could be done about the asymmetric driveway from the gate to the green. Nevertheless the improvements could hardly be sneered at; they had already ensured that the monarchs had the finest gardens in Britain.

Kensington Gardens

William and Mary's other gardening project in these early years was at Kensington. It came about because William was an asthmatic, and found that the coal-smoke of Westminster did not agree with him. Nottingham House, in Kensington, on a higher piece of ground beyond Hyde Park, was thought to have better air, and so was purchased in June 1689.

This was a private retreat, not a palace. The whole property was less than 40 acres, consisting of a large paddock, in the north-east corner of which stood the house approached from the Kensington Highway to the south by an elm avenue. Around the house were the outbuildings and a few small gardens incorporating a mount, a banquetting house and a bowling green. To the east was Hyde Park and to the north was an old orchard taken out of Hyde Park in 1664 and due to revert to the Crown in 1705.

Both house and gardens clearly needed some enlargement, even though they were for private use. The Office of Works set about adding pavilions to each corner of the house and wings to make a courtyard to the west. William

4.5 Kensington Gardens, view of the south garden made in 1690 and 1691 (c. 1705)

wanted a safe passage from Whitehall, his place of business, to Kensington. The preferable route would have been through Hyde Park if it had not been a notorious haunt of footpads. So in November 1689 a contract was signed for the illuminated 'King's Road' or *Rue de Roi* – quickly translated by Londoners as 'Rotten Row' – constructed to the orders of Captain Michael Studholme, the Surveyor of his Majesty's Highways. Celia Fiennes saw this phenomenon a dozen years later:

> The whole length of this Parke there is a high causey of a good breadth, 3 coaches may pass, and on each side are rowes of posts on which are Glasses-cases for Lamps which are lighted in the evening and appears very fine as well as safe for the passenger. This is only a private roade the King had which reaches to Kensington, where for aire our great King William bought a house and fitted it for retirement.

Mary was intent on extending the gardens, so George London drew up some plans for a great southern garden of 12 acres, with the Great Walk on the line of the elm avenue. The King's Road was diverted to enter the garden at its southern end so that the final few hundred yards to the southern steps were through the gardens. By April 1690 London's contractors had laid about 15,000 cu yds of gravel in the gardens and yards – at 2 ft thick this would have made 4½ acres of gravelled area. Meanwhile 3,752 man days were employed prior to April in making minor walks and borders.

The large labour force continued after this date with more gravelling of minor walks, erecting £192 worth of 'reeds and arbour poles', presumably for the hedges, and planting a massive number of 'trees, plants and flowers' worth £700. Flower pots were obtained, and in view of their cost – £238 –

71

they must have been in metal or finely-decorated glazed ware. Garden seats were made by a joiner, and carved stone ones by Edward Pierce. The garden was enclosed by walls on the south and west sides, but it seems that the park paling to the east was left in place. A kitchen garden was made to the west of the paddock with walls and a pumping system, and the gardeners' houses were repaired.

George London also provided a collection of greens from the Brompton Park Nursery, which was not far away. A visitor to several London gardens in December 1691 wrote:

> *Kensington* Gardens are not great nor abounding with fine plants. The orange, lemon, myrtles, and what other trees they had there in summer, were all removed to Mr. London's and Mr. Wise's greenhouse at Brompton Park, a little mile from them. But the walks and grass are laid very fine, and they were digging up a flat of four or five acres to enlarge their garden.

As later views and drawings show, the new gardens at Kensington were a collection of elaborate unsymmetric *parterres* and wildernesses which, although smaller, were even more intricate than any *bosquets* at Versailles. The private approach to the southern steps was soon modified in favour of a more public one from the Kensington Highway to the west gate of the great courtyard. The original intention to treat Kensington as a modest private villa seemed to have been overcome by William's and Mary's love of building and gardening. London's early gravelling and the alterations to the gardens thus cost £12,495, not including the salaries of the Royal Gardens officials.

The state of the Royal Gardens in 1696

Construction of these Royal Gardens was no longer at a feverish pitch by 1693. Expenditure had dropped, from the very high levels of over £20,000 per annum during the period from 1689 to 1691, to about £4,000 per annum. When Mary died in December 1694 her gardens were thus nearly complete, though it might be said that their *genius loci* had fled. New gardening projects then ceased altogether, and without Mary's devotion to her plant collection this went into a decline. As for William, he was heavily committed to his struggle with Louis XIV in the middle years of the 1690s, and showed little interest in further improvements to his palaces while this was the case.

It was time to reckon up. The total expenditure on the Royal Gardens from 1689 to 25 March 1696, it was calculated, amounted to about £83,000. Over three-quarters was attributable to Hampton Court.

The gardens were now under steady maintenance, and small contracts with working gardeners at Hampton Court began from midsummer 1693. Hendrik Quellenburg had a gang working in the Privy Garden and Upper Orangery, whilst Samuel van Staden looked after the grove by the Wilderness; from midsummer 1695 each took on additional areas. Caspar Gamperle began in midsummer 1693 to contract for providing materials and keeping the fires going at the stoves, and also added further areas two years later. Grass and gravel was maintained by Tilleman Bobart, a brother of Jacob Bobart, the keeper of the Oxford Physic Garden. He may have been a foreman organising casual labour under Quellenburg, and it looks as if the Great Parterre was Bobart's responsibility.

The staffing at Hampton Court and Kensington was recorded by the Royal Garden administration on 19 March 1696. At Kensington the incredibly intricate *parterre* and wilderness was contributing to a huge complement of 72 staff. Henrich Timmerman the head gardener required a staff of 40 men and 10 women to keep them. Meanwhile another head gardener, William Kirke, looked after the kitchen gardens with 20 men and women. However nowhere quite surpassed Hampton Court:

workmen	Mr Quellenburg (Privy Garden)	Mr van Staden (Wilderness)	Mr Gamperle (hothouses)	Mr Bobart (grass & gravel)	miscellaneous	total
head gardener	1	1	1			3
foreman				1		1
board wage £15 p.a.	13	11	3			27
men at £14 p.a.	4	4	1			9
men at £9 p.a.	5	4	1			10
men at £7.5s.0d. p.a.	4	3	1			8
women at £5.17s.0d. p.a.				4		4
men at 2s. per day				3		3
men at 1s 8d. per day				3		3
men at 1s 6d. per day				4		4
women at 8d. per day	2 ½	2	½			5
bowling green keeper					1	1
rolling horse keeper					1	1
mole catcher					1	1
	29 ½	25	7 ½	15	3	80

The maintenance of the Royal Gardens was put on a new footing from April 1696. Instead of the various small contracts and other costs being passed to the Treasury, the Royal Gardens administration itself was to enter a contract with the Crown for maintaining all royal gardens. A royal warrant was signed authorising £4,800 per annum to be paid to the Earl of Portland. Out of this all wages, materials, tools and other charges were to be paid, including the officers' salaries amounting to £500. Portland's £200 sinecure was to remain as a separate payment. A few years later, money paid under the contract was being divided thus:

item	allowance per annum
Hampton Court	£1623.4s.0d.
Kensington	£1129.0s.0d.
'The Royal Gardens', St James's	£525.10s.0d.
St James's House Garden	£91.5s.0d.
Richmond	£75.0s.0d.
Windsor	£25.0s.0d.
officers' salaries	£500.0s.0d.
artisans	£831.1s.0d.
	£4800.0s.0d

Since there were 74 acres of Royal Gardens, an average cost per acre was £67.11s.0d. if the sinecure and salaries are included. Of this the Hampton Court gardens alone accounted for 47 per cent of the cost and, at 46 acres, were 62 per cent of the total area, though Kensington, with only 17 acres, was more expensive *pro rata*.

Gardens of the Court

4.6 Bulstrode, in Buckinghamshire, plates 43–44 by Willson and Bowles in *Vitruvius Britannicus*, Vol. IV (1739)

4.7 *Opposite*: Powis Castle, in Montgomeryshire, by Nathaniel Buck (1742), showing the terracing said to be in imitation of that at Saint Germain-en-Laye

During the early- and mid-1690s the English Court was making gardens as feverishly as it had in the 1680s, though the gardening activity of William's Dutch friends seemed rather muted. The closest, Portland, leased the house that Judge Jeffreys had built in 1686 at Bulstrode, in Buckinghamshire, together with some land. South of the main garden front he made a *parterre* and sunken orangery garden. In the awkwardly-shaped field to the west he laid out a series of hedged compartments with pools leading to a cross-canal. The most remarkable feature of the gardens, though, was the rather idiosyncratic winding of paths in the wilderness, seemingly resulting from adapting the layout to the coppice wood he found there. All this is reminiscent of Zorgvliet, and suggests that Portland regarded Bulstrode, too, as a private retreat, rather than his great house.

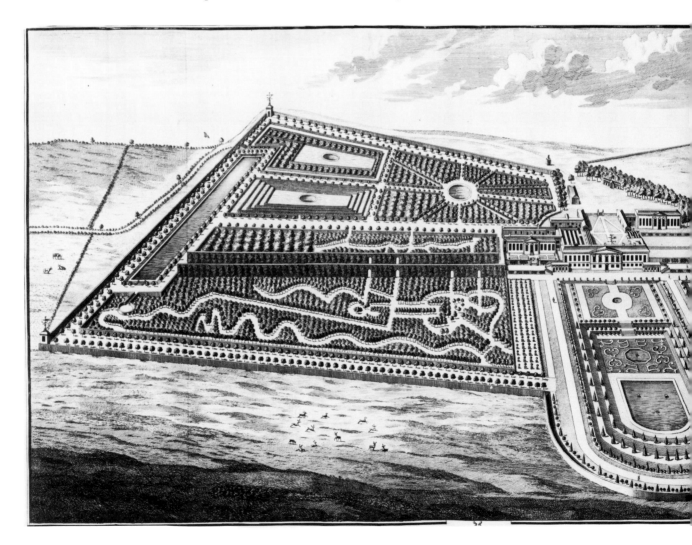

Another Dutch member of the English Court was Willem Hendrik van Nassau, Lord of Zuylestein, a cousin of William's. He accompanied William to Britain in 1689, and soon became an English lieutenant-general. In May 1695 he was made Earl of Rochford and granted part of the estates of the Marquis of Powis. Powis had followed James II to France and was prominent in the exiled Court at Saint Germain-en-Laye, being created Duke of Powis. For these pains he was outlawed in Britain and it was ordered that his estates be confiscated. However it seems as though he had managed to convey them to trustees, and Rochford never took possession. The closest he came to doing so was a visit to the Powis estates when he wrote 'the formal gardens have been greatly extended and filled with waterworks, in imitation of the wretched taste of St Germain-en-Laye'.

What Rochford saw was the upper flagged terrace made by William Winde prior to 1684, to which Winde had added two lower ones and the waterworks in 1697, after they were supposed to have been granted to Rochford. The Jacobite duke's son, reduced in British eyes to the title of Viscount Montgomery, though evidently not so much in his estate, had been continuing the work after his father's death in 1696, apparently confident that Rochford's claim could not be upheld. The central third of the terraces was treated architecturally, with arcades, balustrades, blank windows and an orangery, combined with a series of steps. The remark that the design was in imitation of the terraces at Saint Germain-en-Laye had some justification, although the whole design was very much smaller. Perhaps, though, all terraced gardens looked the same to a man who, despite an English mother and an English wife, cherished his own gardens in the Netherlands made on polderland.

Neither Hampton Court nor Kensington could have been moulded to the ideal form of the garden that London had been able to impose at Longleat and Burghley. After the rush on these schemes was over he was being kept busy by much of the nobility and gentry at such places as Castle Bromwich Hall, the upper garden at Kirby Hall and the terraces at Petworth. Just about

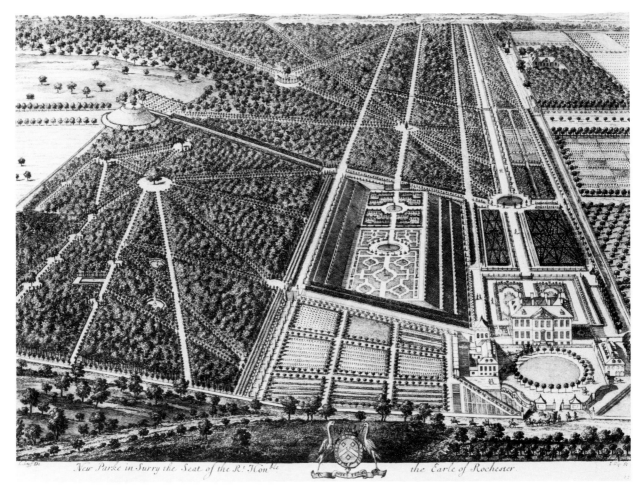

New Parke in Surry the Seat of the R.t Hon.ble   the Earle of Rochester

4.8 New Park, in Surrey, from Knyff and Kip *Britannia Illustrata* (1707). The woodland garden on the steep slope on the left was admired by a follower of Joseph Addison

everywhere London went he once again found that he was altering old gardens, and contending with irrationality and irregularity; he needed to bend his ideas on design. Hence it was that while the gardens of the Netherlands, Germany and Austria continued to follow the Mollet ideal, those with which London was concerned in the 1690s showed a remarkable disregard for it.

At New Park – in other words Richmond New Park, in Surrey – a new house was made for the ranger by the royal master carpenter from 1693. The ranger was Mary's uncle, Lawrence Hyde, the Earl of Rochester, who was the old Earl of Clarendon's second son. The garden layout was very probably London's. The view from the back of the house was traditional enough: a sunken *parterre* garden, beyond which were wildernesses in hornbeam with criss-cross paths, then a circular bason with fountain, and then an avenue to a far corner of the park. However, the striking feature of the layout was the gardens to the side of the house which were so cleverly adapted to the hill that rose steeply to the King's Standing at the highest point of the park.

The lines of the garden were parallel to the contours. On the service side of the house extended a nine-part kitchen and fruit garden, and then, most spectacular of all, halfway up the hill a deep excavation gave a huge terraced platform with a triple *glacis* (shaven, battered uniform slopes) below and double above. Here were two elaborate *parterres*. The whole hill above was converted into a forest garden with walks lined with low hedges. Some of the majestic pollards inherited from the common before the enclosure of the park in the 1630s were set in their own cabinets, and joined by these walks. At the spring line other cabinets sparkled with pools of water and low fountains. The concavity of the hill made the King's Standing a *point d'appui*, or point of view, from which the whole garden hung like a pendant. It was a bold and innovative layout for a difficult site, a forest garden but departing from Cassiobury, by being more empirical in the detail.

Lord Cholmondeley's great gardens at Cholmondeley Hall, Cheshire, were being laid out under London's supervision through the 1690s. London adapted and enlarged an old moated garden empirically, declining to readjust boundaries for the sake of balance and symmetry. The main garden axis is not related to the house at all. It all looks as if it has been assembled like patchwork. This is despite finding the old team here: Tijou making iron gates and Nost making sculpture, as if taken over from Chatsworth. The fruit garden and canal were made in 1693. To one side of the moat was a *parterre*, the orangery garden and the bowling green. Beyond all this was the incredible kitchen garden measuring 450 by 800 ft with 40 compartments, almost as grand as the *potager* at Versailles.

Following the Peace of Rijswijk

Following the treaty that concluded the Nine Years' War, signed in October 1697 at the Rijswijk Palace, the Earl of Portland went to Versailles as William's ambassador to Louis XIV. Taking his duties as Superintendent of

4.9 Cholmondeley, in Cheshire, plates 79–80 by H. Hulsbergh in *Vitruvius Britannicus*, Vol. III (1725)

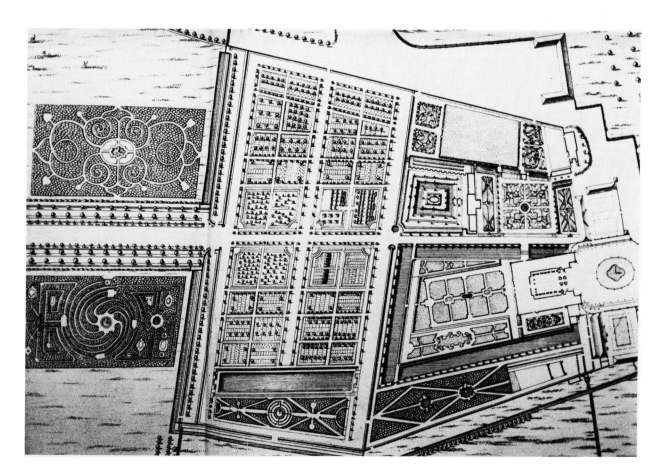

Village

the Royal Gardens seriously, he took George London with him. Between January and June 1698 they saw many of the great gardens of France and, at the *potager* at Versailles, London met De la Quintinye. Portland took the opportunity to ask Le Nôtre for designs for a refurbishment of the Maestricht Garden at Windsor, which he received in June. However Le Nôtre was much too old and feeble to travel to England himself, and sent instead his nephew, Claude Desgots, who accompanied George London on his return. They visited Windsor together in July, and Desgots produced an elaborate design. He also produced designs for Greenwich and Het Loo.

The boldness of the French layouts that London had seen were perhaps reflected later, in 1698, in his suggestions to Charles Howard, third Earl of Carlisle, for Castle Howard, in Yorkshire. Although Talman was displaced by John Vanbrugh, London seems to have continued, even though his initial ideas for a star of walks, as at Longleat, to convert Wray Wood to a wilderness were modified to something like New Park; at least it was here that Stephen Switzer was working as London's 'man', and later eulogised 'his Lordship's superlative genius' in the irregular layout of Wray Wood.

A more modest scheme starting in 1698 was one for William Blathwayt. No doubt Blathwayt's command of the Dutch language, acquired when he was Sir William Temple's secretary from 1668 to 1672, had early brought him to the king's attention. Blathwayt purchased the position as Secretary of War in 1683, and continued this under William, accompanying him to the Netherlands on many occasions. By 1698 Blathwayt had the money to build a new east front and garden at his country house, Dyrham, in Gloucestershire. He turned to the dominant personality in the Office of Works, William Talman, and to the royal gardener, George London. Their other commitments prevented London and Talman from visiting very often, and they designed and supervised Blathwayt's improvements from long range. The stables were constructed on the instructions of Talman's foreman in 1698, but it was the spring of 1700 before Talman's east front went up. The orangery, which was unusual in that it was attached to the house, was erected the following year.

However, the gardens were already well advanced, with the head gardener taking instructions from London whenever he was at Longleat. The house was at the entrance to a coombe in the Cotswold hills, down which a stream ran from a powerful spring at the top end of the park. This situation had two implications. The water gave great opportunities for cascades and fountains, while needing to be culverted past the house. Second, the sloping land of the coombe required extensive levelling if the intended *parterres* and canal at the back of the house were to be made. This was evidently time consuming and expensive for as early as 1698 Blathwayt was writing: 'When will this levelling be at an end?' Next year the *parterres* and waterworks were probably under construction, and lime avenues were planted in the park in the winter of 1699/1700. The completing touches on the fountains and stonework in the garden had to wait till 1704, after the construction of house and orangery.

In December 1700 a relative of Blathwayt's saw the uncompleted waterworks.

> Having past thro the house into the gardens you see on the Right Hand three fountains one above another with a Good Body & Height of Water/ and before you on the top of the Hill about 50 foot High another throwing a good Body of water about 20 foot high/ and under is a large Cataract of water descending the whole hill and coming underground to

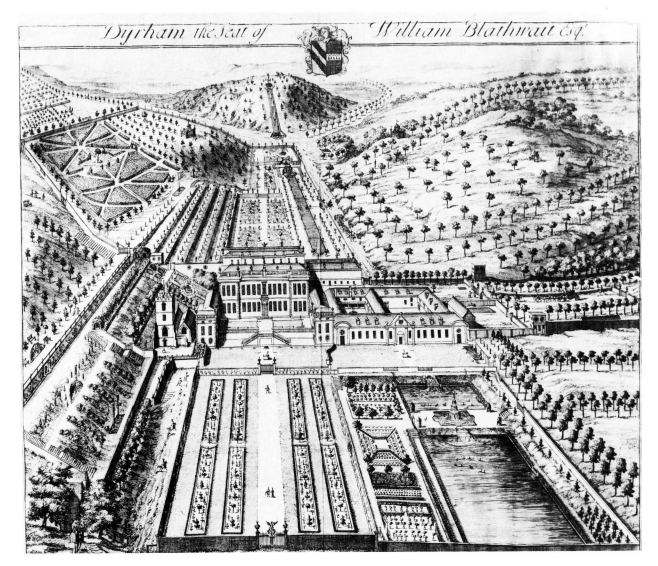

Dyrham the Seat of   *William Blathwait Esq.*

4.10 *Previous page:*
Windsor Castle, copy of a
design by Claude Desgots.
Desgots visited some of the
royal palaces in 1698
instead of Le Nôtre to give
designs, but none were
executed

4.11 Dyrham, from
Atkyns's *Gloucestershire*
(1712), showing the second
finest cascade in England

the Parterre, rising again in a large Fountain to a very Great Height. . ./ &
thence by Three large Basins falls into a large oval from whence it runs
into the Canal. . ./ the whole Disposition of the garden consisting chiefly
in walks and Terraces.

The cataract, or cascade, had 224 steps, thought to be second only to that
at Chatsworth.

Twickenham Park, the seat of the Earl of Albemarle, and William's gift in
1698 to his favourite, was situated on the meadows across the Thames from
Richmond Palace. It had been given some fine gardens after 1610, and
already had an avenue stretching away from the main front of the house
when Albemarle took possession. Whether William thought that Albemarle
would be able to indulge his gardening taste here, as at De Voorst, and as he,
William, was planning to do at Windsor, very little information survives to
inform us. Probably, though, Albemarle confined himself to strengthening
the avenue by further planting and made a wilderness.

5. Het Loo from the air in 1987. The gardens were substantially restored in the early 1980s to their form in William and Mary's time

6. Levens, photograph of topiary. The original symmetry can be discerned, even though the plants have in the past been allowed to grow out

7. Powis Castle, photographed from the south, showing the remaining terraces with the orangery

Finishing Hampton Court

William himself made no positive move to improve his English palaces for over 18 months after the Peace of Rijswijk. At last, though, in mid-1699 William decided to pursue improvements to Hampton Court which soon became almost as expensive as those of 1689 to 1691. It is difficult to ascertain whose designs were being followed in the new scheme of works. London remained Deputy Superintendent of the Royal Gardens, and so one might expect that his ideas prevailed. However, no sooner were the new works fully underway than Talman took control in his capacity as Comptroller of Works. Maybe, though, this shift in leadership did not affect design intentions, because of Talman's and London's close association. What seems certain, though, is that in 1699 to 1702 Henry Wise was at first acting simply as a contractor.

Some of the new schemes had been planned in 1689/90, but had remained unfulfilled. Amongst these were the bason in the Great Avenue and the lengthening of the Privy Garden. However the largest works were newly devised schemes for providing extensive and highly polished walks along which members of the Court could stroll. When the Broad Walk and the Pavilion Terrace were completed it was possible to walk about a mile in the same direction, whilst the gardens' perimeter walling and railing made them quite secure.

Talman was soon employing Wise through the Office of Works although Wise was being directed by London. Planting of additional limes and horse

4.12 Hampton Court, design by William Talman for a Trianon-type retreat. This was probably prepared in 1698 when William III was considering what projects to pursue

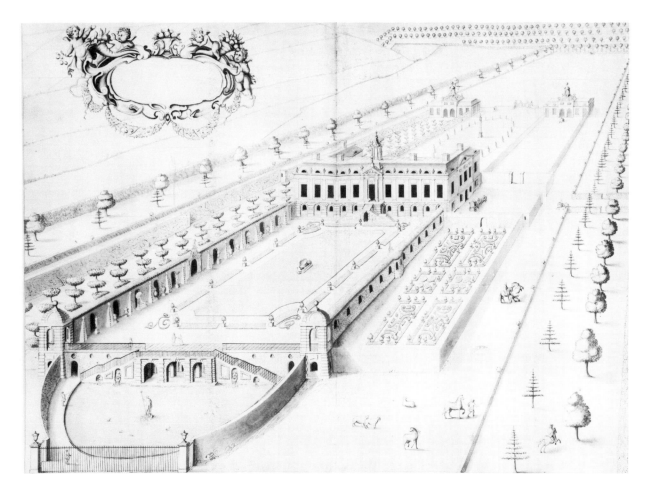

chestnuts inside the Great Avenue in Bushy Park began on 2 August 1699. In October, 5 ft high, triangular tree-guards were being erected and Wise was also employed to make a 60 ft wide roadway down the centre of the avenue and to surface it with gravel. Further, he made the bason of water. These works cost £4,934 after abatements of the contractors' rates. In order to keep the king informed, Talman had to write abroad to William Blathwayt. On 12 September 1699, he wrote that:

> Wee are making a Road of 60 ft. broad through the Middle Park and a Bason of 400 ft. diameter in the middle of the circle of trees, which will be very noble.

At the same time bricklayers' and masons' work commenced on a wall past the tennis court to Hampton Court Road which would match the terrace wall of the Privy Garden. There were also some works in the Privy Garden such as stone steps up onto the terraces, and gravelling and turfing in the Wilderness. These works were all that the Royal Gardens administration took direct charge of.

A programme of works for 1700 was required, and Talman submitted an estimate. Shortly thereafter Wise submitted his own, cheaper, estimate for similar works. The two major items were the Broad Walk across the east front of the palace, to be 39 ft wide and surfaced with 1 ft of gravel, and two levelled and enclosed 'divisions' alongside the Broad Walk. These divisions were to be made into parallel gravel walks, grass and beds edged with box; 168 evergreens were placed in the borders, about 80 of which were variegated holly and the rest yews. A low wall in which iron railings were to be set was built on the boundary of the two divisions with the park, and railings were placed on the wall and joined to those around the Great Parterre. Also the Longford River needed to be diverted out of the northern division into the park. Wise obtained approval for his scheme in February 1699/1700, and carried out his works by about June.

Talman was also carrying out works in the gardens through the Office of Works. One of these was a gate, later called the Flower Pot Gate after the charming figures by Nost on the piers, inserted at the end of the Broad Walk. However Talman found that his works cost over £10,000 instead of the £6,480 that had been estimated. Much of the reason for this was that William was demanding further improvements – in particular a terrace alongside the Thames and the lengthening of the Privy Garden – and completion faster than had been envisaged.

Richard Jones, Earl of Ranelagh, was appointed 'Sur-intendent generall of oure Buildings & of our works in our parks' on 22 June 1700 following Portland's resignation of his superintendency of the gardens. In July, Ranelagh was pressing the Works's officers to prepare an estimate for the terrace, and a few days later he was pressing them to demolish the old Water Gallery. On the last day of July the officers replied to Ranelagh that they were ready to pull down the Water Gallery, and would preserve many of the materials which could be of use either at the bowling green to be built at the east end of the terrace or at the Tudor tower off the Glass Case Garden, which was being expanded into a new banquetting house. On 25 September the officers could report to the Treasury that the banquetting house was nearly finished, and that the wall around the bowling green was being built.

Another unexpected drain on financial resources was the continuing failure of the fountains to function effectively. George London clearly regarded the fountains as a matter for early attention; new lead pipes and

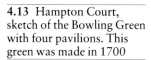

4.13 Hampton Court, sketch of the Bowling Green with four pavilions. This green was made in 1700

brass cocks for them were installed in the Fountain Garden and the fountains themselves were paved. In 1700 Robert Aldersey, an engineer, was called in to give advice. In 1701 he charged £400 for 'bringing the water more plentifully to Hampton Court', and he devised a system for raising water for the fountains. He agreed with Ranelagh and London to maintain the system for £200 per annum as from Christmas 1701.

In the latter part of 1700 Wise made further estimates which were approved and which he acted upon. These included making up the level of the new bowling green and turfing it. There were items for the earthworks for a new Lower Wilderness to be installed beyond the east end of the Long Water, planting an avenue east of the new bowling green, and the removal of 10,000 cu yds of soil from the Mount Garden preparatory to remodelling it as part of the Privy Garden.

Works progressed more slowly in 1701, and at one stage in September, William Blathwayt wrote from Het Loo on behalf of the king to the Treasury urging it to give Talman the money for works to proceed. The foundations were laid to the four pavilions at the new bowling green in April. The other major building work in the gardens this year was the 'new Glass Case', the large greenhouse which replaced three hothouses in the Glass Case Garden. There was also great activity concerning statuary and ironwork.

Wise's estimate for completing the Privy Garden was made in June. He estimated for removing the final 16,751 cu yds of soil from the Mount Garden, lengthening the western terrace in the Privy Garden and laying the gravel and grass of an entirely new design for the whole of the extended Privy Garden as a *parterre à l'Angloise* to replace the *gazon coupé*. The circle in grass at the lower end was a neat solution to a tapering space. It was surrounded by a half-circle of Tijou's twelve panels which at last had a resting place.

The *parterre à l'Angloise* was surrounded by 191 clipped yews and 60 variegated hollies, which, with those in the Great Parterre and others planted in the terrace, in the Glass Case Garden and along the Pavilion Terrace, brought the number of clipped evergreens in the gardens to over 800. The Dutchman, Johannes Kip, in his engravings for this period shows about another 140 yews under the transverse avenues. The number of clipped evergreens in the gardens at Hampton Court thus approached 1,000.

There was also trellis work. A domed arbour was incorporated by a carpenter into the wall between the Broad Walk and Hampton Court Road. This was oiled and painted an iron colour by Thomas Highmore, the painter. Louis la Guerre, Tijou's son-in-law, then decorated it. The small garden south-east of the new Banquetting House was transformed into the king's aviary, sometimes referred to as 'menagerie', the 'vollery ground', 'pheasant yard' or 'hen houses'. This consisted of a semicircle of cages at the broader end which would have contained a collection of exotic birds with clipped wings.

At William's death

The Maestricht Garden at Windsor, first mooted in 1680 by Charles II, was commenced, but to a design from the Office of Works, which was far simpler and more practical than Desgots's, and similar to the Lower Wilderness at Hampton Court. A canal at the centre would provide fill to raise the rest of it above the level of most floods. In 1701 Wise supplied forest trees and '238 Large Spruce Firrs that are Clipt and Shapt into a Pyramid Forme and 8 or 9 foot high' which he promised to clip 'once in a Sumer'. About this time the steep slope down from the castle to the garden was formed into three *glacis* but the canal does not seem to have been dug by the start of 1702.

At Kensington, William did not wait for the Old Ground, the orchard to the north, to revert to the Crown in 1705. He wanted this area to be a 30 acre wilderness. Henry Wise's 'trenching, new making and planting that part of Kensington garden that formerly was an old Orchard' began in September 1701, and by next March he had already planted 3,500 shrubs in 'a Plantation of Evergreene hedges and flowering Shrubbs in the Quarters' at a cost of £371.

William was riding in the House Park at Hampton Court in late February 1701/2, when his horse, Sorrel, threw him. The site of this accident is thought to have been at the Lower Wilderness. A broken collar bone became inflamed and contributed to William's death on 8 March. It is supposed that the horse had stumbled on a mole hill, giving rise to a new toast by the Jacobites – 'the little gentleman in black velvet'.

Mary's sister, Anne, thus became queen. At one point during the ensuing scramble for positions, Anne went to a meeting of the Lords of the Treasury in a mood 'to restrain the expense of the Gardens'. Unfortunately for George London, he chose this meeting to submit his petition for arrears to the

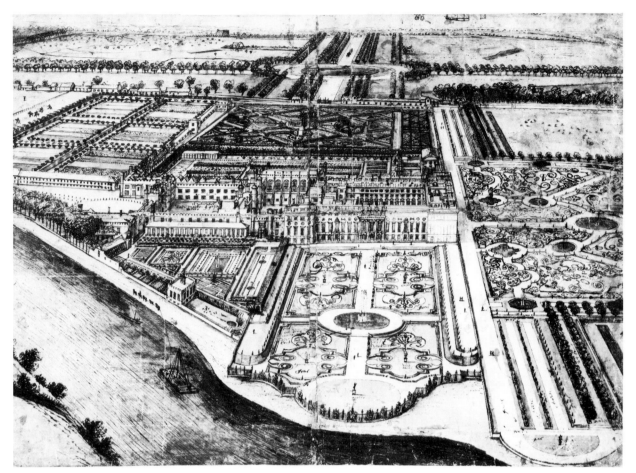

gardeners in the Royal Gardens. London went the same way as the bills, and Henry Wise was called to the next meeting. He told the Treasury that the Royal Gardens could be maintained for £1,600 instead of £4,800, was thereupon appointed the new Royal Gardener as from 1 August 1702. Work at Windsor ceased, uncompleted, and a few minor projects at Hampton Court were abandoned. However, at Kensington, Wise's duties included 'the old Ground as now made and when finished to be kept in Good Order', and it seems that he did finish the wilderness because substantial further amounts were spent.

Anne was ruthless with other petitioners besides London. Robert Balle, a merchant, had obtained £555 worth of statuary for Hampton Court at William's request. He was told 'he may have the statues again'. Jean Tijou petitioned for £1,889 of arrears, but was refused. Tilleman Bobart was still petitioning in 1707 for wages incurred in 1698, and the son of the plumber who had installed the fountain pipework recovered some of the arrears owing to his father only when the pipes were dug up in 1708.

Anne's husband, Prince George of Denmark, must have called upon the services of Leonard Knyff, for Knyff wrote to another patron on 9 January 1701/2 that 'I have done a great many (drawings) of Hampton Courte and Windsor for his Highness which are not yett engraved. I not being payd for them.' However several were engraved, and at least one each of Hampton Court and Windsor was painted, forming a stunning record of the virtually completed gardens.

4.14 Hampton Court, bird's-eye-view from the south by Leonard Knyff (c. 1702). To the left of the privy garden were an orchard, the orangery garden, the auricula garden, the flower garden and the remaining tropical hothouse. The garden adjacent to the banquetting house was the *volière*, or bird garden

5

Perspectives on
the `Dutch´ Garden

Contemporary observers of Dutch gardens

Curiously, most travellers' accounts of Dutch gardens were by foreigners. John Evelyn not only wrote about British, French and Italian gardens, but in 1641 was in Rotterdam where he first saw an elephant and a pelican, and then in Leiden relishing his visit to the *Hortus*, or 'garden of simples', and was delighted to be presented with a register of the contents by the gardener. At Amsterdam and other towns he admired the carefully laid-out streets 'especially, being so frequently planted and shaded with the beautiful lime trees which are set in rowes before every mans house, affording a very ravishing prospect', and appreciated 'the delicious walkes planted with Lime-trees' at the palace of Rijswijk. Honselaarsdijk was another goal, as it was for most visitors, for example Cosimo III de Medici, Grand Duke of Tuscany, who noticed William's early garden improvements in June 1669.

One native Dutchman, Jacob de Hennin, has left a journal of 1680. He described the mathematical layout of Honselaarsdijk:

> Look at all the beautiful *parterres* and flower beds and see how free and smooth everything is, how the curving hedges sway and how gailey they are interwoven, how perfectly everything is clipped and looked after and how a carpet of a hundred scented flowers grow there.

He then went on to describe the flowers he saw: cinnamon, musk, violets, carnations, lupins, African violets, *Anemones*, lilac, cyclamen and many orangery plants and fruit bushes.

De Hennin also described the gardens at the Noordeinde Palace that had been used by Amalia von Solms as a winter palace till her death in 1675. The Princess's Garden had two painted garden houses, designed for the princely couple's relaxation, and many clipped hedges, fruit bushes and a pond. However De Hennin preferred the garden next to the house with its *parterre*, and named many of the flowers he saw there. Among the flowers collected by Amalia herself were *Anemones*, *Ranunculi*, hyacinths, *Narcissi* and fritillaries, while elsewhere in the garden *Campanulas* and sunflowers bloomed. He described how he found orange trees, lemon trees, myrtles and pomegranates in pots, while a banana tree also caught his attention.

Nicodemus Tessin was thought so well of when he visited the Netherlands in 1687 that he was received by William and Mary at Honselaarsdijk. He observed several of the great gardens of the Netherlands, running his eye over the main points of the layout: for example, as in this snippet on Soestdijk:

> Beyond the entrance, to the right of the neat stone-paved courtyard were the stables with the coach houses and offices on the left hand side. Huge oaks stood on the paved courtyard. One could enter the garden from the three sides of the house. On both sides lie *parterres* adorned with fruit trees.

Tessin also admired the country house of Philips Doublet, who beautified the gardens of Clingendaal. Tessin tells how the house is small and the garden, although it has no fountains, has lovely parterres; these consisted of *broderie* patterns completely filled with box while flowers filled the *plates-bandes* placed around them. On the garden axis beautifully-clipped hornbeam hedges led to 'surprises' such as the large pond, statues and a labyrinth.

Walter Harris, who was William III's physician from soon after the revolution, was another keen observer. He was with the king on his campaigns in Flanders where he learned of William's gardening enthusiasms and had 'frequent Opportunities' for visiting Het Loo with him. Mary had to stay in England, and so could not see the improvements that William was making to her beloved Het Loo. At Mary's request Harris therefore wrote a detailed and enthusiastic description of the gardens as they were in 1694 after the alterations. However, before this could be delivered to her she died of smallpox, in fact with Harris in attendance. In 1699 he published his illustrated *Description of the King's Royal Palace and Gardens at Het Loo*, in the hope that

> . . . the Reading it might give some Diversion to the Curious, as the Writing was pleasing to me. Also *Persons* of *Quality*, and Great Fortunes, may here find many things to *Admire*, and also to *Imitate*, if they please, when they are taking their Summer Diversions at their Country Seats.

Walter Harris commends the new awareness of Wren and other architects that 'Buildings, however Noble and Great, do appear very deficient without the Ornament and Conveniences of a Garden'. His summation of those at Het Loo was:

> These *Gardens* in the whole are a Work of wonderful *Magnificence*, most worthy of so *Great* a *Monarch*; a Work of prodigious expence, infinite variety, and curiosity; and after nine years labour by abundance of Workmen they were some years ago intirely finished, and brought to perfection in all respects.

Accompanying William on his visit to the Netherlands in 1696 was Edward Southwell, who made a tour with William Blathwayt and left an interesting account of Het Loo, Dieren, Middachten, De Voorst and other places. For example he described Het Loo as 'at first design'd noe more than a small hunting Seat', so that the 'vast Pile' he saw had

> . . . noe great apartments, nor are the Roofs high. . . But whatever is wanting in the House, is fully made up in the gardens. The Tarrasses are noble, the Parterres very fine, and there is great Plenty of water, which Supplys the Fountains all day long. . . The great Fountain throws up water 50 feet high, & the beauty of It may be estimated by the charge which some talk of to be near £30,000.

The flavour of Portland's gardens at Zorgvliet was given by two more Englishmen. In 1696 Richard Chiswell thought rather ungenerously that 'the garden, for the green House, Forreigne Plants and other Curiousitys in that Art is counted one of the best in these parts, but compared with the Duke of Beauforts at Badminton and severall others in England, it ought not to be mentioned'. On the other hand, Persons, in 1690, recalled:

> Delicate Gardens, Walks, Ponds, Motes, Grottoes, Fountaines and figures, Bridges and gates, and great Plenty of fruit and flowers very Curious and various. . . A place so neatly composed that here Art and Nature seem to go 'hand in Hand'.

When Portland went to France in 1698 as William's ambassador, he related back to the king information on the state of the French parks and gardens. He must have been vastly impressed, but it was a matter of pride to find at least some faults. He described the deplorable situation with the water supply in the garden of Versailles where the fountains were not working because of the cutting off of the water supply. The orangery trees there 'are extremely beautiful and large and numerous, the trunks fine and high, but the heads not like those at Honselaarsdijk. . .' To Portland it was amazing that while colossal sums were spent on these gardens, they were left untouched in winter: 'Of all the thousands of flowers of which your Majesty has heard so much, that the flower gardens were full of them all seasons, I have not seen a single one, not even a snowdrop.'

Celia Fiennes and other observers of English gardens

England had its own, comparatively modest, but more prolific, observer. We must turn to the pages of Celia Fiennes's journals for the true impression that gardens in the reign of William and Mary made on the average traveller. She was the granddaughter of the first Viscount Saye and Sele of Broughton Castle, near Banbury, in Oxfordshire. The Parliamentary conduct of the Civil War, in which her grandfather, 'Old Subtlety', had played a leading role, had virtually been planned at Broughton, and her family were enthusiastic supporters of the Glorious Revolution which finally ended the Catholic sympathies of the Crown. Celia Fiennes was present at the coronation of William and Mary and for 'our Hero King William III's' triumphal entry into London after the Peace of Rijswijk in 1697.

Celia Fiennes took a particular pleasure in visiting Oxford in 1694 as it was her grandfather who had occupied the Civil War royalist capital when Charles I withdrew. As 'Founder's Kin' he had been a Fellow of New College and his granddaughter inspected the college with a patronising air. The Fellows obviously enjoyed garden curiosities and moveable potted plants:

> They take much delight in greens of all sorts Myrtle Orange and Lemons and Lorrestine growing in pots of earth, and so moved about from place to place and in the aire sometymes; ther are severall New Lodgings added and beautifyed here, the gardens also with gravell and grass walkes, shady, and a great mount in the middle which is ascended by degrees in a round of green paths defended by greens cutt low, and on top is a Summer house, beyond these gardens is a bowling-green, and round it a close shady walke, walled round and a cutt hedge to the bowling green.

Celia Fiennes made many journeys, compiling a series of journals during her lifetime with her impressions and observations. Her journeys totalled 3,000 miles, made almost entirely on horseback. She had an eye for the new building and gardening that were taking place in William's new reign and admired the enfilade arrangement of house and garden with 'through glides and vistos'. She dismisses the rather simple, though terraced, gardens at Haddon Hall, which in spite of having 'a very fine Grove of high trees and good Gardens', could show 'nothing very curious as the mode now is'.

The new elements that Celia Fiennes admired in gardens like Newby Hall or Burghley House were the statues, cut-work hedges, stilted and dwarfed trees, the florists' flowers, exotic plants in pots, box labyrinths, avenues of Scots, Norway and silver firs, and 'grates to look through', which enabled a traveller to 'discover the curiosities' within the gardens. Uppark, in Sussex, had just been built for Lord Tankerville, a prominent Whig who already had 'fine gardens, gravell and grass walks and bowling green, with breast walls divideing each from other'. She was clearly amused by joke fountains such as those in the Wilton grotto where hidden pipes and sluices spout up to wet unwary visitors. Sometimes, as at Euston Hall, there was a canal.

'Old Subtlety's' granddaughter took particular pleasure in inspecting the gardens belonging to her numerous relatives. Her grandmother had been Elizabeth Temple and when she visited Stowe she found Sir Richard Temple was just setting out new gardens. She enjoyed walking onto the balcony from the great parlour and viewing the gardens below 'with low breast walls and terras walkes. . . replenished with all the curiosityes or requisites for ornamental pleasure and use'.

Another relative's garden was also in the making, that of St John St Barbe of Broadlands, in Hampshire. Having entered through the blue iron gates and being shown the house she went out into the walled gardens,

> . . . some with brest walls some higher with flower potts on them, severall places with open grates to look through with stone balls or figures. . . a water house that by a wheele casts up the water out of the River. . . to fill the bason designed in the middle of the Garden with a Spout in the middle.

Celia Fiennes gives the historian much detail about the contents of *parterres* and fruit gardens. The main garden was usually divided by gravel paths into four grass plots in the centre of which were a brass or stone statue or some 'dwarfes or Cyprus firs'. At the grand places she saw, such as Chatsworth and Wilton, there would be an ornate fountain at the intersection of the paths, or as at Lowther '4 little Cupids or little boys in each corner of the 4 squares'. At Newby Hall there was one large brass statue and four smaller ones in each of the four quarters. In the Privy Garden at Hampton Court she noticed that the grass plots were 'cutt into flower deluces [*fleur de lys*] and severall devices, with paths of gravell, borders of mould in which are greens of all sorts'.

In most places the flowers were to be found in knots, borders or compartments in a separate hedged flower garden and here she saw 'perpetualls as well as annualls' and singles out for special mention 'fine strip'd stocks double like a rose' and 'white and yellow tuber roses' and 'honeysuckles in a round tuft growing upright'. Orange trees were increasingly to be seen, and Celia Fiennes reported that it was at Braemore, in Hampshire, that she found the 'first oring trees I ever saw' on an early journey from her home at Newton Toney.

Fine fruit particularly pleased Celia Fiennes. At Woburn, having admired the topiary beasts she indulged herself in 'a great quantity of the red carolina gooseberry' and when she went into the cherry orchard she was surprised by what was presumably meant as a birdscarer, 'a figure of stone resembling an old weeder woman. . . and my Lord would have her Effigie which is done like so like and her clothes so well that at first I tooke it to be a real living body'. The orchards in which she walked and sampled apricots, peaches, plums and nectarines often had borders of flowers along the gravel paths. She particularly comments when the fruit trees were 'well-dressed and pruned' and 'nail'd neate' to the walls. She noted that at Basing House the Duke of Bolton was using the derelict gardens of the castle slighted by Cromwell for fruit growing.

At Wolseley, in Staffordshire, yet another relative's house, in a walk named after her mother she ate 'a sort of flatt strawberry like a button which grew on a second crop from the same strawberry's roote which produceth its first crop'. She liked to see 'ornament and use' when 'dwarfe fruit trees and flowers and greenes in all shapes' were intermixed with her favourite strawberries. At Tregothan in Cornwall another relation of hers, Mrs Boscowen, actually used 'gooseberry and shrub trees' as the grass plot features of her main garden near the house.

Celia Fiennes encountered various evergreens used in topiary work: yew, Dutch box, *Phillyrea*, bay, myrtle, laurustinus and *Pyracantha*. She sometimes mentioned that laurel or *Phillyrea* was striped and it is apparent that cut-work gardens were not unrelieved green. There was much variation in colour made by obelisks and globes of gold and silver hollies against dark yew panels, arches and columns, and there was also a variety of shapes. At Mr Chetwynd's at Ingestre, in Staffordshire, she admired 14 tall cunningly-shaped cypresses 'kept cutt close in four squares down to the bottom, towards the top enclined to a point or spire', and at Hampton Court they had 'greens of all sorts, piramids and then round interchangeable'.

The general critical reaction to Hampton Court was very favourable. *Magna Britannia* said that:

> The Gardens are improved to a wonderful degree, not only in the Walks, both open and close, and in the great Variety of Topiary Works, but with the Green-houses too, which have stoves under them, so artificially contrived, that all foreign Plants are here preserved in gradual Heats, suitable to the Climes of their respective Countries, where they naturally grow, and from whence they are brought. In fine, the whole seems to be designed with so much Magnificence, that when 'tis finished, it will equal, if not excel, all the noblest Palaces in the World.

Another lady commentator, later to be the Duchess of Chandos, was Cassandra, daughter of Francis Willoughby of Wollaton Hall, in Nottinghamshire. Willoughby was a friend of the botanist John Ray and a great collector of 'phisicall plants', and Cassandra noted the physic garden and that the advice of 'Mr Prat, who had made the Physic Garden at Chelsea' had been sought. This was the Richard Pratt, the first salaried gardener of the Society of Apothecaries, of whom a member remarked in 1679/80 that he 'hath given a Cattalouge of 1200 Plaints & well understands Exoticks & natives &c & the Garden allready is well plainted. . . hee hath made itt a Garden of a heape of Rubbish and Gravell' within two years. Cassandra was also a keen observer of Badminton, Bretby, Cliveden, Haddon Hall, Melbourne, Newby Hall, Wilton and Wrest Park.

Daniel Defoe claimed 'to have had the honour to attend her majesty, when she first viewed the ground,' for enlarging the gardens at Kensington. He thus spoke of the 'exceeding fine gardens, being now made' with greater satisfaction. In the first edition (1724) of his *A Tour through the Whole Island of Great Britain*, Defoe gave a lengthy description of Hampton Court. He noticed the orange trees and Dutch bays in the orangery, and the vases by Cibber and Pierce outside, and later he noticed the 'fine Scrolls and Bordure of these Gardens at first edg'd with Box'. To the north of the palace he saw that the old Orchard 'is very happily cast into a Wilderness, with a Labyrinth, and Espaliers so high. . . well design'd, and compleatly finish'd, but is perfectly well kept, and the Espaliers fill'd exactly, at Bottom to the very Ground'. Defoe pointed to the evergreens in which the king delighted 'as the greatest addition to the beauty of a garden, preserving the figure in the place even in the roughest part of an inclement and tempestuous winter'.

The topographical artists

By good chance Celia Fiennes's and Daniel Defoe's accounts were made at a time when country houses and other establishments, notably the colleges of Oxford and Cambridge, were increasingly being recorded in the form of paintings, drawings and engraved views. In particular it was a period during which the bird's-eye-view technique was much in favour and was being applied not only to buildings but also to their surrounding gardens and grounds. The great advantage of this technique is that the resulting view is like a three-dimensional map giving a very clear idea of the physical reality of the garden.

The most popular artist to supply such prospects in post-Restoration times was Hendrik Danckerts, from Holland. He is first heard of in England when five prospects were ordered from him by Sir Roger Pratt in 1666. Samuel Pepys also ordered prospects of four royal palaces in 1669, and in 1674 an accountant paid this 'Picture Drawer for sevll prospect Pictures made and sold by him for his Majesty's service at the Dutchess of Cleveland's Lodgings at Hampton Court', one of which must have been that of the Long Water. However, Danckerts also did more expensive single views, such as that of Ham House in 1675 and the drawing of Badminton.

Danckerts died in 1679 by which time other good foreign draughtsmen had been attracted to England. David Loggan, who came originally from Danzig, in Poland, was appointed Engraver to Oxford University in 1669. His *Oxonia Illustrata* was published, presumably by subscription, in 1675 and *Cantabrigia Illustrata* followed in 1685. The first contains a remarkable series of bird's-eye-views of the Oxford colleges and their gardens and grounds, the second is an equally remarkable series showing the colleges of Cambridge. In both of these sets we see the grounds of long-established residential institutions. In the hands of a master like David Loggan one receives a vivid impression of what it was actually like to be in them. Here amongst the masters' gardens, the Fellows' gardens, the communal courts and walks can be seen a pattern of gardening, the origins of which in all probability go back into the previous century and before. It is a type of gardening which can be understood by reference to books such as William Lawson's *New Orchard and Garden* which was first published in 1618. Loggan's views perhaps also provide us with a picture of the type of gardening that was prevalent amongst the majority of gardens in the seventeenth century.

In 1673 two more fine Dutch oil painters arrived. Jacob Knyff, the brother of Leonard, was from Haarlem, and before his premature death in 1681 had carried out several commissions, for example of Durdans in 1673 and Berkeley Castle about 1676 for the Earl of Berkeley. Jan Siberechts arrived from Antwerp and over the next 30 years carried out numerous commissions, including those showing Badminton in 1675 and 1678, Richmond Hill in 1677, Cheveley in 1681, Bretby in 1684, Bifrons and Bayhall in the 1680s and Wollaton in 1697.

A native Englishman trained in the Office of Works, Henry Winstanley, should be mentioned. His engravings of Audley End in 1676 and Wimbledon in 1678 perhaps gave him courage to produce an advertisement:

> All Noble men and Gentlemen that please to have their Mansion Houses design'd on Copper Plates, to be printed for composeing a volume of ye Prospects of ye Principall Houses of England: May have them done by Mr. Hen: Winstanley, by way of subscription. . .

The plate he made for the advertisement showed his own house at Littlebury, in Essex, where he resided as Clerk of Works at Audley End. However, Winstanley never pursued the idea of the volume of prospects and he is best known as the designer of the Eddystone Lighthouse who perished with it in the great storm of 1703.

Sets of engravings that did proceed, and in the well-established tradition of Dutch eye-level views, include those of Longford Castle by Robert Thacker, and those by Michael Burghers, another Dutchman, that were included in the county history of Staffordshire of 1686. Home-grown talent for engraving during the early 1690s sunk to very low levels with Sutton Nichols's two views of Hampton Court.

However, at this time, Leonard Knyff became naturalised, and by 1697 he began his ambitious project of an engraved set of views of England's great houses. This began life as a private subscription series, with each subscriber due to receive two copies of the 100 projected views. By December 1702 only 69 of the plates had been engraved, and in January the following year Knyff made his complaint about non-payment by Prince George. It is doubtful that the series was completed. Eventually in 1707 some 78 of Knyff's views were published in book form under the title *Britannia Illustrata* and in 1708 under that of *Nouveau Théâtre de la Grande Bretagne*.

Leonard Knyff's views show the houses, palaces, gardens and parks of the nobility and gentry of England and indeed of the monarch. In the main they are of country seats, but there are also some town properties amongst them. There are detectable similarities or recurring themes and motifs in some of the gardens but by and large they are remarkable for their variety. All but one of Knyff's views were engraved by Johannes Kip who, like Knyff, had been born in the Netherlands and emigrated to England. Kip was not just an engraver; he was also a draughtsman and it was he that drew and engraved the 64 plates that illustrate Sir Robert Atkyns's *The Ancient and Present state of Gloucestershire*, published in 1712. Most of these are bird's-eye-views of country seats and their surroundings. About 70 per cent of the illustrated Gloucestershire seats belonged to untitled gentlemen or their widows. In the Knyff series this figure had been about 15 per cent, most of the others belonging to higher ranks of society. Knyff and Kip were not the first nor the only artists to use the bird's-eye-view to illustrate gardens, but in England they were amongst the most prolific, and between them they provided a wonderful record of the gardens of the time of William and Mary, and her sister Anne.

We also know what the gardens of Holland looked like, for the Dutch had an even finer tradition of bird's-eye-views and eye-level series. Johannes van den Aveele made a series of fine bird's-eye and eye-level views of Portland's Zorgvliet in 1690, and the same year Daniel Stoopendaal and Leonard Schenk cooperated in a similar venture for Clingendaal which was published by Schenk's relative, Pieter Schenk. Pieter went on to produce further eye-level series at Duinrel in 1681 and then Dieren. There was a spate of prospects of Honselaarsdijk in the mid-1690s, including those by Karl Allard, who also made some eye-level views, and Cornelius Danckerts, a relative of Hendrik Danckerts.

Cornelius Danckerts and another relative, Justus, were two of the many excellent artists who celebrated the gardens of Het Loo in the 1690s. They produced four or more eye-level views, while Pieter Schenk and Karl Allard produced at least ten each. However, the most numerous set, at least a dozen, and the one that is fullest of character, was by Romeyn de Hooghe. In his drawings the characters, even the statues, are highly animated and the amusing touches, like the horse passing water while drinking from the dolphin fountain, leaven the sometimes studied accuracy of his contemporaries. Stoopendaal produced a bird's-eye-view which he followed by another for Zuylestein in 1700.

Daniel Marot also made bird's-eye-views; his for De Voorst was engraved about 1700. Twelve years later he produced an influential book of designs, which included many of his *parterres*, including that for Hampton Court.

Dutch garden style in William's time

The excellent bird's-eye-views made of these late- seventeenth-century Dutch gardens often give an exaggerated impression of their size, but they clearly illustrate the carefully-planned structure of their wholes, and the great intricacy and sophistication of their parts.

The Dutch estates were laid out in such a manner that the house was centrally positioned, and the several parts of the garden were aligned on the house or on axes parallel to that through the house. More complex sections, like intricate *parterres de broderie* and orangery gardens were usually directly by the house, while a bit further away were the orchards, kitchen gardens and *bosquets*. Most Dutch gardens also remained as canal gardens. Only rarely, as at Rosendael, or later and at vast expense at Het Loo, was there moving water; at most places waterworks were of a rather static character.

The usually high level of organisation was generally in plan only, serving to perpetuate the tradition of the rectangular enclosed garden; the various parts were often separated by high hedges giving a number of discreet enclosures. Another consequence of the tradition of the garden rectangle was that cross-axes had been important at Honselaarsdijk, Huis ten Bosch, Soestdijk and even the early phase of Het Loo. The most far-reaching change in gardens of the 1680s was the extended main axis. It encouraged a reorientation of the parts of the garden along a strong axial alignment, opening up views and connections with outlying parts of the estate.

The main axis was often unfolded along a drive starting at a great distance from the house. Along such a drive one would progress through farmland, then woodland and *bosquets* before arriving at the forecourt and the parterres. The progression from the gate to the *broderie* was to ascend a scale of increasing levels of Art. The basic formality of the surrounding polderland ensured that the axially-developed gardens were integrated smoothly into their settings through the avenues linking with estate woodlands and canalside planting. The effect was quite different from the traditional practice of treating gardens as if they were isolated oases of cultivation.

Another trend of the 1680s was an increase in ornamentation. While the sober, classicist, architectural tradition of the Dutch Republic provided the framework, the detail was becoming exuberant. Daniel Marot's French designs for *parterres*, ironwork, vases, wallhangings, ceilings and furniture became popular, and brought a surprising richness in ornamentation, nowhere more so than in the gardens.

The Dutch interest in natural history cannot be overlooked. With the increasing popularity of exotic and rare plants the orangery was an indispensable feature in the William and Mary garden. Also at the greater houses there were deerparks, and, usually just outside the main walled garden enclosure, there were sometimes menageries, and aviaries where the exotic animal and bird collections were housed.

Zeist, Het Loo and De Voorst can be seen as the most oustanding layouts in the Netherlands at the end of the seventeenth century. These were of an enormous scale by Dutch standards, with their systems of interconnected axes. Clingendaal, Heemstede, Middachten and Rosendael were amongst other notable creations of the circle around the stadholder. The question remains, though: Who was the organising genius of these layouts? In the mid-1680s Marot was still too inexperienced and his layouts, for example that for Huis ten Bosch, were many years in the future; Jacob Roman was a sculptor before turning architect, perhaps not the best training for a garden designer; and Daniel Desmarets, although in an influential position, seems mainly to have interested himself in plants, not design. From what little is known, it seems that the most likely source for the layouts was sketches by Roman developed with the active participation of the owner.

So what was particularly Dutch about these gardens besides the obvious use of still water? The axial treatment and the increased ornamentation of the most spectacular gardens could also be seen in great gardens all over Europe. Perhaps, though, something Dutch can be identified in the sense of enclosure, of intimacy, and of the relationship of buildings, especially pavilions, to water, even in the most cosmopolitan of gardens. Also, although keen on botanical novelty, the Dutch retained and elaborated elements from an earlier period like mazes, *berceaux*, arbours, and grottoes. In smaller gardens in particular there exists an ornamental complexity that often harks back to earlier Renaissance sources. This continuation of

5.2 Trinity College, by William Williams in *Oxonia Depicta* (1735). The extravagant use of topiary was the fashion of the 1690s and the 1700s, but by the 1740s was out of fashion and being decried as 'Dutch'

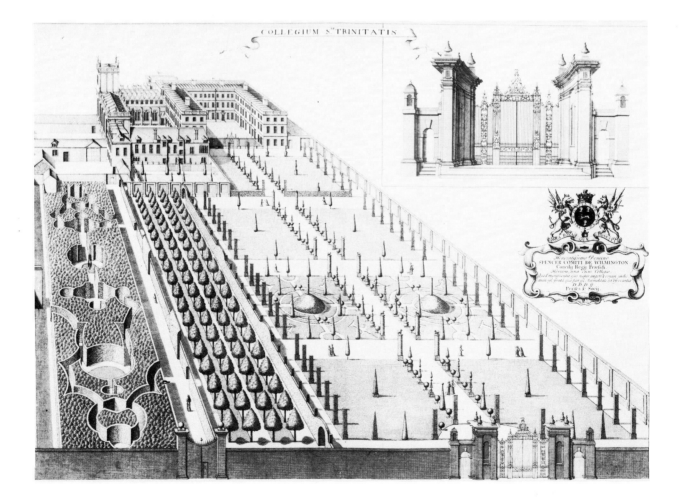

complexity and attention to detail, which extended also to the gardens' complex geometry, may be a Dutch trait.

Dutch gardens in Britain?

Were English gardens, either collectively or in specific cases, 'Dutch'? What about the crimping diminutiveness that Switzer complained about in English gardens of William's reign? The truth is that, despite the scale and pragmatism of George London's layouts, England was still predominantly a country of small walled gardens, and well behind 'that Magnificence which is easily discoverable from the *French* Designs, which certainly yet very much excel ours, notwithstanding those considerable Advantages we have by Nature beyond what they have'. This is what Switzer was bemoaning. So, for example, he could recommend the French manual

> *The Theory and Practice of Gard'ning*, lately Translated by Mr. *James* of *Greenwich*, is esteemed in its Way, the best that has appeared in this or any other Language, and seems to be the best-laid Design, and carried on with the most Judgment; but that being writ in a Country much differing, and very far inferior to this, in respect of the natural Embellishments of our Gardens, as good Grass, Gravel, &c. makes a great Alteration in point of Design.

Excessive topiary is often thought to have been a Dutch vice. Certainly the extreme was Hampton Court with its 1,000 yews and hollies. It can also be observed that, whereas Oxford college gardens in David Loggan's *Oxonia Illustrata* (1675) are devoid of topiary, by the time of William Williams's *Oxonia depicta* (1733) it is ample and complex, and in this conservative society must reflect fashions around 1700. A fairly typical use of topiary at a

5.3 Winchendon House, view from the east of the garden with its topiary (late 1720s)

major house in the last years of the seventeenth century can be seen at the Duke of Wharton's Winchendon House, Buckinghamshire, where we find pyramids and cones on the main *parterres*, interspersed with statuary, and cones and box shapes around the perimeters in front of the topiary arcades.

However, the English weakness for topiary should not be exaggerated. It is worth observing that of the 78 gardens drawn by Knyff, topiary is seldom profuse, and where it does exist the shapes are the standard ones. Also topiary, when it does exist, in France, Holland or England, is of standard shape: the ball, the cone, the cube, or elaborated into a combination of these, as witnessed and recorded by Alexander Edward when he visited Versailles in 1701. While Britain clearly did acquire a good deal of topiary in William's reign, it is not clear whether the model was the Netherlands or France.

The same is true for boxwork. Queen Anne had the box *parterres* at Kensington and Hampton Court ripped out, and this decision is what Switzer said 'cashiers those Interlacings of Box-work, and such like trifling Ornaments, and substitutes the plain but nobler Embellishments of Grass, Gravel, and the like, in which we so much excel other Countries'. The only other *broderie* to be seen in *Britannia Illustrata* was at Bretby and Great Ribston where French influence is suspected. So while the French and Dutch passion for *broderie* did reappear in Britain in the 1680s and 1690s, it had only a temporary stay, and cannot be said to have altered British tastes.

Many Englishmen perceived a national superiority in gravel and grass. Edward Southwell 'saw noe where gravell-wakes' in the Netherlands except at Dieren, and when Richard Chiswell saw Zorgvliet in 1696 he was able to say smugly: 'Here they are forced to cover their Walks with Sand instead of rowled Gravell, which is certainly one of the greatest Ornaments to a Garden.' As for grass, the British thought that everyone acknowledged British superiority, and this perhaps made them unadventurous. Wren had

5.4 Versailles, topiary patterns, recorded by Alexander Edwards (1699)

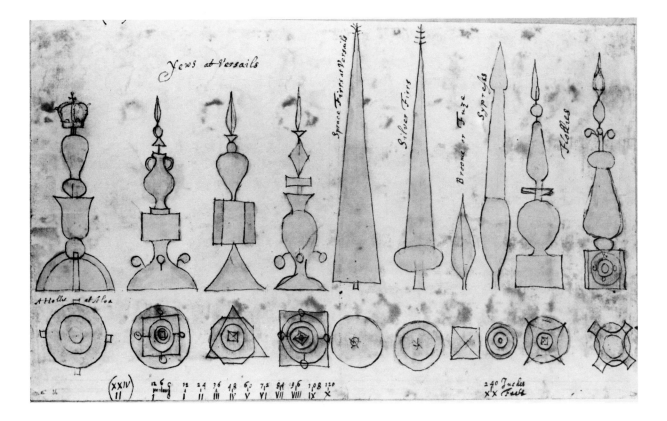

98

not wanted Marot's *broderie* at Hampton Court, preferring instead the grass *parterre* that Anne at last enabled him to implement. The most extravagant British *parterre* normally encountered would be cut-work in grass.

Britain certainly acquired many more canals, and perhaps this was slightly more a result of distinctly Dutch rather than French influence. One looks in vain for more concrete links, though one garden design might possibly have represented a pandering to William's Dutch tastes. This is Talman's project to build a Trianon or pleasure house on the opposite side of the Thames from Hampton Court. Here is something very different from the looser, more articulated, gardens of George London. All is contained within formal boundaries of trees and topiary, and one can surely sense here something decidedly more Continental in flavour, with obelisks, urns, and Baroque garden furniture ornamenting the inner walls of the garden. However this is an isolated and uncertain example, and was not built.

So can one recognise any specifically Dutch traits in England's gardens after 1688? The answer must be a qualified 'No'; with the exception of the Royal Gardens alone, the idea of Dutch gardens in England is a myth. The Knyff and Kip plates were a trophy of the English garden in William's time, but because George London, according to Switzer, dominated the circuits, it is a record also of the London style. Considering that Knyff took eight years to complete his huge task of surveying the gardens, we must imagine that he and London often met on their respective circuits. Seldom would they have recognised anything strikingly Dutch in what they designed and drew.

The princely garden tradition in the Netherlands was represented by their Wilton, Frederik-Hendrik's Honselaarsdijk, or his Rijswijk, and by the strong French influence in decoration, for example through Daniel Marot in William III's time. The Dutch had the greater opportunity to influence the English through their superiority in horticultural matters, but the trade was not entirely one-way. The model of the Earl of Albemarle's De Voorst was probably designed by Talman. But the greatest external influence on both nations, and an eloquent testament to the craving to emulate French achievements, was the stream of French designers – De Caus, Mollet, Beaumont, Marot, Tijou and even Le Nôtre – who worked in or advised upon English gardens, and the number of French architects and gardeners pressed into service for the stadholders. Without denying that distinctive national characteristics existed, which were more marked amongst the second-rank houses, gardens at courtier level in Britain and the Netherlands drew inspiration from the same Franco-Italianate models.

The Reputation of the Dutch Garden – Addison to Arts and Crafts

As in Europe as a whole, regularly laid-out gardens continued to develop and flourish in Britain and the Netherlands for several decades after William III's reign. But the death knell began to sound for topiary works in England when Joseph Addison, the prophet of natural gardening, wrote in the *Spectator* on 25 June 1712:

> Our Trees rise in Cones, Globes, and Pyramids. We see the Marks of the Scissars upon every Plant and Bush. I do not know whether I am singular on my Opinion, but, for my own part, I would rather look upon a tree in all its Luxurancy and Diffusion of Boughs and Branches, than when it is thus cut trimmed into a Mathematical Figure.

Addison felt that Art could not hope to imitate the magnificence or variety of Nature either in its small works such as trees or at the wider scale of the landscape. The best that could be done in garden design was to work with Nature; to 'humour the genius of the place'. Rightness came about when the more-or-less disguised forms of Nature were revealed at their true scale. He reminded the public that the French or Italian garden had

> a large Extent of Ground covered over with an agreeable Mixture of Garden and Forest, which represent every where an artificial Rudeness, much more charming than the Neatness and Elegancy which we meet with in those of our own Country.

In 1713 a young astronomer and keen improver, Samuel Molyneux, visited Hampton Court and thought that the gardens were 'beautifully dispos'd enough' for such a flat area, but the greatest beauty of the place was the Thames, to be seen from the Terrace Walk. In other words he followed the new Addison orthodoxy that Nature outshone all the man-made magnificence of the place. Molyneux 'did by no means think it adequate in the whole to the notion I had of the Palace of a great Prince'. His taste was for the forest garden at New Park:

> I think I have never yet seen any piece of Gardening that has so much as this the true taste of Beauty. There is a certain sort of Presumption appears in the comon restrain'd formal & Regular Parteres & Gardens that one meets with But here art has nothing Sawcy and seems to endeavour rather to follow than alter nature, and to aim at no beautys but such as she before had seem'd to dictate.

Stephen Switzer translated this line of thinking into his theories on 'Rural Gardening' expressed in *The Nobleman, Gentleman and Gardener's Recreation* (1715). He favoured Addison's idea of turning the whole countryside into 'a kind of garden' by walks and frequent plantations, praising French practice and English examples such as Cassiobury, New Park and Wray Wood at Castle Howard.

Some years later the wilderness at Hampton Court, about which Daniel Defoe had commented 'nothing of that kind can be more beautiful', now came under attack in the 1742 edition of his *Tour*:

> To every Person of taste it must be very far from affording any Pleasure, since nothing can be more disagreeable than to be immured between Hedges, so as to have the Eye confined to a straight Walk, and the Beauty of the Trees growing in the Quarters, intirely secluded from the eye. . .

Switzer had objected to topiary and boxwork in *parterres* such as at Hampton Court:

> The *Great Garden*, the *Privy Garden*, the Wilderness, and Kitchen-gardens, were made with great Dispatch; the only fault was, the Pleasure-Gardens being stuffed too thick with Box, a Fashion brought over out of *Holland* by the *Dutch* Gardeners, who used it to a fault.

He preferred the 'plain but noble manner' with grass replacing the *broderie* at Hampton Court and Kensington during Queen Anne's reign. In the 1745 edition of *Ichnographia Rustica* Switzer referred to topiary as 'the *Dutch*

Taste, which came in with the revolution', and of which 'the People of the common level of Understanding grew so fond; being delighted with little Niceties and fantastical Operations of Art'.

Switzer's comments really applied to the extravagant use of box *parterres* and topiary in the Royal Gardens of the 1690s. A quarter of a century later, when he was writing, English fashion had moved towards what he advocated, the 'forest garden'. Enlarged wildernesses had virtually become the garden. Also English grass *parterres*, more likely to be adorned by urns and obelisks than by topiary, had ousted the French boxwork. Switzer probably did not know that Dutch taste was moving that way too. By the early-1720s Dutch forest gardens were being made as alternatives to the French style of decoration being continued in a more Rococo spirit by Daniel Marot.

However, such niceties did not concern the protagonists for the gardening style of William Kent and Lancelot Brown. One of them wrote in the 1760s ridiculing the geometrical style of William III's time:

> Here great Nassau the Belgian gardens spread,
> Yet Hampton-Court th' improving age misled;
> Long gravel walks with puerile knots of flowers,
> Of taste and grandeur still destroy the powers; . . .
> We here fatigu'd the lengthening walk survey,
> That tonsur'd bushes, and *parterres* display:
> And pyramids in yew, that doleful stand,
> Like mutes and mourners in a fun'ral Band.

It was firmly fixed in the Englishman's mind that the landscape garden had triumphed over the false 'Dutch' taste. Hampton Court itself remained unmodernised and so presented a relatively unchanging example of what was regarded as the execrable taste of William's day. No-one of taste, it seemed, had a good word for it while the landscape style prevailed. The still, small voices of the occasional antiquarian about the Tijou ironwork or the maze were lost in the wind.

When fervour for Nature, which had fuelled the landscape garden, subsided, and design principles were being reassessed in the early years of the nineteenth century, Humphry Repton suggested collections of specialised gardens which could satisfy the desire for variety. John Claudius Loudon took up this idea in 1804, and whilst he did not fail to mention the 'absurdities' of the old formal gardens, he also gave the 'Dutch garden' as a possible type of specialised flower garden. 'Dutch' gardens actually constructed in the Regency period included ones at Leigh Park in Hampshire and Bagshot in Surrey. These showed that the epithet 'Dutch' implied geometrically-shaped gardens with beds set in grass for displaying tulips, *Amaryllis* and other bulbs and florists' flowers in masses, surrounded by dwarf box edgings. The designs of Hans Vredeman de Vries and Jan van der Groen were probably the reason for thinking these sort of gardens to be Dutch.

At the end of the century, with the rise of the Arts and Crafts movement, another version of the 'Dutch garden' appeared, but this too had as little to do with the true William and Mary garden as the Regency specialised gardens. Gardencraft, or 'gardenage' as Ernest Law, the historian of Hampton Court, called it, was the essence of Arts and Crafts gardening. There was a yearning in the great landscaped and architectural gardens for the 'nookiness' depicted in the Dutch Old Masters with their intimate domestic courtyard gardens and for the close enjoyment of the 'old-fashioned flowers' in the Dutch flower paintings.

Ernest Law's 'Dutch garden' at Hampton Court, a sunken garden with a wide gravel walk between neat flower borders edged with clipped box, was seen as typical of the Dutch style. Law advocated historical association in gardening and later, in 1924, created an Elizabethan knot garden near the Tudor part of the palace just as the Dutch garden was to offset King William's Banquetting House. A commemorative 'Dutch' pond garden had also been made in 1909 at Kensington Palace. Writing in 1926 in his *Pictorial Guide for Gardens Old and New*, T. G. Henslow felt that the Dutch gardens were eminently suitable for lady gardeners, who could appreciate their trimness and embroidery-like detail and the arrangement of ornamental features.

At the Duke of Westminster's overpowering Eaton Hall, Charles Mallow, an Arts and Crafts designer, laid out a secluded Dutch garden with a tea house. At Broughton Castle, the ancestral home of Celia Fiennes, who loved gardens to be 'neate', 'exactly kept' and 'full of curiosities', Lady Algernon Gordon Lennox laid out in 1898 a courtyard garden known as My Lady's Garden with the *fleur-de-lys*-shaped beds of roses and lavender overlooked by topiary peacocks, which was admired by Miss Gertrude Jekyll, the most famous of lady gardeners. Also in 1898 Jekyll designed with Edwin Lutyens for Arts and Crafts clients a sunken enclosure at Orchards with geometrical beds of roses and lavender and yew hedges and topiary peacocks perched on a very private iron gate to the 'Dutch garden'.

Clearly the English have had some strong prejudices about Dutch gardens. So how justified are they? Very little, it seems. Certainly Switzer was unfair in characterising Dutch gardens as being stuffed full of puerile absurdities, and we see him more truly as the advocate of a new fashion of working with Nature, to whom the previous generation's work would necessarily be anathema, than as the seeker after historical truth.

PART TWO
A TOUR
OF THE GARDEN

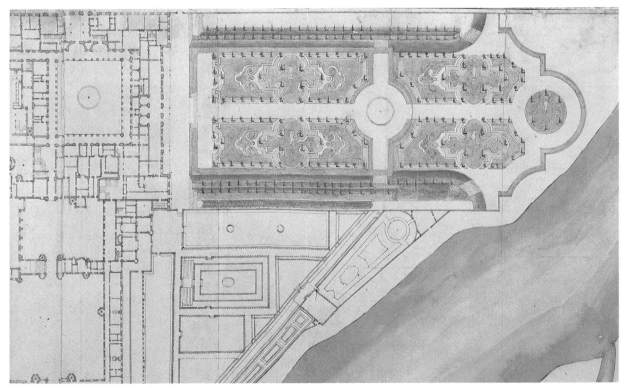

8. Hampton Court, Privy Garden, detail of a survey (sometime 1710–14). This *parterre* was made in 1701

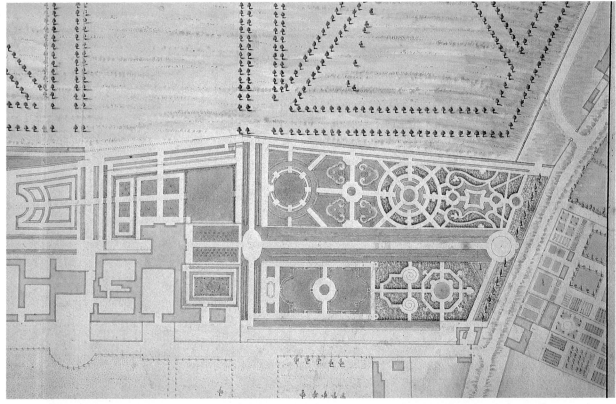

9. Kensington Gardens, detail of a map of about 1715 showing the southern gardens made by William and Mary to an unusual plan in 1691. North to the left, Kensington Highway to the right

10. Kensington Gardens, detail of a map of about 1715 showing the Upper Wilderness made in the Old Ground in 1701–4. This wilderness was in the making when William died. One compartment was an old gravel pit which had been terraced, possibly with the intention of it being an orangery garden

11. Huis ten Bosch, proposal plan by Daniel Marot in the 1720s, illustrating Marot's increasingly Rococo style

12. Hampton Court, photograph of Tijou's screen placed in the Privy Garden in 1701

13. Het Loo, the ironwork doorway onto the garden terrace of about 1685, as restored

14. Castle Howard, gate by John Gardom

15. Middelharnis, the avenue, by Meyndert Hobbema (c. 1680). To the right is a tree nursery

The Approach

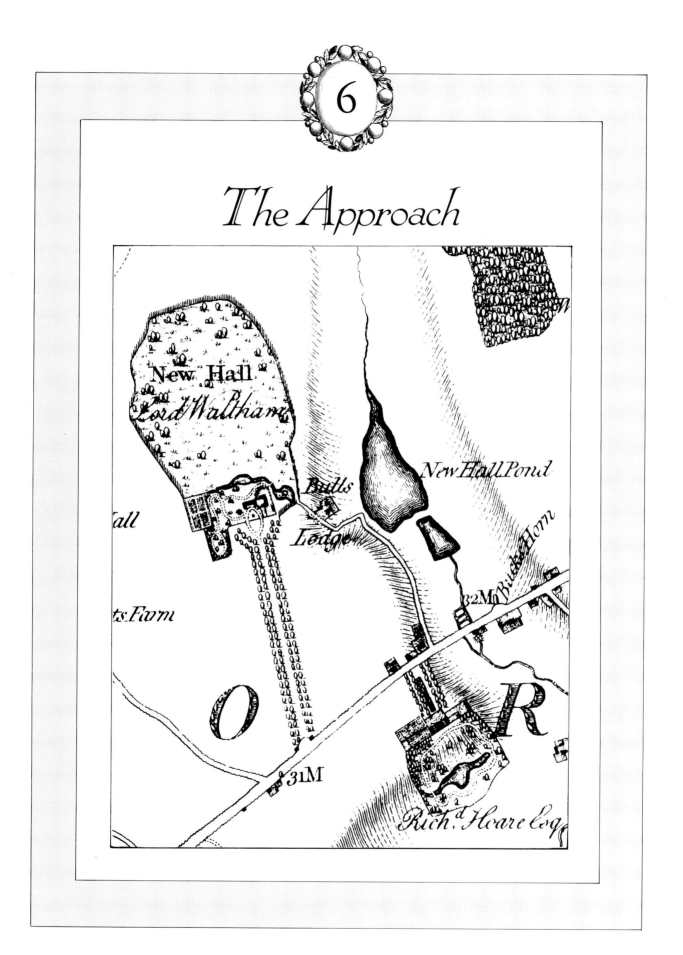

6.1 *Previous page*: New
Hall, in Essex, from
Chapman and André *Map
of Essex* (1777). The
avenue was planted in 1623

When great houses had fortress-like walls, and were shut up by great studded
wooden gates, there was no thought of devising impressive approaches along
axes. Likewise the large internal courtyards allowed the trains of important
visitors to enter the house and so there was no need to plan a forecourt.
Cardinal Wolsey's Hampton Court, for example, was simply set within a
moat in an open park, and the approach was down the most convenient
route which happened to be oblique to the gatehouse.

The axial approach

However, Leon Battista Alberti in his *De Re Aedificatoria* (1452) had
written that

> . . . the Houses of Princes. . . should have an Entrance from the Master
> Way and especially from the Sea or River; and. . . they should have a large
> open Area, big enough to receive the Train of an Ambassador, or any
> other Great Man, whether they come in Coaches, in Barks or on
> Horseback.

In 1615 Vincenzo Scamozzi advised that the line of approach should
terminate at the main façade of the building in order to emphasise its beauty
and grandeur. A large and spacious concourse in the shape of a half-moon is
needed just in front of the building to ensure that entourages could come and
go without interfering with each other. Routes leading to main buildings
must be wide and may be beautified by planting trees on one side, or on both
sides, or perhaps in four rows. Such a four-row avenue has three tracks: a
wide one in the middle for riders and carriages, and two narrow ones on
either side for those on foot. Advantages which Scamozzi cited for an avenue
besides magnificence are shade, and thereby coolness during the heat of the
summer, beauty, and a harvest of timber.

In Britain there had been some Tudor avenues, but axial avenues
terminating at half-moons were probably unknown till that at Twickenham
Park, most probably planted by the order of Lucy, Countess of Bedford,
during her stay there between 1609 and 1618. More impressive still was the
avenue at New Hall, Essex, where in 1623 the Duke of Buckingham laid out
a double avenue 1,310 yds long with a semicircle of 68 yds radius in front of
the mansion.

These Italian ideas were certainly known in the Netherlands too.
Constantijn Huygens possessed a copy of Scamozzi, together with no fewer
than five editions of Vitruvius, and books by Serlio, Alberti and the French
architect Androuet du Cerceau. Also the library of Maurits, Prince of
Orange, contained Italian architectural books, and presumably these were
inherited by Maurits's younger half-brother, Frederik-Hendrik, who in 1625
laid out the axial approach to the palace of Honselaarsdijk. This avenue of
eight rows of trees, 773 m long, terminated in a semicircle just in front of the
moat surrounding the rectangle of the palace and gardens.

Only in the middle of the seventeenth century does this form of
monumental approach regularly occur in France, such as at the pre-André le
Nôtre Versailles. The inspiration for André Mollet's ideas for approaches,
set out in *Le Jardin de Plaisir*, seems to have been Scamozzi and
Honselaarsdijk where he worked in 1633. The second figure in his book
shows a rectangle surrounded by water and avenues with the start of a
monumental central axis. Mollet's English edition says about avenues

... requisite to the decoration of Houses of Pleasure, is to have the conveniency to plant before them a great Walk of double or treble rank, either of female Elms, or of Lime Trees, which are the two sorts of Trees which we esteem the fittest for this purpose; which Walk ought to be drawn by a Perpendicular Line to the Front of the House, and of a convenient and proportionable breadth to the House; and for the Basis of the said Walk, may be made a large Demy-circle, or Square; and in case the place will allow it, there may be also drawn large Walks on the Right and Left of the said front ...

This advice seems to have been followed by Mollet himself at St James's in 1660 and at Hampton Court in 1661, though in both cases he was asked to plant in the parks behind palaces rather than on the approaches. Perhaps this is why he filled the avenues not with roadways, but with grand canals after the Fontainebleau model. There were, though, paths between the double rows to either side, and there were semicircles and walks to the right and left.

Grid planting

A map of Honselaarsdijk dated 1631 shows a grid of walks dividing the area behind the gardens proper into a series of rectangular quarters. These walks

6.2 Honselaarsdijk, map (1631), showing the grid of canals and walks in the area of estate improvement

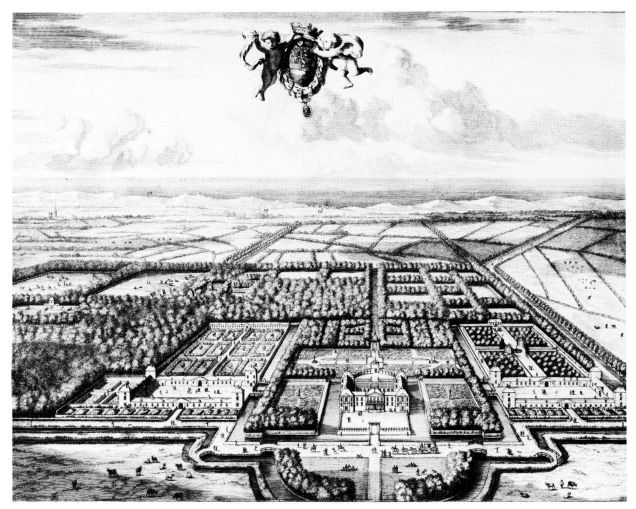

6.3 Honselaarsdijk, 'generale Asbeeldinge van het Princelyke Lust Huys en Hof . . . t'Honslerdyk' by Bega and Blooteling (c. 1680). The grid of *allées* and the avenues beyond as far as the dunes are shown

were the means to make land accessible while parcelling it up, and the quarters were in use as meadows, orchards, vegetable gardens and forest. Beyond this grid, two avenues were extended far into the still irregularly divided farmland. With the walks planted on either side, this was an attractive means of combining beauty with utility, an early essay on the theme of *utile dulci*.

This manner of improvement was also found at other large estates in the second quarter of the seventeenth century, for example on the Schoonheeten estate, the property of the Bentinck family. There is a poem, originating probably from a late-seventeenth-century estate map, on one of 1762. This poem describes the character of this type of layout very well:

This waste field, too low and also too high,
All too wet in the winter, and all too dry in the summer,
Is within twenty years by means of ceaseless labour
With digging, planting and manure prepared in such a way
That high parts feed fish, and the low beautiful trees,
That man and cattle find their necessities and enjoyment
To the eye, the ear, the scent, the touch and the taste;
Air, earth, water and fire, are here united with benefit
In the operations of Nature and of Art upon Her.

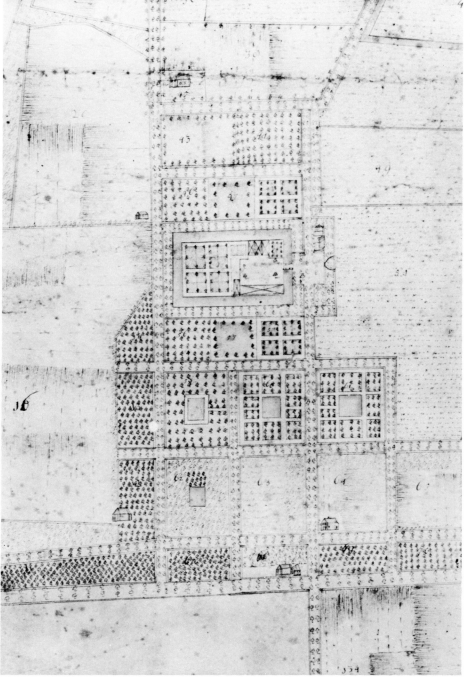

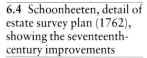

6.4 Schoonheeten, detail of estate survey plan (1762), showing the seventeenth-century improvements

This emphasises that grids of walks such as at Schoonheeten and the furthest part of Honselaarsdijk should be seen as the union of Art and Nature.

A good example of a large improvement scheme in the second half of the seventeenth century was that at Slangenburg, near Doetinchem. Frederik Johan van Baer, the owner, was an officer in William's army. He was familiar with Honselaarsdijk and later with Kensington and Hampton Court. In 1675 he went to considerable trouble to lay out an approach to his castle in the manner of Honselaarsdijk. The old back of the castle was made into the front, and a long monumental approach, which ended in a semicircle

6.5 Slangenburg, estate plan (1774), showing the improvements of 1679 by Frederik-Johan van Baer

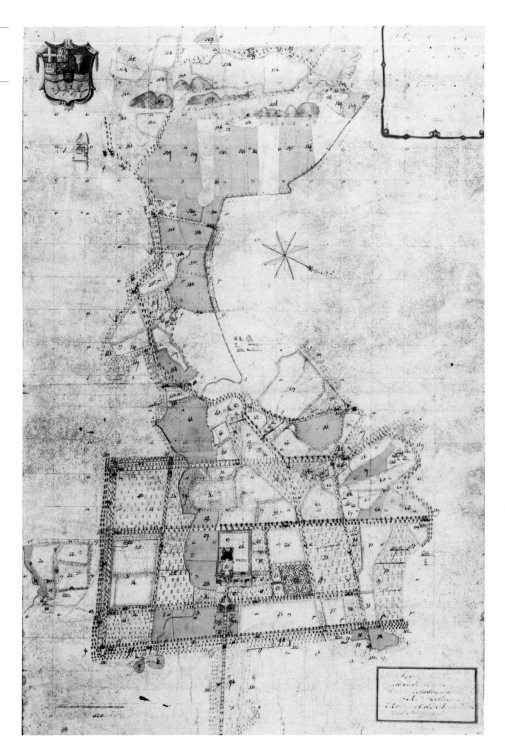

in front of the moated forecourt, was planted on the axis of the house. Van Baer sought to invest his booty in his unproductive land, making it suitable for arable use, meadow and forestry. To do this he had to drain much of it, parcel it up and make the parcels accessible. He did this with the familiar grid of ditched rectilinear walks arranged in conjunction with the approach avenues. In order to lay out the pattern he wanted, Van Baer also had to buy land in the neighbourhood.

An early post-Restoration improvement in a British park was the planting of 'Boreman's Bower', 14 coppice woodlands along the southern boundary of Greenwich Park, in the winter of 1661/2. Sir William Boreman, the underkeeper of the house and park, was presumably chiefly interested in a supply of fuel for the palace. The layout was based on a grid of elm-lined walks, and planting in the quarters was with elms, sweet chestnuts and birches.

Bearing in mind that the English Court's sojourn in the Netherlands was still recent in 1661, it is possible that Boreman's Bower was derived from Dutch examples. However, generally in Britain there were no great hunting forests like the Veluwe, and estates were more likely to be designed for the chase than improvement. Beauty and utility were not so closely interwoven. A natural philosopher like Thomas Browne, despite composing an erudite essay on the quincunx form of planting, was more appreciative of the trees themselves than of layouts.

John Evelyn's famous work, *Sylva*, though written for the Royal Society in order to encourage planting for ships' timbers, concentrated on the trees as well. *Sylva* was enormously popular, and promoted Britain's prestigeous leap forward in forestry and horticulture during the following century. Evelyn did not stand alone: the specialised treatise of Moses Cook, *The manner of raising, ordering, and improving forest-trees* (1676) and that of Anthony Lawrence, *Nurseries, orchards, profitable gardens, and vineyards encouraged* (1677) were influential in a practical way, if not in the layout of estates.

The extended axis

Mollet's *Le Jardin de Plaisir* advocated continuing the axis beyond the house, a comparatively fresh idea to northern Europe at the time:

> At the end of the Garden another Walk in a direct Line to the great Walk, in the midst whereof there may be with conveniency a Door of Railes or Palisado's, through which, when the doors of the House are open'd, one may see from one end to the other, as far as our sight will extend.

An example which was probably also of importance to the Netherlands was the Villa Emo, near Venice, built around 1560 by Palladio, and illustrated by him in *I Quattro Libri dell'Architettura* (1570). The main axis was continued through the farming landscape to the north and south by long avenues of poplars. Although the wings were straight, not curved, the Villa Emo served as a direct source for the amphitheatre and avenue laid out in 1657 for the Stadholder of Cleves, Count Johan-Maurits van Nassau-Siegen. It is suspected that the architect, Jacob van Campen, went to Italy in his youth, and saw Palladio's Villa Emo with its avenues.

The design of the amphitheatre in Cleves was like the Villa Emo: a central main building with a wing with eleven arches on either side. The axis of the Cleves amphitheatre runs from the top of the hill behind it to the Elterberg on the far side of the wide valley of the Rhine in front of it, going straight through the main building. Cleves is one of the few places in the Low Countries where there is plenty of water as well as some marked level differences. These natural advantages were put to use in a series of ponds on different levels on the main axis. A tree-flanked rectangular grand canal on the axis at the foot of the hill may have been another imitation of the canal at Fontainebleau.

6.6 Springenberg, in Cleves, the grand vista from the amphitheatre, by Jan van Call (c. 1680). The extended axis was remarkable for the 1650s

At Cleves the falling ground made the continuation of the axis on both sides of the main building apparent. However on a flat site transparent boundaries to the garden were required. Mollet suggested 'Railes or Palisado's', or even perspectives on canvas at end of *allées* to give the illusion of prospect. Architects and garden designers were quick to see the advantages of iron gates and grilles. Sir Roger Pratt noted in the 1660s:

> . . . every good courtyard should be adorned with some beautiful transparent window niche or gate. . . I mean them to be barred with some handsome ironwork, . . . when immediately behind them is some beautiful object as gardens, woods, walks, fountains, statues etc, and then there can nothing be finer or more beautiful.

Gatesmiths not only provided a highly ornamental means to ensure privacy, but allowed the great wooden gates of the forecourt to be taken down to enable the vista to be continued on the axis of the layout. Awed visitors could glimpse and wonder at the sumptuous palaces beyond. In the gardens, stonework could be pierced by the *clairevoyée* screen in wrought iron, making vistas between and out of the various walled areas possible. Painters were given plenty of work. Walter Harris saw ironwork at Het Loo painted blue and with gilded highlights. Evelyn noticed in 1688 that the gate at Castle Ashby was also 'painted bleu and gilded'. A decade later Celia Fiennes saw that the 'Iron Barrgate' at Newby was 'painted green with gold tops'.

The Het Loo ironwork comprised great lengths of palisade in the Prince's Garden and another one, 2.5 m high, to enclose the forecourt. However, the ultimate expression of ironwork replacing solid boundaries was at Hampton Court, where the whole boundary between the Great Parterre and the House Park was composed of railings. The importance attached to ironwork can then be appreciated; it was vital to the whole idea of opening up the views whilst maintaining security.

In the Netherlands the axial treatment of estate layouts reached its most meglomaniac with Zeist in the 1680s and De Voorst in the 1690s. These had both the monumental approach and the apparently infinite vista, and virtually the whole layout was disposed symmetrically around the axis. In Britain the axial approach was striven for, but the irregularities of the landscape and the past history of the layouts often conspired against the designer. Only occasionally did he triumph against the odds so spectacularly as did Evelyn at Albury, where he continued the axis above the garden by persuading the owner to dig a tunnel through the hill.

When Knyff drew his views of English country houses he saw a bewildering variety of ways in which approaches were managed. There were indeed some axial avenues carrying the approaches at Grimsthorpe, Althorp and Stansted, but the majority of places drawn had not managed this. The legacy of Tudor and Jacobean houses separated from the public highway only by a forecourt made monumental avenue approaches impossible at Newnham Paddox, Chiswick, Temple Newsam, Hutton Hall, Eaton Hall, Dodington, and many other older houses. At some of these places a roadless avenue was planted beyond the highway, purely to extend the axis. Many houses were halfway between; they had their approaches across their own property, but from the side. In these cases the approach was picked up by a transverse walk or road tangential to the forecourt. Some of the grandest houses – Chatsworth, Longleat, Wrest, Wimpole and Dawley – had unsatisfactory approaches like this.

On one of his plates Mollet included a *patte d'oie*, or goose-foot, arrangement of *allées*. This feature seems to have been virtually unknown in the rectilinear landscape of the Netherlands until one was made on the approach to Het Loo in the late 1680s, and in 1651 Mollet no doubt had

6.7 De Voorst, detail of map of Zutphen and its environs by H. J. van der Wyck (1778), showing the interlocking of avenues on adjacent estates

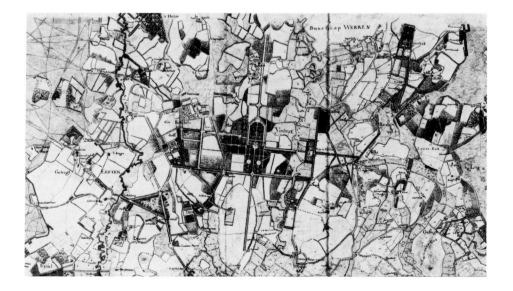

French models in mind. André le Nôtre began to use the *patte d'oie* in the 1650s, and the first in Britain seems to have been that at Greenwich, dating from about 1664. The largest in Britain was that at Hampton Court, made about 1690 by adding two diagonals to the older avenue and semicircle.

Parkland planting of avenues began as a widespread phenomenon in Britain in the 1670s. Evelyn advised that an avenue should be planted to link the park to the house at Euston Hall in 1671, and the Great Park was likewise connected to the castle at Windsor in 1683. Meanwhile the Marquis of Worcester had started on an extensive system of avenues at Badminton sometime before 1679, and when Knyff came to make a view of the place about 20 years later there were over 60 avenues criss-crossing the parks, several of many miles in length. In the Netherlands there was nothing as elaborate as Badminton, though transverse avenues at De Voorst linked up with neighbouring estates to form a cluster of linked avenue systems.

Repoussé ironwork

Ironwork as an element in garden design took a dramatic turn in Britain shortly before 1687, when the French *repoussé* worker, Jean Tijou, arrived at Chatsworth. *Repoussé* was the technique of hammering cold sheet iron on a bed of pitch to achieve a mild relief suitable for decorative elements like masks and leaves. These would then be overlaid on the framework of the gate. This technique, and the much increased use of wrought iron bars for railings, transformed the vistas to the great houses of England.

Tijou's gate to the bowling green at Drayton was a minor but good example. This replaced a solid door in a stone screen and allowed the viewer to see beyond into the next compartment of the garden. At Burghley, Celia Fiennes was stunned by the 'door of iron, carv'd the finest I ever saw, all sorts of leaves flowers figures birds beast wheate in the Carving'. Another country house *habitué* who was impressed was John Evelyn. In August 1688 he visited Castle Ashby in the company of the Countess of Sunderland. 'My lady carried me to my Lord Northampton's seat . . . where they are inlarging the gardens, in which was nothing extraordinary but the Yron Gate opening into the Parke, which indeede is very good worke, wrought in flowers.'

In France, Tijou was of sufficient standing that his daughter married a godson of Louis XIV, Louis la Guerre, the ceiling painter. Tijou was no Huguenot refugee, and seems to have been tempted to England simply by the promise of lucrative contracts. No doubt he would indeed have died a rich man if the English Crown had paid its debts. Tijou worked in England for over 20 years. From the very beginning he seemed to rely on English smiths to create the basic forged framework, but he kept the secret of *repoussé* to himself and his family.

The English were not slow to imitate. Whilst *repoussé* was beyond their capabilities, they became skilled in forging their leafwork hot on the anvil. Almost all of the first generation of English gatesmiths were directly associated with Tijou. At Chatsworth he was assisted by William Marshall of Warwick, who later established a flourishing business in the Midland counties with a clock and gun maker. The estate smith at Chatsworth, John Gardom, built a considerable reputation in the north of England after the master departed, for example in the garden of Castle Howard in Yorkshire. Finally it was at Chatsworth that Tijou found his most famous assistant, Huntingdon Shaw, the son of a Nottingham blacksmith. On his tombstone in Hampton churchyard Shaw was described as 'an artist in his way'.

No doubt at William Talman's bidding, Tijou and Shaw made their way to Hampton Court in 1689, and established a new workshop on Hampton Court Green. The gates made by Tijou and 'the 12 panels for the circle of the Fountain Garden at Hampton Court' were by far the most ambitious use of ironwork in Britain. All this work was prodigiously expensive; in fact Tijou charged £2,160.2s.0d., of which £894.10s.0d. was still owed in 1696. Further work in supplying 172 plainer panels for railing the two new divisions north and south of the Fountain Garden in 1700 created a new debt of £1,782.1s.6d. About the time that he finished at Hampton Court Tijou moved his workshop to the bottom end of Piccadilly by Hyde Park Corner. After he did this a whole school of smiths followed him and set up business in the vicinity. The most famous was perhaps 'the ingenious Mr. Thomas Robinson of Hyde Park Corner' who was responsible for the screen at New College, Oxford, which set a new standard for English smithwork.

In 1693 there was published in London *A new booke of drawings invented and designed by John Tijou*. This slim volume of 20 plates was by far the most prized collection of designs for ornamental ironwork to be published in Britain for many years. Most are derived from published French sources and from the ironwork at Versailles up to about 1680. While Tijou certainly borrowed from his contemporaries in France, he was nevertheless a superb draughtsman himself, judging from a sketch of his that survives. This was a red chalk drawing of the curious wrought-iron Corinthian column which formerly held up the gallery in the House of Commons. The ability to draw well was an essential attribute for anyone who applied to be a gatesmith.

The plates tell us something about Tijou's approach to design. The

6.8 Design for an ironwork gateway for Wimpole, by Jean Tijou in *A new booke of drawings* (1693)

engraved design of the gates for Hampton Court were modified in execution and the proportions considerably improved. This same design was reproduced slavishly by an English smith, probably William Edney, at Elmore Court, in Gloucestershire, but this looks rather squat and certainly less appealing that the Hampton Court ones. Clearly Tijou was a man whose genius was not restricted by a design drawing even when it was his own. The plate showing another magnificent gate appears to have been transposed onto Kip's engraving of Wimpole Hall, near Cambridge, where between 1689 and 1710 the Earl of Radnor was carrying out many improvements. It seems that Radnor was considering commissioning the design from Tijou and had Kip include it on the engraving in order to see what the effect would be. However the gate was probably never erected. Radnor must then have weighed the drawing against Tijou's enormous estimates and found it wanting in the balance.

In time English gatesmiths developed a simpler style of their own, better suited to the English taste and, more importantly, within the price range of many gentlemen. The elaborate masks, swags and eagle heads so beloved by Tijou were replaced with simple acanthus leaves and heraldic coats of arms. The framework of the gate was allowed to show through and play a part in the overall design. Nevertheless Tijou's book, the legacy of his executed work, and of the standards he set in draughtsmanship and *repoussé*, were the vital foundations to the golden age of English smithwork in the reigns of Queen Anne and George I.

Avenue trees

As the seventeenth century dawned the range of trees planted in walks was very limited. Supplies of transplants were also limited, mainly to the strongly-suckering English elm (*Ulmus procera*) which could be gathered from the roadsides and hedgerows, and had been the traditional hedgerow tree in most of southern and midland England for centuries. This traditional practice was applied to ornamental plantations too. At Gray's Inn in 1588 a labourer was put to work 'gathering of younge trees to sett & for plauntinge of them in the Cony Court'. Other common hedgerow trees used for ornament included the ash (*Fraxinus excelsior*) and, less commonly, the oak (*Quercus robur*). The birch (*Betula pendula*) too was regarded as suitably gay for the ornamental orchard, and the walnut (*Juglans regia*) and sweet chestnut (*Castanea sativa*) were in use, though relatively rare.

Some choicer trees were being introduced. Evelyn wrote of a '*Cloyster* of the right *French Elm* in the little *Garden*' at Somerset House. John Gerard, in his *Herball* (1597), thought the sycamore (*Acer pseudoplatanus*) an exotic, 'a stranger in England, only it groweth in the walks and places of pleasure of noble men, where it is especially planted for the shadow sake'. Sir William Brereton noticed sycamores in the forecourt of the Rijswijk palace in 1634. However, by 1664 Evelyn thought that 'the *Sycamor* is much more in reputation for its *shade* then it deserves; for the *Leaves* which fall early. . . turn to a *Mucilage*, . . . and are therefore to be banish'd from all curious *Gardens* and *Avenues*'. Whether due to Evelyn or not, the popularity of this tree was over.

Limes had become fashionable and were the most commonly used trees for avenues. All limes, despite being naturally tall and fast-growing, lend themselves to close planting, to pruning and to training, so that they were often plashed. 'Plashing' is a method of trimming-up woodland trees, and

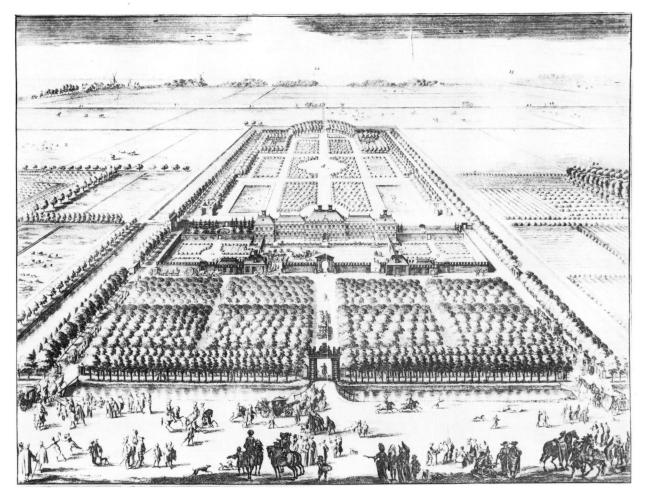

limes treated in this way give a good neat face to an avenue, and grow very slowly. However they also flower very sparsely, so that one of their most attractive features, the heavy sweet scent of their flowers, is largely lost.

There are two species of lime native to central and western Europe, including Britain. The large-leaved lime (*Tilia platyphyllos*) is widespread and locally common in France and Germany, but very rare as a native in Britain, whilst the small-leaved lime (*Tilia cordata*), which had been the wildwood tree in southern and midland England in prehistoric times, was fairly widespread in ancient woodlands there. By the seventeenth century large-leaved limes already had a long history of being planted; in the Middle Ages they were village trees, particularly in what is now Germany, Austria and Switzerland, in eastern France and in the Netherlands. Lime avenues in France seem to have been composed of the large-leaved species.

In Britain, limes appear first to have been planted during the sixteenth century to form walks in gardens and close to houses, rather than in parkland. However, even in England the small-leaved lime was rarely, if ever, used for planting whole lime walks, though occasionally individual trees found their way into avenues of different sorts of lime. The limes planted instead were the large-leaved species, as at Burghley House, near Stamford. One assumes that such trees were imported from France or the Netherlands. Many of the trees planted along the long water at Hampton Court were large-leaved limes, purchased from a boatbuilder and trader.

6.9 Rijswijk, by Van Vianen, 'Maison Royale de Ryswyk' (c. 1700), showing the sycamore grove in front of the house

In the seventeenth century a new lime tree was being propagated in vast numbers in the Netherlands, where it was referred to as the *Hollandse Linde*. This was the common lime (*Tilia x vulgaris*), which is without doubt a hybrid between the large-leaved and small-leaved limes. It grows in a columnar form to a great height, though its advantage at first was its ease of propagation by layering which no doubt accounted for its availability from the nurserymen. There was a considerable demand for street and highway planting for which the Dutch were well known. Evelyn, who had seen the limes of Amsterdam and other Dutch cities, affirmed that

> . . .the People in *Holland* furnish, and maintain whatsoever may conduce to the *public Ornament*, as well as *Convenience*; . . . their *Plantations* in their very *Roads* and common *High-ways* are better preserv'd, and entertain'd then those about the *Houses* and *Gardens of pleasure* belonging to the *Nobles* and *Gentry* of most other *Countries*.

The common lime was imported from Holland to Britain in great numbers in the seventeenth century, so that it became by far the most widely used tree for avenues till about 1750. An early instance was John Tradescant's trip to Holland in 1611, when he purchased 200 limes, presumably common limes, from the Haarlem nurseryman, Cornelius Helin. Evelyn in 1664 lamented that

> . . . we send commonly for this Tree into *Flanders* and *Holland*, to our excessive cost, whiles our own *Woods* do in some places spontaneously produce them, from whence I have received many of their *Berries*; so as it is a shameful negligence, that we are no better provided of *Nurseries* of a *Tree* so choice and universally acceptable.

Evelyn's wish was not granted till the 1690s, by which time the home-grown limes of Brompton Park and other nurseries competed with Dutch imports. Meanwhile, though, they continued; Christiaan van Vranen was given a pass in January 1661/2 to fetch 4,000 lime trees for the king, and Leonard Gurle sent 40 'best Dutch limes' costing £6 to Sir Roger Pratt for his gardens at Ryston Hall, Norfolk, in 1672. Importation was still being preferred, in the north of England, during William and Mary's reign by Peter Aram, who had earlier been one of the gardeners under George London at Fulham Palace. In 1695/6 he went to Holland to buy trees, including limes, in his capacity as the chief gardener at Newby Hall, in Yorkshire; he returned with 2,000 elms, 2,000 beeches and 27 fruit trees, together with seeds, as well.

By the 1660s the variety of trees had thus increased. In *Den Nederlandtsen Hovenier* (1669), Jan van der Groen listed elm and Dutch elm, birch, English oak, ash, sweet chestnut, sycamore, lime, beech, larch, spruce fir, Scots pine, abele and black poplar as the best trees for avenues. All these were known to Evelyn except the Dutch elm, though this was being imported to Britain by the 1690s. The 1776 edition of *Sylva* explained that *Ulmus hollandica* 'was brought from Holland about the beginning of the reign of King William, and was employed in forming hedges in gardens'. However, ordinary elms were not despised in William's time; the great avenue at Wimpole was of them.

Oak was too spreading to be a good avenue tree, being better used in plantations and coppices. Nevertheless it was occasionally found planted as avenues. Evelyn's own brother had a mature oak avenue 56 ft broad and with a 24 ft spacing at Baynard's, in Surrey, in 1664. The 1680s approach to

Het Loo, and the division between the upper and lower gardens, were double avenues of oaks, and the 1690s avenue through the park at Levens was also of oak. Sweet chestnut, Evelyn wrote, was 'a magnificent and royal Ornament. . . for *Avenues* to our *Country-houses*'. Good examples are provided by the avenues at Albury, in Surrey, and Croft Castle, in Herefordshire.

However, a choicer species still was the horse chestnut (*Aesculus hippocastanum*), which had arrived in England from Turkey shortly before it was described by John Parkinson in *Paradisus Terrestris* (1629). Evelyn said that it 'grows into a goodly *Standard*, and bears a most glorius flower, even in our cold Country: this Tree is now all the *mode* for the Avenues to their Countrey palaces in *France*, as appears by the late *Superintendents* Plantation at *Vaux*'. The French fashion was followed at Hampton Court in 1699, when the Great Avenue was lined with horse chestnuts. Curiously, the horse chestnut was not mentioned by Van der Groen, so perhaps this was a rare occasion when England was ahead of the Netherlands arboriculturally.

Abele, or white poplar (*Populus alba*), has the advantage that grass continues to flourish on the ground underneath, and the tree is thus suitable for groves and walks across fields. Evelyn reported that 'in *Flanders* they have large *Nurseries* of them, . . . the *Dutch* look upon a *Plantation* of these *Trees* as an ample portion for a *Daughter*'. Apparently they too were transported in quantity across from Holland to England.

By William's reign various firs were in use as avenues, and prized as evergreens and exotics. An early case was the Scots pines (*Pinus sylvestris*) brought from Scotland by the Duke of Albermarle in 1661 to flank the steps in the hillside at Greenwich. Evelyn's layout at Albury from the late 1660s included a walk of firs along the extended axis. The Knyff views show further examples at Wrest, Bretby, Londesborough and Haigh, and there were groves of them at Newby. Probably most of these later fir plantations were of spruce (*Picea abies*).

The Parterre

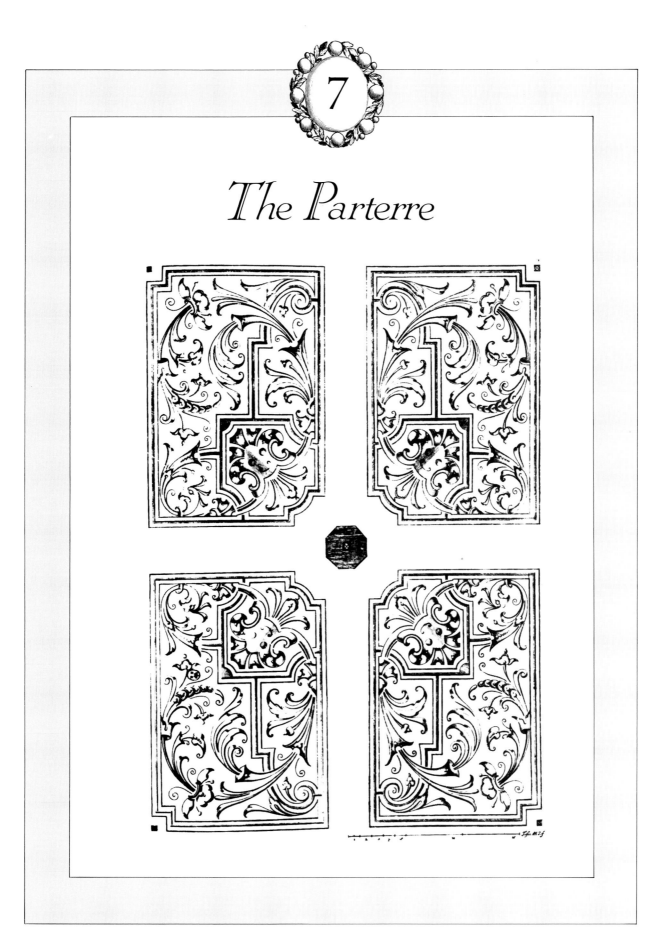

The seventeenth century saw *parterre* design move from rather pedestrian arrangements of flower beds and knot gardens to dizzying levels of sophistication in design and the use of grass, flower beds, gravels of different colours, box hedges, topiary, statuary, plants in pots and fountains.

It was intended that *parterres* should be looked at from the main floor of a building, the first floor, so that the decorative patterns could be seen to good advantage. *Parterres* were also frequently found in sunken gardens, or were surrounded by raised terraces surrounding the garden.

When the previous half-century's practice by the leading nation in this form of design was codified by Antoine-Joseph Dezallier d'Argenville in *La Théorie et la pratique du jardinage* (1709) he categorised *parterres* into five different kinds: *parterres de broderie*; *parterres de compartiment*; *parterres à l'Angloise*; *parterres de pièces coupées pour les fleurs*; *parterres d'orangerie*.

Parterres de broderie and parterres de compartiment

The older form of *parterre* was what Dezallier d'Argenville called the *parterre de compartiment* which was symmetrical about both axes. The term *parterre de broderie* was reserved for the more common form which was the development of the older form designed to be seen from one direction, and symmetrical only about the main axis.

There were various examples in the late-sixteenth century of evergreen plants picking out elaborate designs, often in the form of a flower or branch, on sand or amongst herbs of different colours. These designs could unite a large area in a design, instead of appearing to be a collection of small knot gardens. They were called *parterres de broderie* after their embroidery-like designs. According to Claude Mollet, father of André and gardener to the French king, he had learned about such designs from Etienne du Perac, the king's architect, in the 1580s.

The main problem with using herbs such as marjoram, thyme and lemon balm to pick out the design was that they only lasted a few years. Claude Mollet made another change in practice that enabled elaborate *parterres be broderie* to become manageable. This was the introduction in 1595 of relatively permanent hedges of dwarf box (*Buxus sempervirens 'Suffruticosa'*) into the gardens of Henry IV.

Designs in box on white sand by Salomon de Caus at Heidelburg in 1619, by Jacques Boyceau at the Luxemburg Palace about 1630, and above all by the Mollet family, very quickly became extremely bold. André Mollet introduced this French fashion to England at St James's Palace, and in 1633 went to the Netherlands where he similarly decorated Buren and Honselaarsdijk. Mollet's *Le Jardin de Plaisir* is of special importance as he explains how such *parterres* should be laid out.

Mollet's designs consisted mainly of flower and leaf motif in box, surrounded by white sand which created a sharp contrast with the green box. The finer decorative lines of the flower and leaf motifs could be laid out in stone and marble chippings or black earth. *Grands traits*, bands of grass about six ft wide, could run through the flower motifs in simple geometric lines to contrast with the colour and more intricate boxwork of the main design.

For *broderie*, Mollet's designs were all surrounded by a *plate-bande*, or border, which was of sand, edged with box, and with a central band of flower beds or grass. In either case there could be places at regular intervals for topiary, statuary or tiles for plant pots. The low-growing flowers that

Parterre de Broderie du defsein de Mon— de l'Hôtel de Boucherat— sieur le Nautre

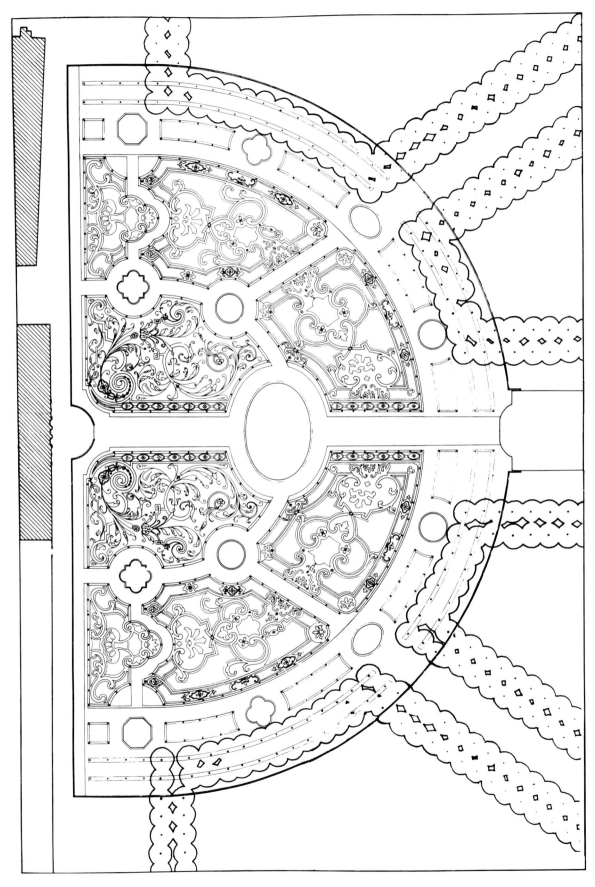

Mollet mentioned as suitable for the flower beds were tulips, *Anemones* and *Ranunculuses*.

Around 1660 André le Nôtre introduced to Chantilly, Fontainebleau, Les Tuilleries and Versailles a less fussy and more elegant form of *broderie*. Whereas Mollet had concentrated on virtuosity in boxwork within simple squares or rectangles, Le Nôtre simplified the boxwork with a pronounced use of wide curves, and opening up the detail more. Meanwhile he made the *plates-bandes* broader and combined them with bolder *grands traits* to give this element of the design a life of its own. Boxwork beds thus acquired complex outlines, and the *plates-bandes* were often themselves finished off as scrolls at corners. The overall effect became more balanced and restful. Daniel Marot and Claude Desgots put these ideas into practice in England and the Netherlands.

Le Nôtre also introduced a greater diversity in the use of plants, giving differences in height, colour and scent, as compared with the Mollets, who used a low and uniform planting. The *plates-bandes*, and the *grands traits* within the boxwork areas, could still be in grass, or they could be adorned with flowering bedding plants in raised beds bordered with dwarf box. The use of topiary was also increasing. The *plates-bandes* were further adorned with small evergreen clipped trees, like yew and box, and sometimes with orangery plants such as orange trees, bay and myrtle. In England it was common to use dark obelisks in yew alternately with silver globes in variegated holly, though there were also examples of spruce fir being used.

Finely ground slag and black earth were still being used for the finer detail of some *parterres*, and other coloured earths were more frequently used as an alternative to white sand. Small areas of grass edged with red stone chippings were frequently used to create an ornamental element. The Dutch *Tracktraat der Lusthoff* (1720), went even further than this; the edging around a *parterre* could be filled with blue materials, and the sand could be strewn with small yellow stones and shells. The flower motifs could, according to the *Tract*, be composed completely of small stones in black, yellow and red.

7.3 *Opposite*: Hampton Court, reconstruction of the *parterre* in 1690.

7.4 Clingendaal, the main *parterre*, by Daniel Stoopendaal (c. 1690)

Parterres à l'Angloise

The use of grass in *parterres* was thought to be particularly English. The purest form of fine turf was bowling greens, and when Leonard Knyff made his bird's-eye-views between about 1697 and 1705 he saw plenty – at Cassiobury in the circle of firs, at Chatsworth next to the West Parterre with a grand temple, at Wimpole in the big square on the distant axis. Indeed most English country houses had a square or occasionally circular one. They were seldom allowed to interrupt a main axis, and were placed to the side, or at a distance along it. Often, though, it was possible to have them under the windows of the house, and where the garden axis was to the side, as was common in England, they could even be placed under the back front.

Where an earth terrace was made in a garden the usual practice in France as elsewhere was to form a turf *glacis*, or slope. The English were again pre-eminent in the decorative sculpturing of such slopes, as can be seen on the slopes down to the Maestricht Garden at Windsor.

The English also preferred grass *plats* with statues and fountains to the elaborate *parterres* of Continental countries. Although cheap to make, the manicuring of these *plats*, slopes and bowling greens was quite an art, and clearly impressed André Mollet. He said that the beautiful effect of English turf depended on frequently mowing it short during the summer, and so not letting the grass get long. Also it was beaten down, or well rolled. Apparently wooden rollers were used for removing wormcasts, while stone ones were

7.5 Het Loo, 'boulegrin met des Koningsthuyn' by Romeyn de Hooghe (c. 1700). This Dutch bowling green was maintained by an Englishman

7.6 Zeist, *parterre à l'Angloise* by Daniel Stoopendaal (c. 1700)

used on walks and the turf to compact the ground to an even surface. Mollet also advised a careful selection of turf, such as could be found on sheepwalks, to avoid coarse or tangled grass. He also thought that a mottled appearance, derived from intermixing different evergreen herbs such as camomile, would give a decorative effect.

Mollet's *parterres à l'Angloise* combined the English love of turf with the French love of patterns. Hence the background was turf bordered by flower beds, and the pattern was made in *plates-bandes* of white sand edged with box hedges and with a central band of grass. The *plates-bandes* formed both the edging around the whole, and wove a symmetrical pattern through the turf interior of the compartment. The grass *parterre* which Mollet designed for Honselaarsdijk in 1633 is a good illustration of this.

Whatever the pattern happened to be, Mollet's *parterres à l'Angloise* kept to a rigid combination of materials in the *plates-bandes*. Later designers did not feel constrained in this way, and a wide variety of combinations using grass were to be found by the end of the century. Marot, for example, preferred to have his flower beds down the middle of his *plates-bandes* instead of bordering the turf, and they acquired box edges, topiary and flowering bedding plants. These beds were thus the same as the *plates-bandes* in the *parterre de broderie*, so enabling unified designs incorporating both *broderie* and turf, so spectacularly illustrated at Hampton Court.

Two simpler forms of *parterre à l'Angloise* were found. One was to dispose of the *plate-bande* within the compartment, though keeping that around the perimeter, thus giving a clear expanse of grass in the interior, perhaps punctuated by a statue in the middle. This simple form was what Mollet had seen in England in Charles I's time, and was still by far the most common *parterre* in England in William III's time. The Knyff and Kip views show various trees in *plates-bandes* – topiary in obelisks and globes, greenhouse plants in their tubs, fruit trees and spruce firs.

The four outer *parterres* of the Great Garden at Het Loo were also like this, though in addition to the perimeter flower bed *plate-bande* there was an inner one as well in a lacework-like pattern. The Het Loo perimeter *plates-bandes* were adorned with pyramids of box and juniper, the local material, and shrubs of marshmallows. The spring bedding consisted of tulips, hyacinths, *Ranunculuses*, *Anemones*, auriculas and narcissus; the summer bedding of poppies, gillyflowers and larks-heels; and the autumn bedding of sunflowers, 'Indian cresses', 'pass-roses' and marigolds.

Another simplification of the *parterre à l'Angloise* was the cut-work treatment, *gazon coupé*, keeping the pattern within the turf, but dispensing with the flower beds, topiary and all, thus composing a pattern in bands of sand alone. On the Continent the bands of sand were usually of uniform width, say six ft wide and were composed in strapwork-like patterns. There were examples in England too, at Chatsworth and New Park. However, in England, gardeners sometimes liked to make their designs in the turf, so that the sand became the background material. George London's *parterres* at Longleat were good examples, and there are others in the Privy Garden at Hampton Court and at Castle Bromwich Hall and Wrest Park. There was an English-style *gazon coupé* at De Voorst, and Marot, too, often sculpted the edges of the turf in his more complicated *parterres* to form scallop, shell and fan shapes either in the grass or in the sand.

Parterres de pièces coupées pour les fleurs

The Italian Renaissance tradition of *parterres* made of ornamental flower beds continued to be appropriate for flower gardening. Hans Vredeman de Vries, in his series of prints *Hortorum viridariorumque elegantes et multi plicis formae* (1583) adopted the Italian taste. His designs consisted of regularly formed, slightly raised, plant beds filled with black earth and separated from the white sand which surrounds them by planks or stones. These designs were clearly meant for exhibiting bulbs and special plants. Sebastiano Serlio's designs were made directly available to the Dutch reader when his *Tutte l'opere d'architettura* was published in Dutch in 1616. The Italian, G.B. Ferrari, and also the German, P. Laurenberg, worked in the first half of the seventeenth century in the same tradition. In *Den Nederlandtsen Hovenier* (1669), Jan van der Groen gives examples of flower beds – these and the examples given by H. Cause in *De Koninglycke Hovenier* (1676) (translated into English as *The Royal Gardener* and published in 1683), all follow De Vries.

Dezallier d'Argenville, working in the tradition of Le Nôtre, called these kind of beds *parterres de pièces coupées pour les fleurs*. In his day the flower beds themselves were laid out decoratively in intricate forms, sometimes in combination with small areas of grass, edged with white sand. Each bed or area was edged with box and the gravel or sand between gave sufficient space to walk between the beds. According to Dezallier d'Argenville these *parterres* were symmetrical on both axes. Daniel Marot's design gives a good impression of what Dezallier d'Argenville meant.

7.7 Hampton Court, Privy Garden, by Sutton Nicholls (c. 1696). An example of English cut-work. The base of the statue of Arethusa had been remodelled and re-erected in 1689

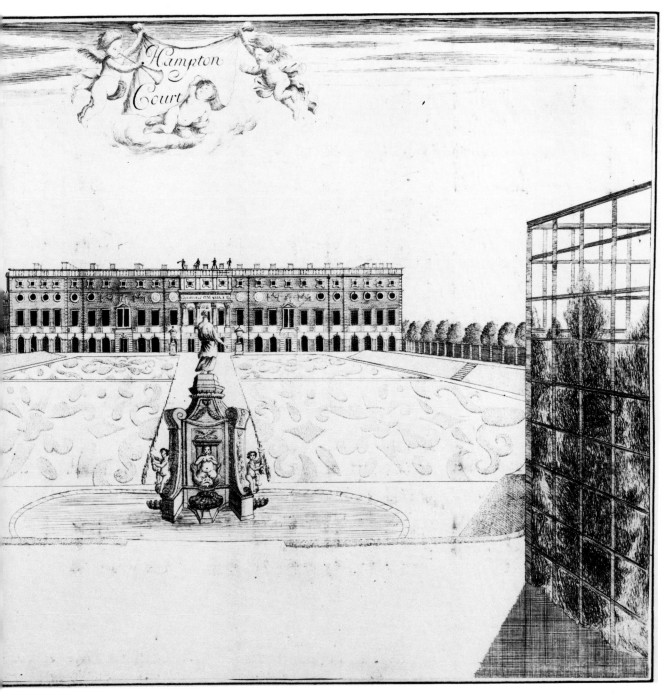

Parterres d'orangerie

These *parterres* were intended for the display of exotics in the summer. They were often circular or semicircular, and the centre was usually simple – a pool or one or more areas of grass edged with white sand. Attention was focused on the *plate-bande* around the *parterre* which was filled with grass, white sand or red stone chippings on which plants displayed in barrels or tubs were set out. The first use for this sort of *parterre* was for setting out the traditional orangery plants – oranges, lemons, myrtle, bay and jasmine.

Well-known orangery collections with such gardens attached included

7.8 Various types of *parterre* from Daniel Marot's *Nouveau livre des parterres* (1703). Above is a *parterre de pièces coupées pour les fleurs,* and below are *parterres de broderie* and *parterres à l'Angloise*

William III's at Honselaarsdijk, Hampton Court and Het Loo. Some other grand ones in England were the semicircular ones with pools at Bretby and Stansted, and the moated one at Wimpole. However, especially after the foundation of the new botanic garden at Amsterdam in 1682, the assortment of exotic plants in the Netherlands was greatly increased and their proud owners required means to display them too. The best Dutch ones were the circular ones with pools at Zeist, Heemstede and Zorgvliet.

Fountains and statues

Like many European countries, the sixteenth-century Netherlands and England had traditions of elaborate fountains, and, in Dutch gardens at least, human bodies and faces were carved at the top of the wooden stanchions supporting arbours. The next wave of Italian fashion in the early seventeenth century brought statuary and cascades into northern European gardens. New work of this nature was very expensive. This was not too great a constraint to Louis XIII or Louis XIV, and most of André Mollet's published designs for *parterres* indicated positions for figures. Indeed many French royal gardens of the late-seventeenth-century were positively crowded with statuary.

There were urns and vases, but the principal subjects of fountains and free-standing figures were gods and goddesses from Roman and Greek mythology. These were suitable for demonstrating that the garden belonged to a refined and classically-educated patron. Sometimes the statuary was arranged in a programme in order to provide a narrative or an allegory; at Marly in the 1690s it expressed the parallels between the reigns of Louis XIV and the Emperor Augustus. Designs for statues besides gods and goddesses included subjects from hunting, such as antelopes and wild boars, while dolphins and equestrian statues were also found.

Outside France this fashion was necessarily exclusive, being principally confined in the Netherlands to the stadholders, and in England to the monarchy. The visits in the 1600s of the young Frederik-Hendrik with his mother, Louise de Coligny, to the French Court must have been a formative experience. He afterwards had several statues erected in the Princessetuin, the garden laid out at the Noordeinde Palace, in The Hague, after 1609. Here figures of Diana, Neptune and Aquarius were placed in a flower garden in front of a wall covered with apricot and peach trees.

The Huis ter Nieuwburg at Rijswijk had many statues erected on the axis of the *parterres* made about 1630. For its time, the placing of so many ornamental objects on the main axis was remarkable. In the middle of the first *parterre* stood a large elaborate fountain, then in the middle of the second and third *parterre* gardens enormous statues on high pedestals. Further statues were placed in the *parterres de broderie*.

During alterations to Honselaarsdijk in 1639 the bases for a group of statues were placed in the garden and nine statues and busts cast in metal were imported from France. Another of Frederik-Hendrik's gardens to be liberally furnished with statues was the Huis ten Bosch, begun in 1645 by Pieter Post. Four statues mounted on high pedestals stood at the crossing of the paths between the four *parterres de broderie*. The path leading from the house was flanked by flower bed *plates-bandes* further beautified by pedestals supporting pots filled with flowers. White painted trellis obelisks stood at either end of the flower borders and were covered with climbing plants.

Meanwhile, in London, the Earl of Arundel and Charles I had been assembling collections of antique and modern Italian statuary, some of which were placed in their gardens. St James's Palace housed the lion's share of Charles's collection, including the bronze gladiator, cast by Hubert le Sueur from moulds taken from one at the Borghese Palace in Florence. This gladiator was placed at the Whitehall end of the canal when it was made, though it was moved again to Hampton Court in 1701. Another copy was placed in the garden of Wilton in the 1630s.

Queen Henrietta Maria, added several bronze statues to Somerset House, including an elaborate fountain surmounted by a figure of Arethusa, the nymph of the fountain at Syracuse. This was designed by Inigo Jones and made by Le Sueur in 1635. In 1655/6 it was taken by Oliver Cromwell to the Privy Garden at Hampton Court, where it joined other bronze figures of Venus and Cleopatra on stone pedestals, marble statues of Adonis and Apollo and four large leaden flower pots. Arethusa and her supporters were described in 1663 as

> . . . four syrens in bronze, seated astride on dolphins, between which was a shell, supported on the foot of a goat. Above the sirens on a second tier, were four little children, each seated, holding a fish, and surmounting all a large figure of a lady – all the figures being bronze and the basin of marble.

The few examples of garden sculpture by native Englishmen in the 1630s included the stone figures by Nicholas Stone at Wilton. The four *parterres de broderie* each had a central fountain with Venus, Diana, Susanna and Cleopatra. Behind the *parterres* the wilderness had large figures of Flora and Bacchus. Besides these examples at Wilton, there was the stone Venus presiding over a fountain at Bolsover, in Nottinghamshire, and the statuary at Hadham Hall. None of these were as sophisticated in style or execution as Le Sueur's or the imported Italian ones, and the Civil War effectively put an end to high-quality garden sculpture in England till the 1680s.

William III introduced considerably more statuary in adapting all the palaces he inherited. For example, at Honselaarsdijk statues were erected around the new *parterres de broderie* directly behind the house, while a fountain stood in the middle of the main axis. This was described by the Swedish garden architect, Nicodemus Tessin, as consisting of four dolphins, on which there was a seated cupid. The *parterre* gardens that had been designed by Mollet on either side of the house were also replaced by *broderie* surrounding grass plots with statues in the centre of each.

In addition to statues, vases also held an important place in gardens. Daniel Marot designed many vases for Het Loo, while Van der Aveele designed the ornamental vases for Bentinck's Zorgvliet. At Zeist, Nassau-Odijk had many ornamental vases in the large *parterre de broderie* garden. These were fitted with lids so that no water could get in and, in the winter, form ice which could cause them to burst.

By the time that William III arrived in Britain in 1688, several of the nobility had begun to introduce statuary to their gardens in numbers. These were principally in the great country house gardens designed by Talman and London. The sculptor most in demand at these places was Caius Gabriel Cibber, originally a Dane. Following work at Thoresby in 1686, he went on to Chatsworth where from 1687 to 1690 he made sphinxes, a triton, and a Flora.

However, Cibber's greatest test was at Hampton Court. Here he found himself pitted against Edward Pierce who was carving a redesigned base for Arethusa in white marble, which was set up in a pool at the end of the Privy Garden, and a small fountain of two entwined dolphins in the same material. In 1690 each man carved a great vase with a matching pedestal to be set up under the south front overlooking the Privy Garden. Although each vase was identical in shape, Pierce carved a relief of Amphitrite and the Nereids, and Cibber carved the Triumph of Bacchus. Two years later each carved very elaborate urns; Pearce's subject being the Judgement of Paris and Cibber's Meleager hunting the Calydonian boar. At Kensington in 1691 Cibber

7.9 Zorgvliet, two vases (c. 1690). Pairs of monumental stone vases were also installed at Hampton Court

provided four great stone flower pots. It was Cibber who was made 'sculptor to his majesty' in 1693, but the exquisite workmanship exhibited by both men had proved that either was worthy of the title.

William's statuary at Het Loo was as ambitious. In the forecourt Walter Harris was greeted with the sight of entwined dolphins spouting water into the horse fountain, but this was merely a foretaste:

> The *Lower Garden* has a *Terrace Walk* on three sides of it; and here we behold straight before us the *Fountain of Venus*, and beyond it another *Fountain* of a young *Hercules*. In the Cross-walk that goes between those two Fountains, here is on the right hand a Fountain of a *Celestial Globe*, and on the left such another *Terrestial Globe*. And at the end of the same Walk on the right hand, upon the side of one Terras Walk, there is the *Cascade* of *Narcissus*, as also on the left, upon the side of the opposite Terras Walk, the *Cascade* of *Galathea*.

Venus was accompanied by a cupid and stood on a rock surrounded by four tritons blowing water from conch shells. Placed centrally in the outer four *parterres* of the lower garden were marble statues of Apollo, Pomona Bacchus and Flora. Just beyond the infant Hercules

> . . . on the two *Pilasters* next to the Steps are placed two Beautiful *Sphinxes* with their Riddle express'd or carved; and on the two others are

133

seen two *Wolfs* in Stone, each of them giving suck to a *Romulus* and *Remus*.

At Middachten Castle, completely restored and embellished by the Earl of Athlone between 1695 and 1698, statues were erected in the large *parterre de broderie* behind the castle. The Baron Van Arnhem's garden at Rosendael was lavishly decorated with sculptures, fountains, grottoes and garden pavilions. The sloping ground required terracing between the *parterres de broderie* which gave an opportunity for a grotto. On arrival at the viewing point above the *parterres*, a gilded lead statue of Fortune standing on a blue globe awaited the stroller, and from here a wonderful view was discovered down the *parterres* and the cascades to the moated castle.

When William returned to the embellishment of Hampton Court in 1699 to 1702, he concentrated upon the Great Parterre. Cibber made stone figures of Flora, Pomona, Ceres and Diana but died in 1700. This created an opening for John Nost whose speciality was lead, as at Melbourne Hall, in Derbyshire, where boys, Perseus, Andromeda, Mercury and Psyche were supplied in 1699. For Hampton Court he made the 'flower pots' on the gates of this name supported by four boys each, and a statue of Bacchus. He also made a model of an intended great fountain with four mermaids on dolphins and other embellishments, to be cannibalised from the Arethusa fountain which was removed from the Privy Garden at this time. He moved Cibber's and Pierce's urns and vases, and the Borghese gladiator in St James's Park, to the Great Parterre. The new statuary delivered to Hampton Court in 1701 included the lion and unicorn at the Trophy Gates by Grinling Gibbons who is better known for his carving in lime wood.

In the Netherlands, statues were usually painted as the cold and dampness of the winter would have a damaging effect on the materials – stone, marble and wood. The paint could be white or stone-coloured. Frequently the statues were given a new layer of lime in the spring to freshen them up among the greenery. In the winter, marble statues were brought indoors and covered up to protect them from extremes of frost and sunshine which could damage them.

Trellis and arbours

Although originally meant merely to support climbing plants, lattice work became an artform in itself. Jan van der Groen illustrated *Den Nederlandtsen Hovenier* (1669) with many excellent models for lattice work in obelisk or pyramid form, many of which one suspects lasted for less than 20 years. Even more ephemeral were the triumphal arches and other trelliswork erected for special occasions, for which Jean Marot, Daniel's father, was known. Daniel himself was able to take this fine French style of decoration, which reached its peak during Louis XIV's reign, to the Netherlands.

Trellis pyramids and obelisks were used at the centre of the *parterres* or, as at the Huis ten Bosch, marking the beginning of the paths. Marot liked to provide elaborate eyecatchers at the end of axes and these generally were in trellis, mimicking classical architecture, unless they were in stone in the form of a portico.

Another use for trellis was to construct bird cages. These were placed in *volière*, or aviary, grounds. William and Mary had several such areas – at Honselaarsdijk, Het Loo and in a small garden adjacent to the Glass Case Garden at Hampton Court.

7.10 *Opposite*: Trellis arch and pyramids, by A. van Langelaar (1685)

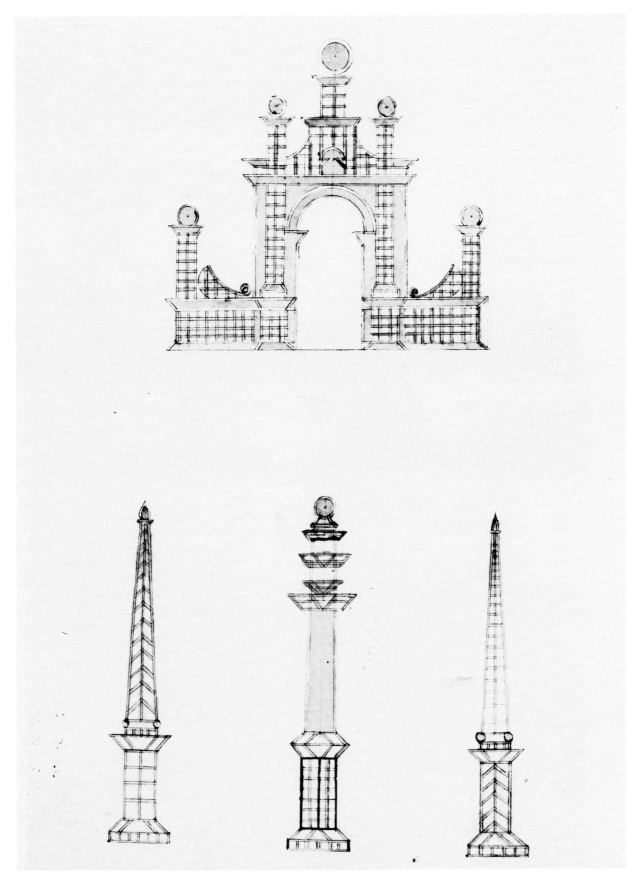

7.11 Zorgvliet, tunnel arbour

Arbours, which consisted of hedges, usually of elm, arched over paths to knit together into a tunnel, were inherited from the Renaissance garden of the sixteenth century. The tradition was maintained particularly strongly in the Netherlands into William and Mary's time; indeed one of the most elaborate was made for Mary herself as 'the Queen's garden' at Het Loo. Training the hedges required extensive trellis work, often with domed rooms at the corners which formed substantial pavilions in their own right. The trellis was sometimes painted; at Het Loo the carpenters' work was painted blue. The ground was meanwhile treated as a normal flower garden, viewed through windows in the trellis. There were many other examples, and Zorgvliet had perhaps the greatest length of tunnel arbours in the Netherlands.

However, the Dutch also favoured another form of arbour – that when only the roof was formed, such as at Dieren and Zeist. This gave a form of gallery when one side was closed off by a wall. To make these arbours, trees were trained upwards, and the side branches removed, while the upper branches were trained onto a trellis framework.

English examples were far fewer, and were not so splendid. Tunnel arbours, or 'bowers', included the Dutch elm 'Queen Mary's Bower' in the Privy Garden at Hampton Court, and others at Grimsthorpe, Newnham Paddox and Longleat. Domed trellis arbours were extremely rare; there was one terminating a walk at Hampton Court and decorated by Louis la Guerre,

two in the wilderness at Wimpole, and four small ones in the wilderness at Dawley.

7.12 Hampton Court, arbour from the 'Fort Album' (c. 1718), which was decorated by Louis la Guerre

Pavilions

The summer houses at the corners of the old arbours were continued in more permanent form in stone at the end of walks in the more expansive classical gardens of the 1640s onwards, and some were installed at Zeist in the 1680s. Corner turrets and pavilions were quite usual, though at Huis ten Bosch a pair of two-storied summerhouses were placed halfway along opposite sides of the *parterre*, closing off the cross-axis. Here balconies on the first floor gave views over the *parterre*. Towards the end of the century Zorgvliet acquired a pavilion to terminate the main garden axis, and Marot designed a pavilion for Rosendael. Also, garden pavilions were built at the water's edge along the Vecht, a river along which many of Amsterdam's rich built their villas. There was another pavilion of this type at Heemstede.

In England the traditions were slightly different. There had been banquetting houses since the previous century, and some of these survived. A new one was made from a turret at Hampton Court for William's use. Promenading to take the air was an English obsession, and facing pairs of

7.13 Zorgvliet, the pavilion beyond the *parterre*, by Johannes van den Aveele (c. 1690)

summerhouses were to be found at Gray's Inn and some country houses. The hexagon at the extremity of the garden axis at Longleat was an unusual example of a small pavilion at a distant viewpoint provided for the walker. Yet another English recreation requiring its own buildings was bowling; William Talman built a bowling green pavilion at Chatsworth, there was a similar one at Wollaton, and a pair at Grimsthorpe, and William's own bowling green at Hampton Court had as many as four pavilions.

Grottoes

The English were reluctant to follow Salomon de Caus's lead in making grottoes, but the Dutch were more enthusiastic. In one part of Count Johan-Maurits's garden made in the 1630s there was a famous grotto at the centre forming a refuge to a colony of herons. They and other water birds were allocated plenty of room. The grotto was decorated with whelks and other kinds of shells and glass.

Later in the century there was a grotto at Rosendael; one of the most admired buildings at Zorgvliet was the grotto, reached via the labyrinth. In front of the pavilion in which the Zorgvliet grotto was built water jets spouted from the ground making a spectacular display. On the exterior, rocks were piled up on top of each other, and on the interior there were shells

and fountains, as well as stone baskets of flowers and busts decorating the walls. Finally, Queen Mary had a grotto in the basement of Het Loo which was passed through on the way into her private gardens. This was adorned with shells, and there was a cage containing songbirds.

7.14 Dieren, grotto, by Pieter Schenk (c. 1690). Such grottoes were more symbolic than real

8

Waterways and Waterworks

8.1 *Previous page*:
Zorgvliet, the canal
surroundings the *parterre*,
by Johannes van den Aveele
(c. 1690)

Antoine-Joseph Dezallier d'Argenville expounded on the sensual value of water in gardens in the 'Une Traité d'Hydraulique' in *La Théorie et la pratique du jardinage*.

> Water and fountains are the most important ornament in gardens; they add life to them and are lively in themselves. Their clear and sparkling movement dispels loneliness, and we can enjoy endlessly their refreshment and murmuring in peaceful tranquillity.

Still water canals

However, let us start with the more prosaic canals of the Dutch polderland and build up to an understanding of the more sophisticated hydraulics of Dutch and English gardens. Most of Holland is former seabed, reclaimed with great ingenuity and expense over centuries. Being below sea level, all the rainfall onto polders had to be drained away across a virtually flat landscape to windmills where it could be pumped up to sea level. Dutch skill in practical hydraulics is thus easily understood, as is the characteristic landscape intersected with a lattice of canals.

Circumferential canals were inevitable around all Dutch castles and country houses in and around the margins of polderland, but the Dutch always made a virtue of this, creating substantially broader canals then necessary in order, perhaps, to evoke the appearance of old moated sites. Honselaarsdijk and Rijswijk are early-seventeenth-century examples, whereas Clingendaal, De Voorst, Zeist and Middachten are examples from the time of William III. It is probably no coincidence that André Mollet's plans of ideal layouts in *Le Jardin de Plaisir* include circumferential canals, since he worked for Prince Frederik-Hendrik from about 1633 to about 1635, certainly at Honselaarsdijk, and perhaps elsewhere in Holland.

As early as 1653, Dutch engineers in England, led by Cornelius Vermuyden, had completed the drainage of the Lincolnshire and Cambridgeshire Fens. Vermuyden died in 1677 by which time drainage canals and polder windmills were well known in Britain, but there is no evidence to connect him or his colleagues directly with any garden waterworks. In fact England's first major ornamental waterworks were axial, not circumferential, being the canals flanked with limes and laid out by Mollet at St James's in 1660 and Hampton Court in 1661. Neither were they connected with a drainage project; each had a supply of running water – the Tyburn Brook for St James's and Charles I's Longford River at Hampton Court. A more likely source of the idea for these English canals was the Grand Canal at Fontainebleau begun in 1607 and flanked with elms. A few imitative axial canals could be seen in the following decades, such as at Wrest Park and Melton Constable. Chatsworth had one parallel to the river, but not on an axis.

Though not mandatory, it was usual for the French garden designer of this time to include water. Dezallier d'Argenville advised that a garden should contain plenty of water. Burghley and Longleat were the main English examples of the use of canals within the gardens, but there were many minor examples too. Westbury Court, in Gloucestershire, was typical – walled and geometrically regular, babbling streams being replaced by still, box-edged straight waterways whose flat surfaces reflected statuary, topiary and the outlines of the summerhouse. Another use to which George London put still water was as reflecting surfaces along the approaches to a mansion, which

8.2 Dieren, view of the
large pool from the grotto,
by Pieter Schenk (1702)

seems to have been the purpose of the basons at Woburn Abbey, Wanstead and Bushy Park.

In terms of construction, the garden canal was nothing more than a straight-sided pond. Hand dug, and using horses and carts for transport, the canal required a major outlay on labourers. The canals would be lined with puddled clay, a technique that was to become common with the early builders of transport canals. The 'puddling' consisted of compounding lumps of clay, using the bare feet of the workers, until a homogeneous lining had been obtained. Sometimes, it is said, a herd of cattle was used, their cloven hooves having the desired effect.

Pools, rockwork and cascades

The French had been elaborating pools with artificial rockwork for many years well before about 1598 when Italian engineers were sent by Ferdinand, the Grand Duke of Tuscany, to construct grottoes and automata at Saint Germain-en-Laye for Henry IV. These Italians, Tommaso and Alessandro Francini, were soon at Fontainebleau constructing rockwork with jets of water in a balustraded pool, and on top of the rocks was placed a cast of the river god Tiber. The French engineer, Salomon de Caus, took his skills in this sort of work to the English court of James I from 1608 till 1613, then to

143

Heidelberg in the service of James's daughter, Elizabeth, and her husband the Elector Palatine.

De Caus built a Mount Parnassus in a pool at Somerset House. He had also seen the rockwork giant at Pratolino, in Italy, and, combining the ideas of the giant and the river god in a pool, planned a series of huge stonework river gods reclining on vases from which their rivers flowed. De Caus designed one for Richmond Palace, and used the same model for the figure of the Rhine in a pool at Heidelberg. Holland shared in this tradition, though rather late if Rijswijk was made about 1630. Two almost identical river gods in pools, and the old-fashioned fenced *parterres*, strongly suggest De Caus or his craftsmen. Another French *grottier*, Joseph Dinant, was permanently employed at Rijswijk and Honselaarsdijk on the grottoes and fountains throughout the 1630s and 1640s.

The French did not let this sort of work die out, but England did not see much of it after De Caus. The faint echoes to be seen in the rockwork fountains of Bretby and Chatsworth were unusual, and it may be no coincidence that the Frenchman Grillet worked at both these places. In the Netherlands the interest in grottoes and fountains grew, and there were two statues of river gods at Het Loo, but the De Caus-like rockwork with its river gods had disappeared from Rijswijk by the 1690s.

Only occasionally was it possible to use a natural spring as a source of water. However pools were quite simple to arrange as long as a supply of running water was available and a system of channels and culverts could be

8.3 Het Loo, 'de Terras Cascade op Zyde' by Romeyn de Hooghe (c. 1700). The lack of substantial water level differences meant that no more than this short flight could be achieved

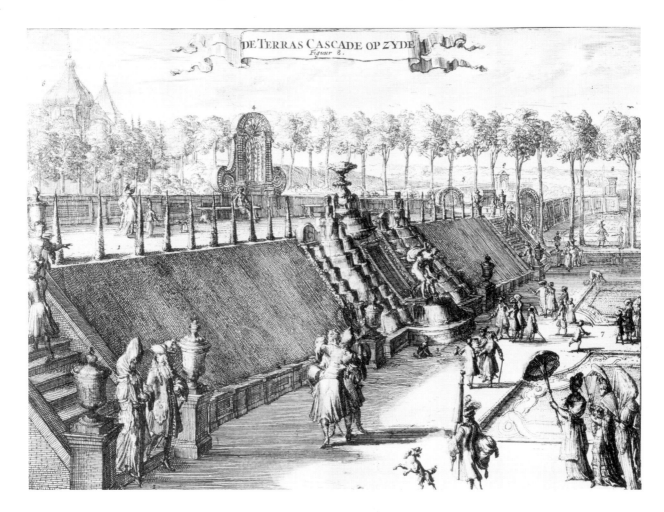

arranged. The same was true of the more spectacular cascade, of which England only had two of note, at Chatsworth, with which Grillet was involved about 1687, and Talman's at Dyrham ten years later. The main challenge of cascades was that the effect depends upon huge quantities of water, and so it was necessary to construct reservoirs for storage, and to release the water by opening a penstock. In the Netherlands the only cascades that were at all impressive were those at Rosendael, where streams could be conducted to a position above the terraced *parterres*. Even those at Het Loo had very short flights.

Jets d'eau

Water had to be piped in order to force a jet of water from a fountain nozzle. It was not adequate simply to arrange for a large enough reservoir; skilful hydraulics were often required. De Caus knew how to achieve jets, because the river god at Heidelberg had them rising from a rocky island. So did the Rijswijk ones, and the last recorded payment to Joseph Dinant included monies for three fountains at Honselaarsdijk.

The principle of hydrostatics was set down by Simon Stevin, Quartermaster-General and Director of Waterworks in Holland, and by Blaise Pascal, a French mathematician, in his *Recit de la Grande Experience de l'Equilibre des Liqueurs* (1663). This was simply that interconnected bodies of water will come to rest at the same level. This was useful, in conjunction with a survey of levels, in the design of slow-moving canals and channels along contours to the higher points of a garden. However there was not yet any formula to enable the fountaineer to juggle the 'head' (or height) of the reservoir, the size of the pipes, the flow and the pressure at the jet. This had to be judged from the experience of obtaining better results from a reservoir high above the fountains, but at as little distance away as possible.

Jan van der Groen, writing on the pleasures of country life in his *Den Nederlandtsen Hovenier* (1669) gave advice to the modest fountaineer thus:

> The fountains of the pleasure garden are quite delightful and graceful, especially when supplied with sparkling water brought down from the mountains or hills above or below ground. But this is not possible everywhere, so that rain water has to be collected in the gutters and stored in lead tanks high up on roofs and lofts. A tap in the pipe can stop the flow of water and cut off the fountain. From this tap different lead pipes are led to the places where the water jets are wanted. If the jets are not to reach the same height, separate taps have to be fitted on to the lead pipes. These fountains can be placed in ponds, on islands or hills and can be made out of valuable carved marble or grey or blue Ardwin stone – or even of copper, lead and wood, which can be attractively painted. . . [a beautiful fountain is illustrated] of which the lowest basin is of stone. With all basins whether they be 3, 4, 6 or 8 sided, wood can also be used, but it must be lined with lead. Because of the continuous dampness, the pedestal or base must be of stone.
>
> The topmost bowl can be made of beaten copper or gilded or painted wood. This fountain can, however, be made completely of stone and on it can be mounted all kinds of statues of gods, people, animals, fish, birds and other subjects.

An engraving shows another bowl made of scalloped beaten copper. This stands on a base of rocks standing in a brick-edged bason, from which water

8.4 Longleat, the fountain, detail from Knyff and Kip *Britannia Illustrata* (1707)

shoots out of little lead pipes. Van der Groen suggested that objects could float on the main jet, such as birds, fish, cupids, and human figures.

The English took to single jet fountains enthusiastically in their *parterres* and forecourts after the Restoration. Bretby had one just outside the forecourt gates, while Badminton and Longleat each had a pair in the forecourt itself. Hundreds more were made at the focal points in English *parterres* and wildernesses, even in quite modest gardens. Bretby had another ten fountains in the gardens, some with multiple jets. However nowhere surpassed the 17 at Hampton Court, including 13 in the Fountain Garden alone.

Longleat was the first of George London's gardens where he displayed a prowess and delight at constructing grand and complex fountains. The Great Fountain in the centre of the canal bason was carved by John Harvey of Bath and literally dwarfed, if not drenched, the onlooker. Progressively we can

8.5 Zorgvliet, *jets d'eau* below the pavilion, by Johannes van den Aveele (c. 1700)

observe the evolving artistry of London's fountains and waterworks, and how he valued the role of the reflection and movement of water in the overall design, as important as the geometry of gravel and grass and the enlivening and beautifying of flowers. Bretby, Chatsworth, Dawley and New Park are demonstrations of these.

Daniel Defoe noted that William III was personally concerned with the fountains at Hampton Court:

> While the Gardens were thus laid out, the king also directed the laying of Pipes for the Fountain and *Jette d'Eau's*; and particularly the Dimensions of them, and what Quantity of water they should cast up, and encreas'd the number of them after the first Design.

This shows the king in the role of an engineer, and the *jets d'eau* indicate that a good working pressure was hoped for. However, William was obviously more hopeful than experienced, and the fountains never worked properly. The problem was that the head of water was only 13 ft, and the source was so far distant that most of the pressure was dissipated in the pipework.

In Dutch gardens of William III's time, *jets d'eau* were popular though elaborate systems of pumps were usually necessary. William had a rather extraordinary example of waterworks made in the *bosquet* at Dieren. Each little room was given a *jet d'eau*, and channels ran down the *allées* to take the water away.

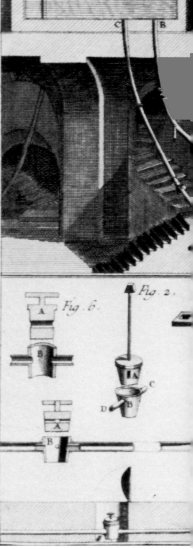

8.6 Het Loo, 'Fontaine de Venus', by Karl Danckerts (c. 1700)

Pipework and stopcocks

Timber pipes would still have been used in the early-seventeenth century. Solomon de Caus had an illustration of a machine for boring out 9 ft long tree trunks with an augur in his book *Les Raisons des forces mouvantes* (1615). They were bored so as to fit together with a spigot and socket joint. Wooden two-way stopcocks, possibly lined with brass, which would give a degree of control over the flow, were also available at this period.

However, lead was also commonly used, and by the late-seventeenth century its use in hydraulics seems to have been universal. In 1699 the plumber who installed the pipework in the Fountain Garden at Hampton Court, Matthew Roberts, laid another 566 yds of '7 inch burnt pipe' weighing 50 tons and 12 cwt across the Wilderness and Fountain Garden. The joints required another 70 cwt of 'sodder' (solder), and there was a large brass stopcock weighing 4 cwt and costing £30. Lesser piping was of 3 in and 2 in diameter, and there were six more brass stopcocks at each size.

That some system of valves must have been included in the elaborate system in the gardens of Versailles is shown by the fact that Claude Denis, the *fontainier* was ordered to make sure that the fountains started up just before Louis XIV moved into any particular part of the gardens.

Pumps

When a reservoir at the desired height could not be filled by gravity, the engineer had to resort to a pump. The seventeenth century was a period in which the quest for improving pumping methods was of consuming interest in mining circles. At the same time in Britain the founding of the Royal Society in 1660 focused men's minds on scientific principles, and the Great

Fire of London in 1666 laid even more stress on the need for efficient pumping equipment. Nevertheless, until the turn of the eighteenth century, there was no effective means of driving a pump except by man, animal, wind, or water power.

Throughout the period there were many attempts to harness the expansive power of steam to drive water pumps or to use the weight of the atmosphere to fill a vacuum created by the expansion of steam. The ancient Greeks had invented ingenious devices using steam and hot water to produce dramatic effects at their temples, but the idea lay dormant until Salomon de Caus wrote of 'little devices for raising water by the power of steam' in *Les Raisons* in 1615. De Caus's book set other minds thinking, among them

8.7 Plate XIII from J. E. Bertr and *Descriptions des Arts et Métiers . . .* (1776)

Edward Somerset, Marquis of Worcester. Somerset certainly built a machine which could raise water 40 ft and be operated by one man, but his description in *A Century of the Names and scantlings of the Marquis of Worcester's Inventions* (1663), is too vague to assure us that it was steam-powered. Sir Samuel Morland, 'Master of Mechanicks', to Charles II, also built a model of a steam pump.

Whilst the goal for a steam engine to pump the water remained unfulfilled water wheels were the most usual means of raising water. Salomon de Caus had planned a waterwheel-driven pumping system for Hatfield House. In 1671 John Evelyn noted at Euston, in Suffolk, that:

> The Water furnishing the fountains is raised by a pretty Engine or very slight plaine Wheele, which likewise serves to grind his Corne, from a small cascade of the Canale, the invention of Sir *Sam: Morland*.

Celia Fiennes wrote of her visit to Broadlands, near Romsey:

> The gardens are walled in, some with brest walls some higher with flower potts on them, severall places with open grates to look through with stone balls or figures on the pillars each side the gates every way; there is a water house that by a wheele casts up the water out of the River just by and fills the pipes to serve all the house and to fill the bason designed in the middle of the Garden with a spout in the middle.

The most spectacular, grandiose, and costly seventeenth-century waterwheel installation was that at Marly to supply Louis XIV's garden fountains at Versailles. Water was pumped in three stages up to 162 m of hillside, 5,000 cu m of water per day serving 1,400 fountains. This installation was also one of the least efficient, largely on account of the distance to which the water had to be pumped. In 1681 Charles II sent Sir Samuel Morland to France to assist, but his advice does not seem to have been welcomed by Louis XIV and Morland returned to England.

Another foreign observer of French hydraulics at this time was Christiaan Huygens, the Dutch scientist. After a visit to a country house outside Paris he offered to send drawings of the ingenious pump installations there in case this would be of help for the fountain machine at Honselaarsdijk. He was also in touch with the Francini family, which had settled in France following their works at the start of the century. At this time François de Francine was *Intendant de la Conduite et Mouvements des Eaux et Fontaines*, and was heavily engaged with the waterworks at Versailles.

In the absence of running water one assumes the Honselaarsdijk machine to have been animal- or wind-powered. Windmills were used exclusively for polder drainage in conjunction with the scoop wheel or the Archimedian screw, thus moving high volumes through short vertical distances. The same technology could supply a fountain which merely poured rather than one that spouted. However, most garden designers wanted jets for which the power and pressure requirements were entirely different, and so windmills were rigged up to higher pressure pumps.

One Englishman who employed windmills for pumping water in garden settings was Henry Winstanley, the topographical artist who had proposed a volume of prospects in a 1678 advertisement. He was an inventor and designer as well as an artist, inviting tourists to view his house near Audley End, which was full of trick effects and illusions, many water-operated, for which he charged 1s. entrance fee. One of the visitors to these marvels, in

1697, was Celia Fiennes. In about 1690 Winstanley set up in Hyde Park 'Winstanley's Waterworks' – 'the greatest curiosities in Waterworks, the like never performed by any' – a series of mobile *tableaux* in which trick effects were achieved by fountains and waterspouts, and the mingling of fire and water. After he died in the great storm of 1703 the entertainment was carried on by his widow who petitioned Queen Anne for a pension.

Hydraulic devices

A favourite trick of hydraulicians was to devise stopcocks under paving stones that were tripped by visitors stepping on them. These familiar 'deceivers' were described by Jan van der Groen in 1669:

> Water jets can be installed in various corners of the garden and from paths – also from the balustrades, hand rails, stairs, doors and seats, from home-made creeping snakes and frogs, from flowers, rocks, grottoes and hills. You can also, by using a jet of water, surprise the passers-by by making birds fly up out of the shrubs.

A good impression of the pleasure which these 'little conceits' gave can be obtained by studying early drawings of Zorgvliet; water jets spout from the ground and surprise the ladies. The same trick was employed at Hutton-in-the-Forest, in Cumberland, where visitors could be trapped on an island, and would have to brave the jets in escaping.

Another elaborate waterworks, the work of Grillet, was found by Celia Fiennes at Bretby Hall. She wrote of fountains playing through pipes

> . . . in one garden there are three fountains wherein stands great statues, each side on their pedistalls is a dial, one for the sun, the other a clock which by the water worke is moved and strikes the hour and chimes the quarters, and then they play Lilibolaro on the chymes – all this I heard when I was there . . .

The waterworks at Het Loo

William's interest in the fountains of Hampton Court in 1689 and 1690 shows how close waterworks were to his heart. When he enlarged the gardens of Het Loo in the following years he was even more concerned to have some exceptional fountains. The earlier gardens already had a system giving jets up to 2 m high, partly from the garden having been excavated, and partly because the reservoir in the park was raised by about 2 m above ground level. However, he wanted jets much higher than this for his spectacular 'King's Fountain' in the Upper Garden. His achievement should not be underestimated. It was a technical feat requiring great inventiveness and involving high risks. There was little prior experience to draw upon in the use of the several materials and in devising the different solutions of the problems, and the pipes had to be taken across hilly country.

The King's Fountain had 16 jets in an outer ring, fed from the 'High Lake', the reservoir in the park, and so giving jets about 2 m high. For the higher jets two more water pressure levels were obtained. The lesser was from a well called Orden about 5 km away and with a fall of about 10 m. After the losses of pressure through friction in transmission, the 16 jets of the inner ring

8.8 Het Loo, 'de Cyfer Founteynen Cascades' by Romeyn de Hooghe (c. 1700). This shows the reservoir supplying the cascades and fountains in the gardens

could spout 4 m high. The highest pressure level was in pipes conducted from wells at Asselt, situated about 10 km away, and with a fall of 38 m; they supplied enough water and pressure to give a powerful central yet 13.5 m high. This was higher than the most powerful jet at Versailles, truly the King's Fountain! Furthermore the water was fresh, clear and without odour, which could not be said for that at Versailles. Sad to relate, the waterworks deteriorated soon after William's death.

At Het Loo there were about 20 other garden waterworks of various kinds including jets, fountains and cascades. The garden also had a shell grotto, much beloved by Mary, with walls covered by exotic shells and with two niches, in each of which were three fountain jets. On the slopes of the terraces and in the grass path on top of the terraces were the so-called 'deceivers' to surprise unwary visitors, but also to irrigate the grass.

A variety of materials was used. The nozzles of the jets were made of bronze, and for special water effects, such as the peacock tail fountain and the tritons, moulded lead was used. All the pipework in the garden was of lead, much of it of very heavy calibre, and some, according to tradition, was stamped 'William Rex'. The English spelling could point to English manufacture. Outside the garden some pipes were made of baked unglazed clay, 75 cm long and 15 cm wide, many with the king's emblems in relief such as the harp, the thistle, the lily and the rose. Finally, some wooden pipes were used, held together every 3 m by iron rings with a diameter of 30 to 50 cm wide and width of 5 cm. Most likely these were made from hollowed out tree trunks. To seal rotten or split patches, lead plates were nailed on.

16. Hampton Court, Great Parterre, photograph of one of the pair of vases by Cibber and Pierce of 1690

17. Het Loo, trelliswork on terrace above Lower Garden

18. Het Loo, the Konigsfontein ('King's Fountain') as restored

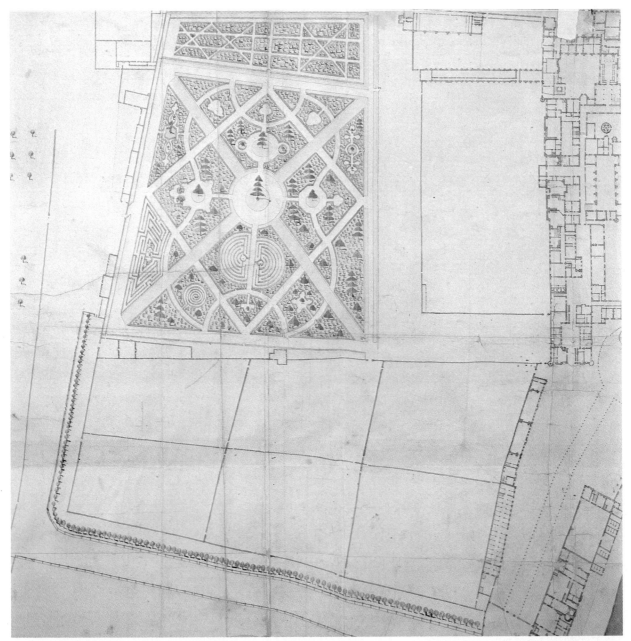

19. Hampton Court, a plan of the wilderness, detail from a survey plan (sometime 1710–14). This wilderness was made about 1688, probably just prior to George London's alterations for William and Mary

20. A Delft orange-tree vase with the arms of William and Mary, at Erddig, in Wales

21. Zorgvliet, the orangery c. 1690. Hans Willem Bentinck's orangery was perhaps derived from the amphitheatre at Cleves, and itself inspired many other orangery gardens

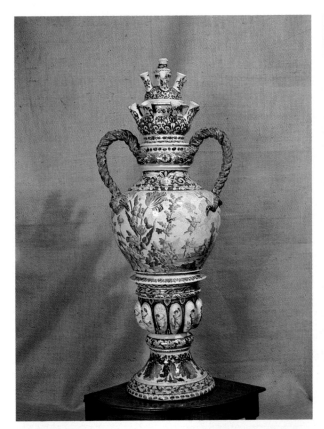

22. A Delft tulip vase, at Uppark in Sussex

23. Red-flowered polyanthus in the Badminton *florilegium*, by Everard Kick (c. 1704)

24. Het Loo, tunnel arbour in Queen Mary's flower garden

9

The Bosquet and Wilderness

9.1 *Previous page*: A Cabinet from John James's *The Theory and Practice Gardening* (1712)

John James begins a new chapter in his 1712 translation of Antoine-Joseph Dezallier d'Argenville's *La Théorie et la pratique du jardinage* (1709) by writing:

> This chapter contains all that is noble and agreeable in a garden, namely woods and groves, for no garden without these can be accounted handsome, since they make the greatest ornaments thereof.

In France and the rest of Europe this wooded part of the garden was the *bosquet*, in Britain the 'wilderness' or grove. Many other words have been used in Britain to indicate the same area, namely 'thicket', *boscage*, 'coppice', 'wood' or, rarely, 'forest'. Nevertheless it is the word 'wilderness' which epitomises the designed woody area as part of the seventeenth- and early-eighteenth-century garden.

John James describes the usual form of a wood or grove as a star, a direct cross, a St Andrew's cross and a goose-foot. Groves may be varied in different ways, the general rule being to 'pierce them with alleys as much as possible, not making so many walks and returns in them as to waste the whole area of the wood; nor so few as to leave the great squares of wood naked and without ornament'. In his 1728 edition James adds a list 'as to the names and different figures of walks' for the secondary path system. These included 'the parallel walk, the straight walk, the cross walk, the winding or circular walk, the walk returned square and the diagonal or level walk in respect of that at right angles'.

James goes on to list elements which could be admitted to the design:

> Cloisters, labyrinths, quincunxes, bowling greens, halls, cabinets, circular and square compartments, halls for comedy, covered halls, natural and artificial arbours, fountains, isles, cascades, water galleries, green galleries, &c.

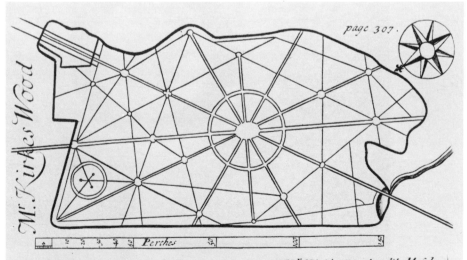

9.2 Cookridge, in Yorkshire, Squire Kirke's wood. Plan in the 1706 edition of John Evelyn's *Sylva*. Thomas Kirke was a contemporary of Evelyn's in the Royal Society

The lines in this Platforme represents the Walkes in M.ʳ Kirke's Wood (call'd Moseley) neare his House at Cookeridge, (betwixt Leeds and Otley) in Yorkshire. The whole containing about Six Score Akers.
The Double line Walks are about 20 Foot wide, and if Single lines about 8 Foot wide.

The next advice is 'to make something noble in the middle of a wood as a hall of horse chesnuts, a waterwork, a cascade or the like'. The walks in these places should be 'something wider than ordinary' and he gives an example as to the required width.

A number of types of wilderness were listed by James, and his list is the basis of the following parts of this chapter.

Forests and great woods of tall trees

'Forests, or great woods of tall trees' are 'wild and rural, do not form part of the pleasure garden, and have neither hedges nor rolled walks. They are usually planted in a star with`a large circle in the middle where all ridings meet'. This type of design was very popular in the Netherlands, where many estates had their *sterrebos* (star-wood), and a good English example of this type of wood is known through John Evelyn's description of 'Mr Kirk's Wood (cal'd Moseley) near Cookeridge (betwixt Leeds and Otley)'. These woods may have been slightly less wild than James suggested, and the manner of planting often had similarities with the groves of middle height.

This type of wood became popular in Britain. Stephen Switzer referred to it as 'forest gardening', giving 'such natural and rural, yet noble and magnificent decorations of the country villa'. In *Ichnographia Rustica* Switzer emphasised both the profit and the pleasure of planting such woods

9.3 Zuylestein, 'Vue de la maison de Zuylstein, de ses jardins et plantages', by Daniel Stoopendaal (c. 1700), showing the extensive *bosquets* of tall trees

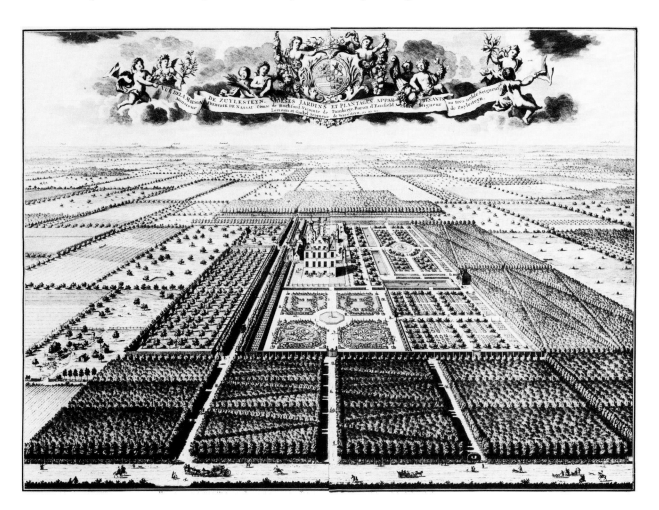

of tall trees, and suggested that they guarded country houses from winds and provided shady walks. A characteristic of this kind of forest garden is the planting of one tree species in large plots. An early English example of a forest garden was Cassiobury. A later example of this type of garden is Bramham Park, near Wetherby, Yorkshire. This garden was laid out by Robert Benson after he acquired the site in 1699. About this time the forest gardens of New Park and Wray Wood at Castle Howard were also in the making.

Groves opened in compartments

These groves have a layout of *allées* and rooms, but the quarters between the *allées* have no trees or shrubs, but are left open. According to John James the *allées* of these groves are 'planted with lime trees or horse chesnuts, persuant to the design'. Underneath these trees are low hedges 'kept trimm'd to about three foot or breast-high'. This

> ...renders the lower part of the grove free and disengaged, and in walking, gives you the advantage of the prospect, and a sight of persons that are on the other walks, which can't be done in the common wood, where the palisades [hedges] and under-wood grow very high.

The quarters were laid with grass with a 'rolled path of two foot wide running everywhere'. The best example was the wilderness at Ham House, which was laid out in 1671 to a design which has been ascribed to John

9.4 Acklam, Knyff & Kip *Britannia Illustrata* (1707), groves opened in compartments probably with fruit trees

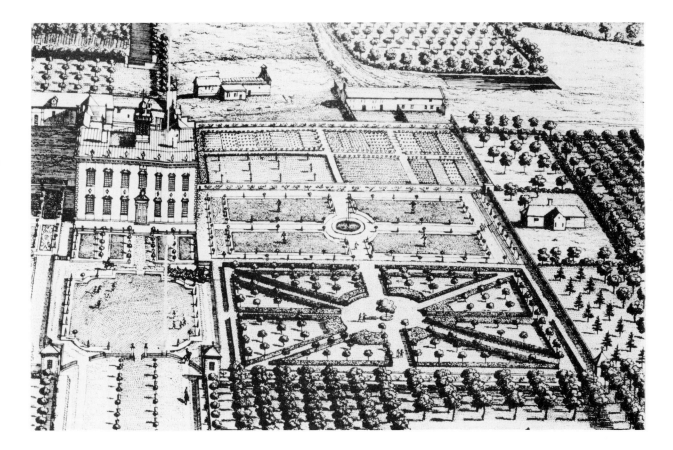

Slezer, a German engineer, and Jan Wijck, a Dutch painter. James thought that some quarters could be 'adorned with yews and flowering shrubs'. In the engravings of Johannes Kip, published as *Britannia Illustrata* (1707), only that of Longleat shows something vaguely resembling this description. There are, however, some very good examples of this type of grove without embellishment. Acklam had such a grove on the left-hand side in front of the house. In his description of Boughton, in Northamptonshire, John Morton in *The Natural History of Northamptonshire* (1712) describes a 'wilderness of apartments', by which he might have meant this type of grove. This Boughton wilderness had, incidentally, been laid out by another Dutchman, Van der Meulen.

Open groves

In 1706 the open grove was described by London and Wise in *The Retir'd Gard'ner* as that which is 'neither inclosed with borders of hornbeam, without, nor tufted within, but consists only of trees with high stems, such as elms, or horse chesnut trees, &c planted at right angles'. The alternative way of planting was in quincunx, where the diagonal placing of the trees bears resemblance to the 'cinque-points of a die'. By the late-1720s in England these two ways of planting became more popular until preference was given to the irregular way of planting.

The surface of the ground underneath the trees in an open grove had either to be 'kept smooth and well rolled', which probably meant a soil surface without vegetation, or 'covered with grass'. The choice of trees was generally

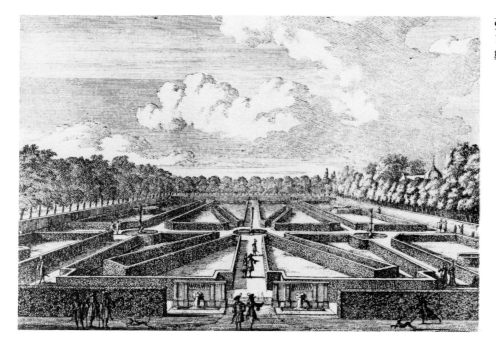

9.5 Het Loo, wilderness (c. 1700), being of the open grove sort

limited to one type of deciduous forest tree, but sometimes evergreens were used, and occasionally mixed together. For their open groves London and Wise favour elms for the desirable provision of shade. They advise a planting distance of 15 ft and consider the tallest elms with high crowns the finest.

Groves of a middle height with tall hedges

The grove of a middle height with tall hedges was the most popular and frequently planted type of *bosquet*. The main body of the planting consisted of low trees, not envisaged as exceeding 30 or 40 ft in height. The *allées* were confined by hedges and lattice work. Being of an architectural nature, such *bosquets* could be adorned with halls, cabinets, galleries, fountains and so on.

The list of trees and shrubs used in this type of grove was large and varied. When James explained how the quarters should be planted he envisaged a thickly planted wood with elms, chestnuts, and so on, 3 ft apart in the rows with the rows 6 ft apart. The 'rows of rooted plants will, in time, form the head of the grove, if care be taken to trim their branches, and conduct them to their proper height'. Additionally, all kinds of seeds of trees and shrubs should be sown to form the understorey. Cassandra Willoughby described the wilderness at Badminton as 'very fine, ye trees so large as to make it very shady: they are all Ash and Elm except shrubs to thicken it in ye bottom'.

The advice from London and Wise would have given a slightly different effect; the quarters should be filled with little wild trees, the tops of which could be seen above the low enclosing hedges, and which resemble a low copse. Meanwhile, tall trees would grow out of the hedge at equal distances.

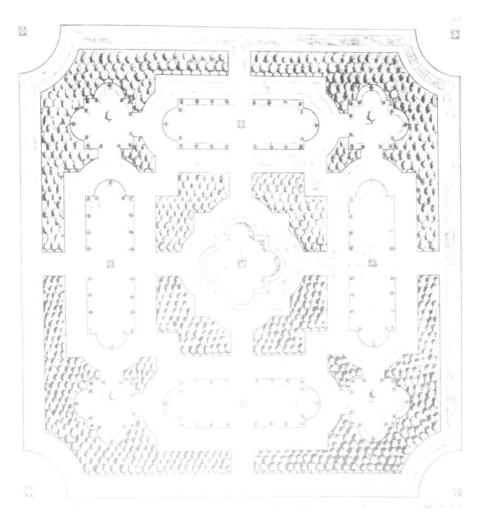

9.6 Grove with borders, by André Mollet in *Le Jardin de Plaisir* (1651). An early form of the grove of middle height with tall hedges

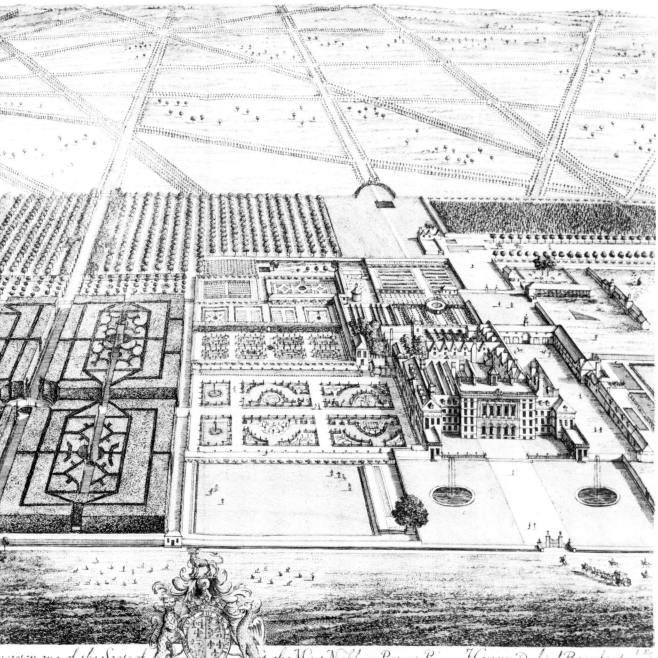

ucester one of the Seats of ... the Most Noble & Potent Prince Henry Duke of Beaufort
...ter Baron Herbert of Chepsto... MVTARE VEL TIMERE SPERNO Raglan & Gower, and Knight of the Most Noble order of the Garter

Another author to give advice on the planting of the quarters was Timothy Nourse in his *Campania Foelix* (1700). He wrote that a wilderness should be 'natural-artificial, as to deceive us into a belief of a real wilderness or thicket'. The quarters should be planted with different kinds of trees and shrubs as well as fruit trees, and furnished with 'all the varieties of nature'.

Captain Charles Hatton may have helped make the wilderness like this at Kirby Hall, and in 1698 Lady Bridgeman consulted him about her intended wilderness at Castle Bromwich Hall. Hatton pointed out that her wilderness would be too small to waste the space on common fruit or wild forest trees,

9.7 Badminton, wilderness, by Knyff and Kip *Britannia Illustrata* (1707). The wilderness on the left was of the tall hedge sort, with groves filling the interstices

159

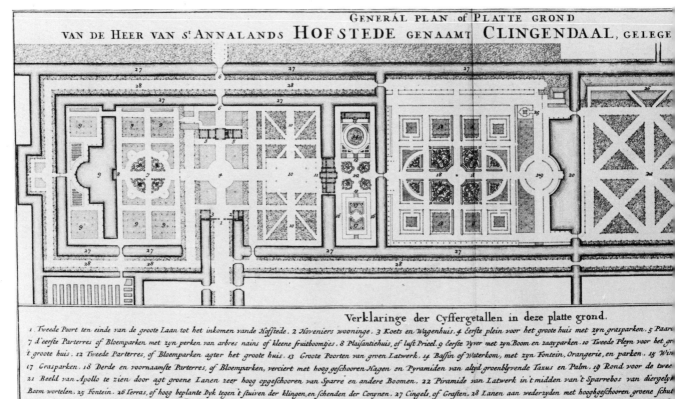

GENERAL PLAN of PLATTE GROND
VAN DE HEER VAN St ANNALANDS HOFSTEDE GENAAMT CLINGENDAAL, GELEGE

Verklaringe der Cyffergetallen in deze platte grond.

1. Tweede Poort ten einde van de groote Laan tot het inkomen vande Hofstede. 2 Hoveniers wooninge. 3 Koets en Wagenhuis. 4 Eerste plein voor het groote huis met zyn grasparken. 5 Paar
7 d'eerste Parterres of Bloemparken met zyn perken van arbres nains of kleene fruitboomtjes. 8 Plaisantiehuis, of lust Prieel. 9 Eerste Vyver met zyn Boom en zaayparken. 10 Tweede Pleyn voor het gr
t groote huis. 12 Tweede Parterres, of Bloemparken agter het groote huis. 13 Groote Poorten van groen Latwerk. 14 Bassin of Waterkom, met zyn Fontein, Orangerie, en parken. 15 Win
17 Grasparken. 18 Derde en voornaamste Parterres, of Bloemparken, verciert met hoog geschooren Hagen en Pyramiden van altyd groenblyvende Taxus en Palm. 19 Rond voor de twee
21 Beeld van Apollo te zien door agt groene Lanen zeer hoog opgeschooren van Sparre en andere Boomen. 22 Piramide van Latwerk in 't midden van 't Sparrebos van diergely
Boom wortelen. 25 Fontein. 26 Terras, of hoog beplante Dyk tegen 't stuiven der klingen, en schenden der Conynen. 27 Cingels, of Graften. 28 Lanen aan wederzyden met hooghgeschooren groene schut
Na't leven getekent en in 't Koper gebragt door Daniel Stoopendaal. 't Amsteldam uitgegeven door Niccolaus Visser met Octroy van d'E

9.8 Clingendaal, plan by Daniel Stoopendaal (c. 1690). Note the elaborate wilderness to the right

though he made an exception for the wild cherry for its flowers, the rowan for its berries and native everygreens – holly, yew and pine. He advised that the space should otherwise be planted with exotics. The evergreens mentioned were bay, laurel, *Phillyrea*, *Rhamnus alaternus*, *Pyracantha*, laurustinus, Spanish broom and the cypress. On the latter, he advises letting it grow naturally, not tied up or pruned except for the lower branches, so as to make it a spreading standard. He also advised gilded varieties of holly and *Phillyrea*.

Amongst the exotic deciduous trees that could be planted, Hatton mentioned the horse chestnut, *Robinia*, tulip tree and the occidental and oriental planes. All kinds of flowering shrubs should be planted amongst them: *Laburnum*, white, blue and purple lilacs, Persian, white and yellow jasmines, the trumpet flower (which should never be pruned because the flowers are at the tips of the branches), all varieties of roses, bastard and Italian sennas, bladder nut, Gelder rose, spindle tree, ladies' bower, althea frutex (*Hibiscus syriacus*), dwarf almond tree, *Hypericum frutex*, *Spiraea hypericifolia* and sumach.

At Melbourne Hall there was an instruction 'to make the little grove of trees on the left hand of the lower garden fit to walk in, to make thickets in it of roses of several sorts and honeysuckles, lilacs, syringas and in the middle a close arbour'. The honeysuckles were probably planted against trees, as at Wrest, in Bedfordshire, where Cassandra Willoughby noted that 'to run up ye bodys of ye Trees are planted Honeysuckles and Sweet Brire'.

As to the hedges, Hatton advised yew or holly. On the other hand, London and Wise advised large trees, preferably elms, set at equal distances along the hedges, and trimmed up. Hampton Court had hornbeam like this, and

Melbourne Hall had hornbeam and Dutch elm. When the tops were too tall for the gardener to reach they spread over forming a tuft or plume. The effect this gave was described by Celia Fiennes when she visited the wilderness at Ingestre, in Staffordshire, which was very fine

> ... with many large walks of a great length full of all sorts of trees, sycamores, willows, hazel, chestnuts, walnuts, set very thicke and so shorn smooth to the top which is left as a tuff or crown – they are very lofty in growth which makes the length of a walk look noble.

This was the trimming-up method called 'plashing', and several woods remain in England today called 'plash wood'.

In some wildernesses attention was given to flowers. At Melbourne Hall a bed of violets was planted 'behind the espalier but close to it'. Cassandra Willoughby said that in the Badminton wilderness 'Ye earth is covered with a variety of plants and primroses, periwinkle, etc.'

Wildernesses of fruit trees

Hatton's recommendation not to have fruit trees in the quarters at Castle Bromwich Hall introduces a variant type of wilderness. Though not mentioned by James, it was referred to, for example, by William Temple in his description of Moor Park in *Upon the Gardens of Epicurus* (1692). He writes about 'a lower garden, which is all fruit trees ranged about the several quarters of a wilderness'. At Het Loo in the Netherlands there was also a labyrinth or wilderness of fruit trees next to the King's Garden described by Walter Harris. There were hedges surrounding the quarters, about 7 or 8 ft tall, and the fruit trees were arranged in squares, planted in right angles within the bodies of the quarters. Though more complicated than Temple's, the walks in this Het Loo wilderness shared the same general form of St Andrew's and direct crosses combined.

Woods of evergreens

An early Dutch example of an estate with groves of evergreens is Nimmerdor ('never dried out'), near Amersfoort, which was finished in 1655, and about which its owner Everhart Meyster wrote an extensive poem. A variant on this type of grove is the golden or gilded grove with variegated evergreens. These were mentioned by, for example, John Worlidge in *Systema Horti-culturae* (1677). Celia Fiennes noticed another use of evergreens at Ingestre:

> ... there is also a row on the outside of firs round every grove 2 yards or three distant – some silver firs some norroway [Norway] – some scots and pine trees; these hold their beauty round the groves in the winter when the others cast their leaves.

Coppice woods

As with forests and great woods of tall trees, James only found coppice woods suitable in the open country or in large parks. He wrote that in France

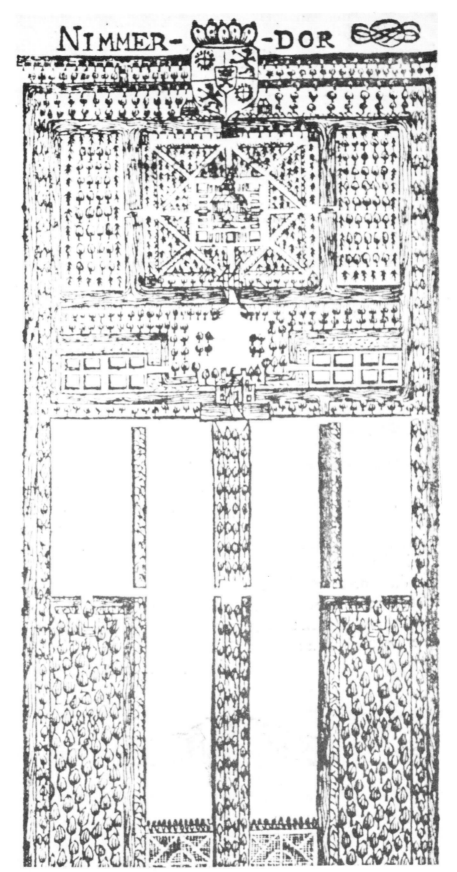

9.9 Nimmerdor ('Evergreen'), plan by Everhart Meyster. This evergreen grove was finished about 1655

these woods were divided in nine parts, one of which was cut down every year, and they were obliged to leave 16 tillers (standard trees) per acre. James only referred to coppice as a commercial wood, as Evelyn did before him in *Sylva*.

Switzer, however, was of the opinion that 'a young wood springing up one two or three foot high is the pleasantest view in nature, much more than what it is at full growth'. He preferred coppices, which are more natural and rural than 'set [planted] wildernesses'. Some standard trees were considered an additional advantage. From this it is unclear whether coppice was used in wildernesses in England, though in the Netherlands coppice does seem to have been the most important form of planting in the quarters of *bosquets*.

Hardy trees and shrubs available

In Britain the number of hardy plants commonly grown in wildernesses, which can be charted from lists by nurserymen, was still quite small in the 1680s. At Leonard Gurle's death in 1685 the inventories of his three nurseries show that, apart from fruit, the only hardy trees stocked were chestnut, elm, horse chestnut, lime, mulberry, plane and walnut. Other lists of the time show a few fir and arbor vitae, *Pyracantha*, lilac and pomegranate.

Within a few years hornbeam, sycamore and yew had been added, especially the last, with the occasional cypress. The evergreen shrubs alaternus (*Rhamnus alaternus*), bay, *Phillyrea*, the holm oak, Spanish broom, laurustinus and *Pyracantha*, also enjoyed some popularity. For colour there were only a dozen or so favourites: *Clematis*, *Cytisus*, Gelder rose, honeysuckles, jasmines, two *Laburnums*, lilacs, the althea frutex (*Hibiscus syriacus*), mezereons, bladder and scorpion sennas, two *Spiraeas*, sumachs and syringa (*Philadelphus coronarius*). From this it can be seen that Hatton was suggesting to Lady Bridgeman almost the entire range available from nurseries at the time.

(A list of plants recommended for wildernesses, compiled from contemporary literature, is given in Appendix B.)

Mazes

Mazes are identified by their most distinctive quality which is their ability to confuse and puzzle. The most famous one from antiquity was the labyrinth of Knossos, constructed by Daedalus in order to contain the Minotaur. Hence a maze could be referred to as a 'labyrinth' or a 'Daedalus'. Confusingly, though, a wilderness could also be referred to as a 'labyrinth'.

The plan of a maze could be either compact or diffuse. The former was the traditional form, familiar from the Hampton Court one, with paths tightly packed together and separated only by hedges in order to obtain the maximum length of path in the area available. The shape of the area could be square, round or even, as at Hampton Court, trapezoidal. The diffuse type consisted of paths laid out irregularly within a *bosquet*. This was a seventeenth-century development, the most famous example of which was the labyrinth at Versailles made in the 1670s. The water maze at Dieren was also like this.

When thinking of a maze, one normally thinks of a hedged labyrinth with a hidden centre, and its discovery is rewarded by an elevated view, a bench, a

9.10 Dieren, water wilderness, by Pieter Schenk (c. 1700). This was a labyrinth layout with the unusual feature of water channels along the paths

tree or some ornament. However there were flower bed mazes too in the sixteenth century. Thomas Hill depicted some in *The Gardener's Labyrinth* (1577), and he was followed by William Lawson's *The Country House-wife's Garden* (1677). In the Netherlands Hans Vredeman de Vries showed several in *Hortorum viridariorumque elegantes* (1583), and Jan van der Groen also gave designs, at least one copied from De Vries, in *Den Nederlandtsen Hovenier* (1669). Whether many flower bed mazes were actually made is not clear, but they were intended for the many smaller gardens in the Netherlands, which may explain why Van der Groen's book remained in print for 50 years.

Of much greater antiquity were the turf mazes of England, medieval features perhaps related to religious devotion. These typically consisted of a single path winding back and forth around the centre in an expanding pattern of concentric circles. They are thus distinguished from the true multicursal labyrinth in which the visitor had the choice of many paths. These were the mazes popularly called 'Troy Towns', probably after the 'game of Troy' described by Virgil, in which the boys of that city rode around the walls one way and then the other. There was a Troy Town in the wilderness at Hampton Court, and the pit at Kensington shaped into many small terraces and planted with yews and hollies was referred to as 'The Seige of Troy'.

Some hedged mazes are suspected in the first half of the seventeenth century in Britain, for example at Nonsuch, Theobalds and Wilton. One in the Netherlands was described by Sir William Brereton in *Travels in Holland . . . England, Scotland and Ireland* (1634) as

> . . . a remarkable garden in the shape of a square with high trimmed hedges forming a maze. The hedges were trained on to wooden supports and were composed of yew, box, elm, privet, juniper, thorns, dogwood, pears, apples, arbor-vitae, tamarisk and barberry.

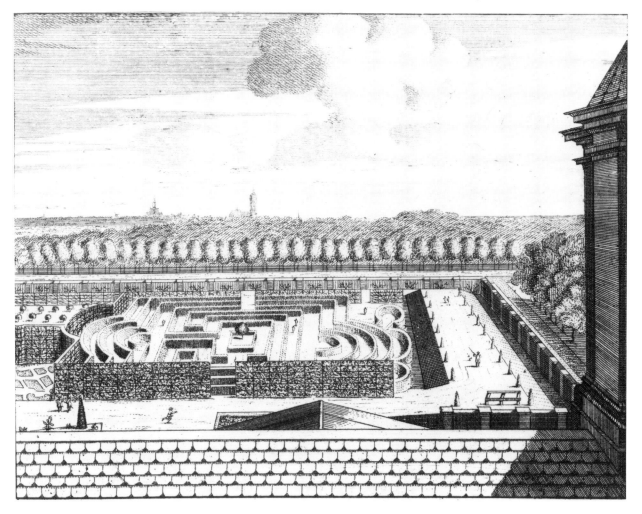

André Mollet gave some designs for labyrinths in *Le Jardin de Plaisir* and advised:

9.11 Huis ten Bosch, maze (c. 1690)

> Pallisadoes are to be planted in double ranks, that they may be thereby the stronger and thicker, to hinder the going through them . . . the alleys are to be 12 foot in breadth or more . . . it is to be noted that the most of space that can be given to a labyrinth is the best; therefore it will be necessary to chuse some convenient place out of the garden to contrive them in, where one may have space enough as 60 or 80 toises in square. [A toise is 6 ft.]

Mollet designed one for Wimbledon in about 1641, and its general form was portrayed in a survey of 1653:

> The maze consists of young trees, wood, and sprays of a good growth and height, cut out into several meanders, circles, semicircles, windings and intricate turnings, the walks or intervals whereof are all grass plots.

In the second half of the seventeenth century mazes became quite popular in the Netherlands, but the British interest in them died away. The Hampton Court maze can perhaps be viewed as part of the Dutch tradition in them. Models for compact hedge mazes were illustrated in Jan Commelin's

Nederlantze Hesperides (1676), and a well known one was that at Huis ten Bosch made about 1686.

An extraordinary design for a multi-branched spiral maze, which would surely have disorientated everyone in it, was given by Dezallier d'Argenville. By a curious coincidence *bosquets* were made exactly copying this design, at both Rosendael in the Netherlands and at Cholmondeley Hall in England.

10

Exotics

10.1 *Previous page*:
Dawley, in Middlesex, the
orangery, detail from Knyff
and Kip *Britannia Illustrata*
(1707). This was one of
many orangeries erected in
the 1680s and 1690s. In
front were ten flower
gardens

Early introductions

The fashion for growing orange and lemon trees from the Mediterranean had existed in northern Europe since about 1600. Salomon de Caus had built a removable greenhouse around orange trees planted in the ground at Heidelberg about 1618, but the usual practice became that of having the trees in tubs and moving them in and out of a permanent orangery. There were numerous orangeries, especially in the Netherlands, by the 1670s, and Jan Commelin, a wealthy merchant from Amsterdam, produced a book on citrus culture, *Nederlantze Hesperides* in 1676, translated into English in 1683. Another, later but more influential, Dutch book, by Hendrik van Oosten, was not published until 1700 in Leiden; but was soon translated into English as *The Dutch Gardener* (1703).

However, the Dutch were not content with countries' exotics from the Mediterranean once their shipping reached Japan, the East Indies (modern Indonesia), India, Ceylon, Mauritius, the Cape of Good Hope, West Africa, the Cape Verde Islands, Canary Islands, Azores, Morocco, Brazil, Surinam, the West Indies, Mexico and North America. Not surprisingly they also became pioneers in introducing these exotic species, especially from the East

Indies and the Cape of Good Hope. The physic garden, or *Hortus*, belonging to several Dutch towns played an important role in the upkeep of these imports. The earliest of such gardens were at Franeker (founded 1589), Leiden (1590), Amsterdam (1638), Utrecht (1639), Breda (1639), Groningen (1642) and Harderwijk (1649).

The Leiden *Hortus* was attached to the famous university, and was pre-eminent until the 1680s. The director during the 1680s was Paul Hermann, who had been a botanical collector at the Cape of Good Hope in 1672. Hermann was responsible for extensive collections from Ceylon as well as from the Cape. Not far from Leiden, at Warmond, Hieronymus van Beverningk, a diplomat, was developing his own much admired collection. Some of his plants from the *Hortus* and Warmond survive in an herbarium made about 1665 by the Leiden apothecary Anthony Gaymans. Van Beverningk's garden at Warmond was also repeatedly mentioned by Van der Groen in *Den Nederlandtsen Hovenier*. When Van Beverningk retired in 1679 he became the university's trustee with special responsibility for the *Hortus*, and, for example, was the first to grow *Tropaeolum majus* in 1684. Serious competition arrived from the Amsterdam *Hortus* after the move in 1682 to the *Plantage* where it grew under the supervision from 1683 of Jan Commelin.

At such places at this time the slightly sensitive species were kept in pots in the orangery and set out in the garden in the summer only. Of those from the tropics, at first only the bulbous plants and those that could be cultivated as annuals from seed, or cuttings, could be kept. So, for example, several *Passiflora* species were multiplied from annual cuttings and cultivated on the melon ground.

Two events made greater progress possible. The first was a change of heart by the Dutch East India Company in the early 1680s. Up to that time they had had a rather restricted policy on the transportation of plants. This was in spite of the great demand for exotics, especially from among the highly-placed enthusiasts who very often had close ties with the Company. However, William of Orange's request, made in 1675, to be honoured yearly by the East India Company with animals and plants and other curiosities from far countries was difficult to refuse. Joan Huydecoper van Maarsseveen, a director of the Company, a burgomaster of Amsterdam, and, later, one of the initiators for the foundation of the *Hortus* in the *Plantage*, organised the Company's activities in the search for plants. The principal Dutch commanders in the Far East and the Cape were asked to organise collection of animals and plants for William, and botanists and draughtsmen were employed in those far-away countries to send plants and herbaria back to the Netherlands in large quantities, especially to the Amsterdam *Hortus*.

The second event was the construction, about 1685, of the first tropical greenhouses in the *Hortus* of Leiden, the *Hortus* of Amsterdam, and most probably in the private botanical garden of Gaspar Fagel, the Grand Pensionary of Holland, at De Leeuwenhorst, which was near Noordwijkerhout and not far from Leiden. These provided facilities to cultivate perennial tropical plants, and the building of these greenhouses was just in time to receive the plants flooding in.

In Britain, the Oxford Physic Garden was a bit slow to take an interest in exotics, and stocking of the Society of Apothecaries' new Physic Garden at Chelsea was not under way in earnest until 1677. The garden was quickly stocked by Richard Pratt till 1679/80 whereupon John Watts took over till 1693. Also, in 1680, a committee was formed in order to promote the construction of a greenhouse which seems to have been serviceable about

10.2 Jan Commelin's orangery, from Jan Commelin *Nederlantze Hesperides* (1676), showing two 'stoves' and the means of transporting the plants

four years later. This left Henry Compton, who seems to have started with exotics when he became Bishop of London in 1675, as

> . . . one of the first that encouraged the Importation, Raising and Increase of Exotics, in which he was the most curious Man of that time . . . and by the recommendation of Chaplains into foreign Parts had likewise greater opportunities of improving it as any other Gentleman could.

After a few years Compton 'had above 1,000 species of Exotic Plants in his Stoves and Gardens' at Fulham Palace.

Compton had jurisdiction over the Anglican Church in North America, and had plants, seeds, drawings and specimens sent from the West Indies and Virginia by the Reverend John Banister in the years 1678 to 1692. On one occasion in 1684 a consignment of Virginian plants and seeds, sent by John Banister, had just arrived. John Ray, one of the bishop's botanical friends, wrote in 1684 to Hans Sloane to tell him: 'There is a vast number of East and West India seeds come over this year.' Compton was very willing to show his achievements to others. For example, his *Aeonium arboreum* was admired by John Evelyn who, on 11 October 1681, went 'to Fulham to visite the Bish: of Lond: in whose Garden I first saw Sedum arborescens in flowre, which was exceeding beautifull'. The bishop also invited the flower painter Alexander Marshal to live at Fulham Palace, though he died in 1681.

Compton's collection included the most important hardy additions to the

10.3 Fulham Palace, from John Rocque *London . . . and the Country near 10 Miles Round* (1745), showing the gardens that had been Bishop Compton's. The exact whereabouts of his 'stoves' is unknown

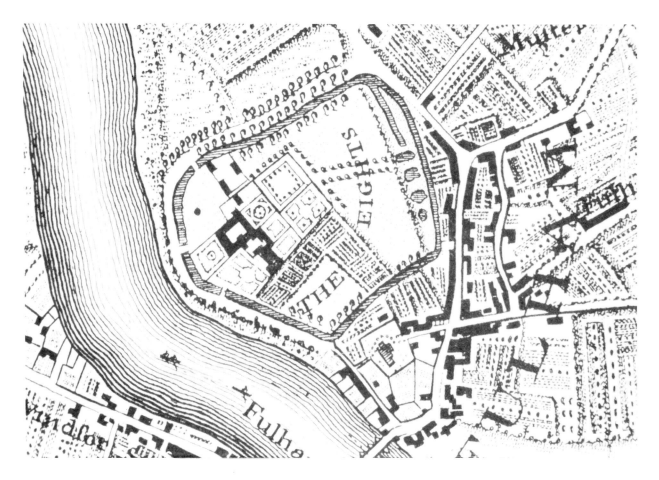

British flora at this time. He collected many North American trees and shrubs, such as cedars and the first specimens of magnolia (*Magnolia virginiana*) and azalea *(Rhododendron viscosum)* in England, in effect forming the first British arboretum.

Other British plant-collecting expeditions included one mounted by John Watts, who sent James Harlow to Virginia, and Hans Sloane's journey to Jamaica as physician to the Duke of Albemarle, when the latter was appointed Governor in 1688. Although Albemarle died within a year, Sloane remained in Jamaica and while he was there he studied the natural history of the island and returned to England in 1689 bearing 800 specimens of Jamaican plants and seeds.

Dissemination

The physic gardens were collectively the most important means of distributing exotics to collectors and nurserymen. In the Netherlands Paul Hermann made Leiden an important early clearing-house for introductions, and then the Amsterdam *Hortus* disseminated many of the East and West India Companies' imports. In England the botanic gardens of Oxford and that at Chelsea had a share in the distribution of exotics. They also exchanged plants between themselves. For example Paul Hermann was in England in 1682 to arrange an exchange of plants with the Chelsea Physic Garden, which John Watts effected on a visit to Leiden the next year.

William's request for plants and animals was being honoured in 1676 when Joan Huydecoper in Amsterdam received some flowers and bulbs from the Governor of the Cape of Good Hope for the prince. Huydecoper sent these on to Daniel Desmarets, who besides being William's agent in these matters was the pastor of the French Church in The Hague. Desmarets seems to have arranged for the onward transmission and installation of such imports at Honselaarsdijk. Although these offerings from the Dutch East India Company were very often duplications of those sent to the gardens of Amsterdam and Leiden, Honselaarsdijk was important as the centre of distribution to other palaces and to William's circle, including presumably to Bentinck at Zorgvliet where the huge orangery was built probably in the late-1670s.

At this date the British nursery trade was just commencing. In Britain, individual collectors, especially Henry Compton, were more important than the physic gardens were, and the nursery trade followed, usually a bit later and to a broader clientele.

John Rose had been of early importance as a nurseryman in that he was able to combine a trade in plants with office under the Crown. From his appointment at St James's on 14 October 1661, he had charge not only of the Royal Garden but of the 'green-house' to be erected there with the oranges and other trees and greens (evergreens) therein. One of Rose's apprentices was George London, who at one point was sent into France, where he is thought to have worked with André le Nôtre as one of the many (over 300) gardeners employed at Versailles and elsewhere for Louis XIV.

London later recalled an incident during his apprenticeship in a letter written in 1710. He gave an account of the almost miraculous survival of the 'Duble-flore'd Indian Almond' (apparently *Prunus glandulosa roseo-plena*) captured among other botanical specimens in 1673 during the Third Dutch War, from a 'Dutch East Indie-Man Cald the Patricks-boon'. Sir Charles Middleton, 'a Lover of plantes' was on board the victorious British man-of-war and managed to get some plants to the Royal Garden where London 'wase then Apprentice' and succeeded in bringing the flowering almond 'to flourishe and is tht wch is soe Increas'd'.

The centre of the English nursery trade remained in and near London until well after 1700. There had been nurseries before Brompton Park was founded in 1681, but few of them boasted exotics. The first large-scale one was that of Captain Leonard Gurle who was exploiting an area of some 12 acres between Spitalfields and Whitechapel by 1660 or earlier. Principally he would have sold fruit trees, and by the 1670s he was selling laurustinus, spruce, cypress, jasmines and some other introduced ornamentals, but there is no evidence that he sold tender exotics.

For less common species the chief suppliers before the founding of Brompton Park were mostly at Hoxton, in Shoreditch, and exotics seem to have started amongst them about 1680. It is perhaps significant that William Darby, of Hoxton, who did not begin to stock his nursery until 1677, was remembered as 'one of the first in England who chose the Culture of Exotic Plants'. George Rickets had a famous nursery at Hoxton for over 40 years, and his catalogue, printed by John Worlidge (or Woolridge) in the third edition of *Systema Horti-culturae* (1688), showed that Rickets had a selection of 'Housed-Greens, Winter-Greens, Flowering-Shrubs, Flowering-Trees, Flowers, and other curious Plants, as well Exotick as English'. Among the 20 tender exotics named were oranges, lemons, myrtles, oleanders, 'Indian Jucca' *(Yucca gloriosa), Amomum Plinii (Solanum pseudocapsicum), Lentiscus (Pistacia lentiscus)* and the Indian Fig *(Opuntia vulgaris).*

George London, as Henry Compton's gardener from the start of the collection at Fulham in 1675, was, from 1681, in a position to disseminate the bishop's latest exotic introductions through the Brompton Park nursery. Keen gardeners, from the Duchess of Beaufort downwards, looked to him for their supplies. London was again acquiring plants from the Dutch, though in more peaceful circumstances than those of 1673, when making a list of plants at Gasper Fagel's garden in 1684, and the next year when he visited Honselaarsdijk, Amsterdam, Haarlem and Leiden, where he described himself as a student, and was kindly received by Paul Hermann, the director.

The craze for exotics

William's circle included some of the most ardent private collectors of exotics. William and Mary had the enormous orangery at Honselaarsdijk, and Bentinck, in his Zorgvliet orangery, had another large collection of exotic plants. Daniel Desmarets too had his own collection, catalogued in 1688 by Dr William Sherard, an English student at Leiden, and a close acquaintance of Paul Hermann.

Some government officials joined in the craze. In The Hague, Simon van Beaumont, the Secretary of the States of Holland and West Friesland, had a rich collection noted for its West African and West Indian plants, catalogued in 1690. However the most important collection of an official was Fagel's at De Leeuwenhorst. This garden was rented by Fagel in 1676 and must have been built up to something quite exceptional by the time of George London's visit in 1684, and Fagel was still collecting hard. In this year he obtained permission from the Dutch East India Company to send a collector to the Cape of Good Hope, and in 1687 he received plants from the Company via Huydecoper.

Fagel was a *confidant* of William's. None of the princely palaces seems to have had a tropical greenhouse, but Fagel seems to have had one. This is known because between 1685 and Fagel's death in late 1688 William commissioned a botanical artist, Stephanus Cousijns, to depict Fagel's plants in beautiful gouaches. These were collected together in 1692, after William had become King of England, into a volume entitled *Hortus Regius Honselaerdicensis.* From Paul Hermann it is clear that Fagel had succeeded in getting the West Indian orchid *(Brassavola nodosa)* to flower as well as the pineapple. William's motive for commissioning paintings of plants in another person's greenhouse may have been that Fagel was housing William's most tender exotics.

The accession of William and Mary as joint sovereigns in 1689 brought closer the already strong horticultural links between Britain and the

Netherlands. A combination of the East Indian and Cape species from the Netherlands, and Sloane's recently introduced West Indian plants, gave a wonderful opportunity for further expanding collections in both countries. The changes at Hampton Court included Mary's for the cultivation of her plants. As Stephen Switzer wrote, 'that active Princess lost no time but either measuring, directing or ordering her Buildings, but in Gardens Especially Exotics, she was particularly skilled'.

At the same time she continued to receive advice from the Superintendent of the Royal Gardens, Bentinck, and she could call upon the services of George London the Deputy Superintendent. Mary also wanted to appoint a botanist, thus reviving the post previously held by Matthias de l'Obel, John Parkinson and Dr Robert Morison. The contenders were William Sherard, Dr Leonard Plukenet, and Daniel Desmarets. Plunkenet secured the appointment at £200 per annum in late 1690 or 1691, possibly because of the recommendation of John Ray, the leading British botanist of the day.

Gaspar Fagel's collection was purchased from his executors by William on a valuation by Jan Commelin and another, and moved temporarily. Dr Gray, who saw it later at Hampton Court, wrote that it was 'a gift from Soesdyke, a house belonging to Mr Bentinck . . . about the year 1690 and given by him to King William'. There is no record of Soestdijk having had a tropical greenhouse, so perhaps Gray meant to say 'Zorgvliet'. In any case, an estimate for building a hothouse at Hampton Court was obtained as early as April 1689, and soon the three 'glass cases', which gave the Pond Yard a new name – 'Glass Case Garden' – were made. These were more like the glass frames on hotbeds than traditional brick orangeries. Fagel's collection must have been transported over the Channel as soon as the new 'glass cases' were ready.

When a noted gentleman botanical collector, Charles Hatton, visited in April 1690 he was told that the collection had been made by 'mine Heer Fagel'. He saw 'about 400 rare Indian plantes wch. were never seen in England'. A catalogue of the collection, entitled *Stirpium . . . quibus hoc anno 1690 Horti Regii Hamptoniensis Hybernacula sunt ornata*, was made on 2 March 1690/1 by Cornelius van Vliet. Perhaps this was at the request of the Earl of Portland, as he paid for Van Vliet's passage home out of Royal Gardens funds.

Not content with her East Indian and Cape collection, Queen Mary and Portland sent collectors to the Canary Islands and to Virginia. It is said that Portland had 'so much relish for exotics, as to have repeatedly sent James Reed to the west Indies to collect curious productions' for the new stove houses at Hampton Court. In October 1690 Portland obtained a customs

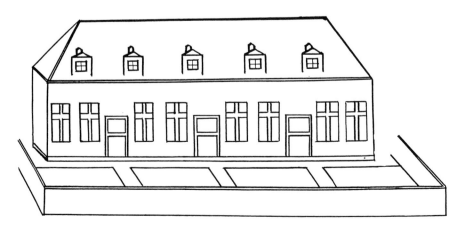

10.5 Badminton, detail of the view by Thomas Smith (c. 1700), showing that the Duchess of Beaufort's orangery was of conventional form

pass for Reed's plants from Barbados to be delivered into the hands of George London.

Queen Mary's collection of hothouse plants at Hampton Court was certainly celebrated, but it was not unique, as there were others who grew exotics on a similar scale. It was at Badminton, in Gloucestershire, that the Duchess of Beaufort's 'stoves' outshone them all. The duchess also assiduously noted the sources of her plants. Her notes, together with her herbarium specimens and correspondence with Hans Sloane, provide an almost complete account for her horticultural methods and her stoves. A catalogue of her Badminton collection, dated 1699, contains 750 species and 90 kinds of variegated varieties – largely acquired through George London and collected from many parts of the globe. Perhaps gardening was in her blood; she was born as Mary Capel, the daughter of Lord Capel of Hadham, and was sister to the Earl of Essex.

In describing her 'orangeree', the duchess told Sloane that it had two borders, one in the middle and one against the wall and in the latter she grew *Adhatoda rus* (now *Justicia*) while on a shelf she kept other plants in pots. She engaged the artist, Everard Kickius, who had already worked for Sloane, to make drawings of her plants. Kickius also taught the duchess's footman, Daniel Francom, how to draw and their work, in two volumes, may still be seen at Badminton.

It comes as a surprise to find that in the early 1690s at Moira, County Down, which was then a remote and troubled corner of the British Isles, Sir Arthur Rawdon constructed a hothouse, which was probably the first in Ireland. As Ulstermen, Sloane and Rawdon were acquainted, so when the latter was in England in 1689, he went to see Sloane's specimens of West Indian species and was so impressed, that he engaged James Harlow to go to Jamaica to bring home West Indian plants and seeds. While Harlow was abroad, Rawdon built the stove-house in which he successfully raised the plants with which Harlow returned in 1694. These 'grew and came . . . to great perfection' as Sloane wrote, and many of them were given to the Bishop of London, Dr Uvedale at Enfield, the Chelsea Physic Garden and the Duchess of Beaufort. In addition, the botanic gardens at Amsterdam, Leiden, Leipsic and Uppsala, 'shared these rarities'.

No one in Ireland had had any experience at all in the management of hothouses and exotics. Rawdon engaged an Englishman, Thomas Harrison, as gardener, but his cargo of West Indian plants called for greater skill than Harrison possessed. At this time William Sherard had returned to England after the Revolution hoping to be appointed to the post of Queen's botanist, but had been disappointed. When Rawdon turned to Sloane for the name of someone who could supervise his 'stoves', William Sherard was recommended. Sherard agreed, and helped Rawdon until the latter's death in 1695. Sloane afterwards persuaded Sherard to go to Badminton, where the Duchess of Beaufort required a tutor for her grandson, a task which Sherard undertook from 1700 till 1702, combining it with the supervision of her 'stoves'. Of these he wrote 'that truly in a few years they will out do any yet in Europe being furnished with all ye conveniences imaginable and a good stock of plants'.

The heyday of growing stove-house exotics may be associated with the reign of William and Mary, but it was not long-lived, for the expense of collecting on such a scale was too great to be sustained. Queen Mary had died the year before Sir Arthur Rawdon, after which their collections declined. Bishop Compton, having lost the services of George London, engaged another gardener 'who very well understands the true Culture of

Exotic Trees and Herbs', William Milward, but in the 1700s the stove houses at Fulham Palace were costing more than Compton thought he could justify. He even thought of parting with his collection so that he could give more to charity. However, at Badminton the Duchess of Beaufort continued to collect with a passion until her death in 1714.

The plants

The influx of plants into the various Dutch collections was very numerous. (An impression of the countries of origin is given in Appendix C.) From the original lists of plants which grew at Hampton Court and Badminton, from herbarium specimens and contemporary accounts, it is clear that collections of tender exotics in England shared many of the same species with each other and with those in the Netherlands, and that many of the individuals involved were indebted, to some extent, to Sloane.

10.6 *Pelargonium zonale*, a plant from the Cape of Good Hope, in the Badminton collection, by Daniel Francom (c. 1705)

Of the various lists of plants which grew at Hampton Court the most extensive was Van Vliet's. This with two others, one of which was compiled by Dr Gray, included 235 species amongst which he mentioned the pineapple *(Ananas comosus)* and the cashew tree *(Anacardium occidentale)*. These lists give an idea of the contents of the queen's stove-houses and show that her interests werre not confined to species from the East Indies and the Cape, but included West Indian plants as well. Gray mentioned that his list was taken from a catalogue lent to him by the 'intendent' at Hampton Court.

Plants which grew at Hampton Court, the custard apple *(Annona reticulata)*, the cotton tree *(Gossypium arboreum)*, the banana *(Musa paradisiaca)*, aloes, *Apocynum, Phaseolus, Solanum,* and so on, also grew at Badminton. The duchess raised Cape figs *(Mesembryanthemum)* there, and *Cacti,* and also the guava *(Psidium guajava)* ripened its fruit: 'Her Grace . . . had them brought to Table fresh from the Tree and some other ripened in Sugar'. The duchess, too, received the credit for being the first person in England to grow the zonal *Pelargonium (P. zonale);* at Badminton, too, the North American sweet fern *(Comptonia peregrina)* was first raised in England and was later described and named in honour of the bishop.

10.7 *Comptonia peregrina*, named after Bishop Compton, by P. J. Redouté

Less well documented is the bishop's collection at Fulham, for any records that he kept have disappeared. None the less, writing in *Phytographia*, Dr Leonard Plukenet referred to a number of the bishop's plants. Otherwise, John Ray, in *Historia Plantarum*, gave an account of his visit to the bishop's garden and noted the hardy plants he found. Ray was, at the same time, allowed by Hans Sloane to include information, not fully published until 1725 in *The Natural History of Jamaica*, in the third (1704) volume of *Historia Plantarum*.

In spite of the problems of tracing Compton's stove-house plants, there is evidence to show that his collection of tender species did not lag behind those of the duchess or the queen, for in his 'stoves' there was a coffee tree *(Coffea arabica)* and night-flowering or torch thistle *(Cereus):* 'The first of this plant that was in England, was in the garden of the late Reverend Father in God Henry Compton Bishop of London at Fulham . . . and the curious from all parts were invited to see it.' Besides these his *Aeonium* (which also grew at Badminton) was immortalised by John Evelyn.

It was among the half-hardy plants that the Dutch connection was prominent. Several species of *Pelargonium* came in to England during the 1690s, though most of those significant for later hybridisation not until 1710 or later. By about 1705 George London's daughter Henrietta had painted *Nemesia strumosa* in flower at Badminton. This is an annual usually supposed to have come from South Africa only around 1890. Various *Mesembryanthemum* from the Cape were arriving too in 1690, and *Lampranthus coccineus* in 1696, with further species, starting a collectors' craze which involved other succulents, notably *Cactus* from the West Indies and tropical America such as *Cereus (Aporocactus) flagelliformis* in 1690, and in the same year the first *Stapelia (S. variegata)* from the Cape.

Hothouses

Exotics from warmer climates were not generally hardy, and would be killed by the frost or the general climate in northern Europe. Moses Cook related what happened when his employer, the Earl of Essex, received some unknown exotics:

> My Lord had thirteen sorts of strange Seeds sent him, as I remember, from Goa; I never saw the like . . . I rais'd ten of the thirteen Sorts, tho some of them lay almost a year in the Ground; but I also must tell you, I lost all my ten sorts the first Winter, but one Sort, and that the second, for want of a Green-house.

The lesson was obvious: buildings with an artificial climate more suitable for the plants were required. So when Charles Hatton, fired with enthusiasm by

10.8 Brenhelen, in Gunterstein, orangery garden and its hothouse, by Mulder and De Lespine (c. 1690). The angled glass and the chimneys behind suggest that the frames were for tropical plants

the latest craze for growing tender plants, wrote to his brother, Christopher, 1st Viscount Hatton, of Kirby Hall, Northamptonshire: 'I have settled a correspondence with Mr Bobart, and he hath . . . promis'd me some curious plants wch I designe for yr Lordshippe', he also warned him, 'without a stove you cannot keepe them.' He told him that the Bishop of London planned to visit Kirby: 'I wish you'd have discourse [with] my Ld Bpp as to ye making ordering and advantage of one'.

Some exotics like the citrus plants – orange and lemon trees – were safe

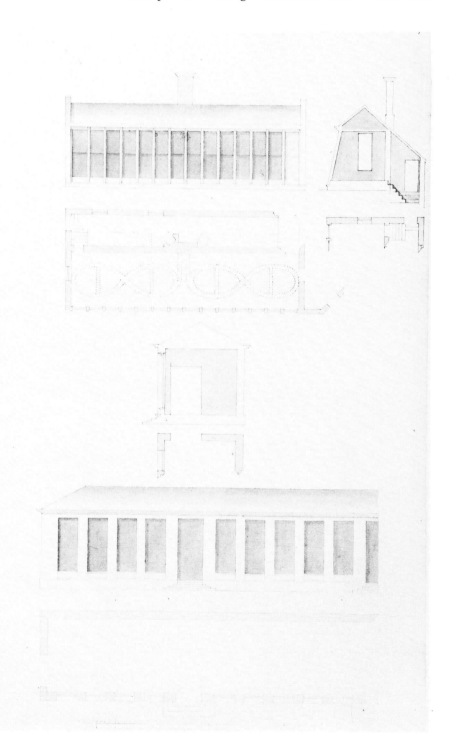

10.9 Hampton Court, one of the glass cases of 1689 (above), and the orangery of 1701 (below), from the 'Fort Album' (c. 1718)

from the worst of the frost in a greenhouse with some primitive form of heating, but many tropical plants required higher and more constant levels of heat. The scale of the problem was compounded by the diversity of the plants' origins: lists of plants received by George London between 1693 and 1701 include material from Barbados, New England, Virginia, Africa and the Cape of Good Hope. There was also the size of some collections to consider, the largest of which was the Duchess of Beaufort's housed at Badminton and at Beaufort House, Chelsea.

The difficulty of dealing with these introductions from tropical climes can hardly be over-estimated. The primitive methods of heating greenhouses with stoves, braziers and pans of charcoal were extremely unsatisfactory because of the fumes generated. There was no effective thermometer until after 1714, so that only subjective assessments of warmth were available, and many plants were lost through excessive heat as well as from smoke. Even at Leiden it was not until the time of Hermann Boerhaave, after 1701, that serious experiments were undertaken into better methods of heating the greenhouses. Systems of heating by steam or hot water were unknown until around 1800.

In the early 1680s English gardeners still had little experience in the management of hothouse plants. Although professional help was available at the Oxford and the Chelsea physic gardens, in the form of Jacob Bobart and John Watts respectively, this was very limited. It was thus a credit to English gardeners that they were able to learn how to preserve such large numbers of tropical plants in so few years. The early collections must have been housed in hot, steamy, atmospheres provided at much skill and labour by their owners. The form of Compton's stoves is not known, but in describing her 'orangeree', the duchess told Sloane that it was built against an 18 ft wall and the building was 110 ft in length. It was essentially an orangery adapted for use as a hothouse.

Adoption of the ancient Roman hypocaust, heating by means of flues embedded in walls and floors, was the principal expedient throughout the latter part of the seventeenth century and the early years of the eighteenth. Hothouses were heated with stoves fed on peat, from which the hot air was conducted through a subterranean system of heating channels. The hothouses of Amsterdam and Leiden seem to have been heated this way, and at Chelsea in 1685 John Evelyn admired 'what was very ingenious the subterranean heate, conveyed by a stove under the Conserveatory, which was all Vaulted with brick; so as he leaves the doores & windowes open in the hardst frosts, secluding only the snow &c.' However, this method seldom gave a uniform heat, and was difficult to control.

The Dutch seem to have hit upon another idea in the 1680s. The glass frames placed on hotbeds seemed to work well in trapping heat from the sun, so why not try ones with the glass surface perpendicular to the sun's rays on the shortest day, and large enough to walk inside? They could also be heated by underground flues. The Amsterdam hothouses, totalling 35 m in length, followed these principles. They were made of glass resting against a brick back wall, and were only 1.74 m wide. This was likewise the idea behind the three 'glass cases' at Hampton Court built by the specialist Dutch carpenter, Hendrik Floris, for Queen Mary. Hatton described these glass cases as 'much better contrived and built than any other in England'.

These glass-cases also attracted the attention of the Duchess of Beaufort, who had been making enquiries through John Bale (or Ball), a servant of the duke's at Beaufort House, and in September 1692 he was able to make a very full report on 'ye Queens new stoves'. 'There are three separate Stoves', Bale wrote, 'standing in a range wth their fronts Direct South'. Each building was 55 ft in length, and the front sloped – 8 ft broad at the bottom and 5 ft at the top: 'All ye front is glass windows, of wch there are 14 doors to each'. These doors opened to enable the plants to be moved. The houses were backed by a wall behind which was a shed 'to shelter those yt make ye fires under ye stove'. Each house had '4 fire plases to each of wch is a grate in ye forme of a little wagon'. The 'wagon' had four wheels, and 'when ye fire is made in it & Burns Clear it is Runn into ye Valt' by means of rails and pushed or pulled by 'an Iron Crooke'. Careful precautions were taken to ensure that fumes could not attack the tender greens.

It must be added that the Oxford and the Chelsea physic gardens maintained their stoves and hothouses well into the eighteenth century. At Oxford the long, low greenhouse, built early enough to have been shown on the Loggan view of 1675, acquired two small glass cases, one at each end, by 1710. Perhaps until 1837 there was still a wagon in the replacement greenhouse 'intended to hold glowing charcoal . . . was placed first in one corner of the building, then in another and was occasionally drawn to and fro throughout the house . . . the apparatus was in use in the old conservatory or orangery'.

The physic gardens thus continued, albeit on a lesser scale, skills in the cultivation of exotics, but the rapid advance in collecting exotics at Badminton and Hampton Court was not to be surpassed for many decades after.

10.10 Oxford Physic Garden, heating apparatus in use until about 1837. When filled with red-hot coals it would be pulled to those parts of the hothouse that required warming

11

The Flower Garden

Tulipomania and the Dutch trade in bulbs

In 1554 the Austrian Ambassador to Turkey, O.G. de Busbecq, saw a strange and beautiful flower, the tulip, near Constantinople, and by the end of the decade they were in cultivation in Augsberg. About 1578 they reached faraway England. By 1583 the botanist Charles de l'Ecluse from the Spanish Netherlands could describe 34 varieties, and when he was put in charge of the building of the Leiden *Hortus* in 1593, selling his tulips was a profitable sideline. In 1601 De l'Ecluse described tulips in broken colours (variegated tulip) for the first time, alongside florist hyacinths, *Anemones*, auriculas, *Ranunculuses* and *Narcissi*.

From Emanuel Sweerts's *Florilegium primus et secundus* (1612) and Crispijn van der Passe's *Hortus Floridus* (1614) it becomes clear just how many tulips and other bulbous plants were already in cultivation in the Netherlands early in the seventeenth century. Sweerts's preface indicated that, besides his books, he offered his bulbs in a market, the *Herbstmess* in Frankfurt, and subsequently in his shops in Amsterdam. His flower books may, then, be considered almost as a nursery catalogue.

Another form of nursery catalogue found in the Netherlands in the 1630s was the 'tulip book'. This contained watercolours and gouaches of tulips, painted for the florist to serve as an illustration to his customers of the flowers that would shoot from his bulbs. One was painted by Jacob Marrell between 1637 and 1639 for the florist and merchant F. Gomis del Costa in Vianen. Another dating from 1637 belonged to the florist P. Cos of Haarlem. Also Anthony Claesz and Judith Leyster painted tulips for these catalogues. Their lavishness suggests that large sums were being spent on collecting tulips in this period. In P. Cos's tulip book the tulip varieties are mentioned and the weight of the bulbs and the individual prices.

The most expensive tulips were the 'Viceroy', the 'Bruin Purper', the 'White and Red Boode', the 'Brandenburger', the 'Goemermert van Kaer' and the 'General Verijck'. The 'Viceroy' was sold by Cos for 4,200 guilders, whilst the cheapest tulip the 'Asientier' was only 15 guilders. The planting of these expensive tulips was undertaken with extra care, as befitting their status as exotic rarities. Each was displayed individually, at very large planting distances by today's standards. Every bulb had to be able to develop fully and be seen from all sides.

In 1637 tulipomania was declared illegal by the States of Holland. The exorbitant prices then decreased somewhat – but, nevertheless, in Holland bulbous plants have remained good merchandise from the seventeenth century onwards. Clearly the state of the Dutch nursery trade in bulbs was strong as early as the 1620s or 1630s. Most nurseries were located in the province of Holland – Haarlem, Leiden, Amsterdam, Alkmaar, Hoorn and Enkhuizen were well-known centres. Dirk Voorhelm, Barend Cardoes, Pieter Gerritsz and P. Cos were some of the well-known florists.

In Britain, there was only one florist nurseryman of note in the 1620s, Ralph Tuggie of Westminster, praised by John Parkinson and others; in the following 30 years the nursery trade seems to have been very low-key in comparison to that in the Netherlands. One florist nurseryman to have provided continuity between the days of Parkinson and the Restoration period was John Rea, a gentleman from Kinlet, in Shropshire. His *Flora* (1665), reissued in 1676 and 1702, dealt exhaustively with ornamental gardening and the cultivation of flowers, especially bulbs. On his death in 1677 he left his nursery to his daughter, who married the Reverend Samuel Gilbert, author of *The Florist's Vade Mecum* (1682). By this time London

11.2 Tulips, from Sweerts's *Florilegium* (1612)

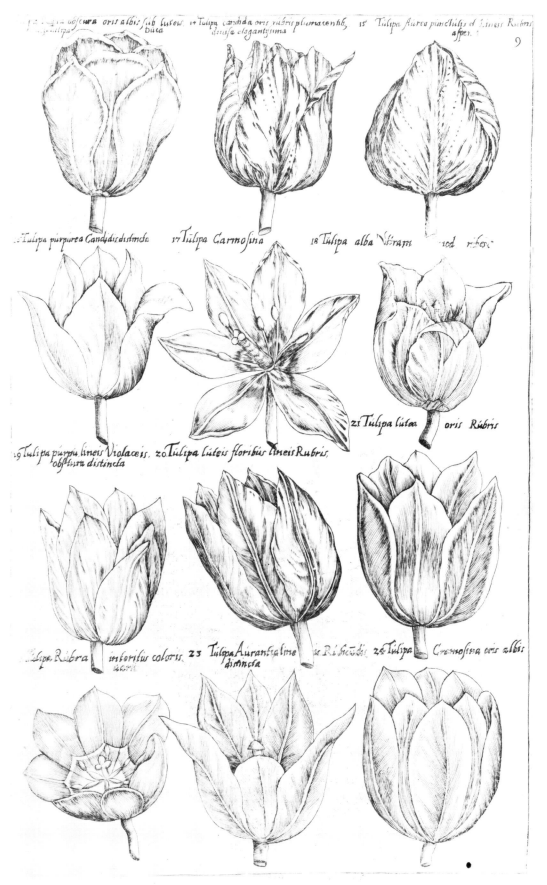

183

nurseries were selling a wide variety of flower seeds; William Lucas's catalogue of 1677 advertised the seeds of over 70 different flowers. Another of the Hoxton nurseries was specialising in *Anemones* in 1691; this was Mr Pierson's, 'accounted very honest'.

Although Holland specialised in bulb-growing, it was to Paris that Gabriel Mollet turned to stock the Royal Garden at St James's in 1661. Indeed English plant lovers were still buying largely from Paris until the end of the century, as for example the Hatton family for their gardens at Kirby Hall, Northamptonshire. On the other hand, there may have been links with Holland in the seed trade, for William Lucas of the Strand, one of the leading seedsmen in London until his death in 1679, had a brother-in-law named Peter Vandenancker, merchant of London. Lucas's catalogue of 1677 is the earliest known English trade list and includes a wide selection of seeds for kitchen and flower gardens, as well as many bulbs and other plants.

During the second half of the seventeenth century, gardeners in the Netherlands started to set their experience down in handbooks. The clergyman, P. van Aengelen from Alkmaar, was the first in his *Herbarius: Kruyt- en Bloemhof* (1663) followed by *De verstandige hovenier* (1665). The physician P. Nijland wrote *Den verstandingen hovenier* (1669) and *Den Nederlandtse herbarius* (1673). These are concerned primarily with the medicinal properties of plants, and written in the tradition of the herbal. However, many garden plants were mentioned with maintenance advice for each plant, so these books are useful because they give an overall impression of horticulture in the Netherlands during this period.

Jan van der Groen, gardener to William at Honselaarsdijk, was the first one to describe plants for ornamental gardens and he hardly mentions medicinal properties at all. His book, *Den Nederlandtsen Hovenier*, was the most popular gardening book in the Netherlands. First published in 1669, it was reprinted until 1721, and was translated into French and German. After the success of *Den Nederlandtsen Hovenier* others tried to market similar books. Cause's *De Koninglycke Hovenier* appeared in 1676, published simultaneously in one volume with *Nederlantze Hesperides* by Jan Commelin. The illustrations in Cause were copied from Crispijn van der Passe and were now published in mirror image.

The last Dutch handbook in the period of William and Mary to tell us about flower gardening was the *De Nieuwe Nederlandse Bloemhof* (1700) by the nurseryman Hendrik van Oosten of Leiden. This book gives a detailed account of how tulips, carnations, hyacinths, *Narcissi* and other plants are grown. The treatises about tulips, carnations and orangery trees were translated from French sources, though Van Oosten himself seems to have written the chapters 'De Nederlandse bloemhof', about perennials, and 'De naauwkeurige hovenier', on fruit and ornamental trees, perhaps indicating that he had special experience himself in these areas. Van Oosten's handbook was much translated, for example into English as *The Dutch Gardener* (1703 and 1711), and in the Netherlands it remained popular during the whole eighteenth century.

Florists' and other flowers

Van der Groen mentioned a huge variety of bulbs in use in the Netherlands of such species as *Colchicum, Crocus, Cyclamen, Fritillaria imperialis, Fritillaria meleagris, Hyacinthus orientalis, Narcissus, Ranunculus asiaticus, Scilla bifolia* and of course tulips. In the chapter about perennials it is clear

that there were also many *Allium, Campanula, Iris,* auricula (*Primula*), and *Ranunculus* species in those days. In the Netherlands, *Anemones,* Turkish *Ranunculi, Narcissi* and tulips were the plants with the most cultivar names. Carnations too had romantic names such as 'Prince of Orange', 'Emperor Augustus', 'Count William', 'King and Queen of France'.

When Alexander Marshal was making his lovely watercolours of flowers, which tell us so much of what they looked like around the middle of the seventeenth century, only tulips, carnations and some *Anemones* had as yet been given cultivar names in Britain, whereas auriculas were still known by descriptive ones, such as 'Black Imperial' or 'Mistress Buggs her fine purple'. However by the time the Duchess of Beaufort's *herbarium* was made early in the next century auriculas also had such cultivar names as 'Glory of England', 'Duke of Beaufort' and 'Royal Widow': these, and many of the others she named, appear in other lists of the period and some were illustrated in Furber's *Twelve Months of Flowers* (1730).

Any new development in flowering plants was quickly exploited as is shown by the rapidity in which the polyanthus became available. As far as is known, the polyanthus arose as a hybrid between garden forms of red-flowered primrose and cowslip and was only known as a distinct kind of plant in the 1650s. However it was already being sold in quite large numbers by the nurserymen, Rickets, Lucas and Looker in the 1670s. In 1676 40 polyanthus were bought for 10s. from William Looker for the gardens of the Earl of Bedford at Woburn Abbey, and the following year 'a fine poleyanthis' was obtained for 1s. as well as some striped auriculas.

Similarly new forms of hyacinth superseded the kinds which had been introduced from the Ottoman Empire. Bulbs of *Hyacinthus orientalis* had arrived in the mid-sixteenth century from Turkish gardens where its graceful sprays of single blue or white bells had been much admired. Semi-double kinds, in which the florets had a second row of petals, were known and illustrated from early in the seventeenth century, but Pieter Voorhelm of Haarlem is generally credited with developing fully-double hyacinths in the 1680s; yet, by 1702, the remote garden of Westbury Court, in Gloucestershire, had obtained '50 hyacinths double'.

One of the most famous and long-enduring of Voorhelm's cultivars was raised by him in 1698 and called 'King of Great Britain' in honour of William. It had fully-double white florets with red inner petals forming an eye arranged to make a pyramidal inflorescence, different and more graceful than our modern dome-shaped varieties. So many kinds of these popular hyacinths were being sold early in the eighteenth century that for a time it was feared there might be a craze for them to rival the tulipomania of the 1630s.

The tulips grown by Queen Mary and her contemporaries would have included some of those dating from the days of tulipomania, for the purple-striped 'Viceroy', one of the most highly priced of that era, was still advertised late in the eighteenth century. Those grown at the end of the seventeenth century were mostly single flowered and finely striped, often with two or three colours on a paler ground colour.

Numerous as these tulip cultivars were, there were probably even more kinds of carnation available. John Rea, in the 1676 edition of his *Flora*, could name more than 360. The most favoured had stripes, speckles or spots of a darker colour on the paler petals of the fully-double flowers. Two kinds of *Anemone*, also with double and often striped flowers, were widely grown and were then more admired than the *Ranunculus asiaticus* which was to outstrip them in popularity by the middle of the eighteenth century. Many species of *Narcissus* were seen in gardens, including some double yellow, and white varieties.

Some of the other flowering plants which would have had a place in the late-seventeenth-century garden have altered little over the centuries; such as 'Crown Imperials' and species of *Crocus* and *Cyclamen*. Others, like the many *Iris* and lilies so well-loved then, have since been joined by even more species and their cultivars. A few widely grown then, particularly for their late flowering, are less so now: plants such as Marvel of Peru (*Mirabilis jalapa*) and various kinds of *Amaranthus*. Some more ordinary garden plants that were certainly grown in the period would have included pansies and forget-me-nots.

Most of these hardy plants in British flower gardens had been known since before the Civil War, and there were few new annuals or biennials being introduced. However, before the British evacuation of Tangier, seed of the colourful local pea (*Lathyrus tingitanus*) arrived in England in 1680, and *Sutherlandia frutescens* arrived from the Cape of Good Hope in 1683. From Virginia came the Prince's Feather (*Amaranthus hypochondriacus*) in 1684, and in 1686 the Dutch blue annual lupin (*Lupinus angustifolius*) and the large nasturtium (*Tropaeolum majus*) from Peru.

To the reign of William III there belong only the first *Dimorphotheca* (*D. pluvialis*) from South Africa in 1699, followed by the Purple Jacobea (*Senecio elegans*). The year 1700, however, deserves to be famous in horticultural annuals for the introduction of the Sweet Pea (*Lathyrus odoratus*) from Sicily. Few bulbs or tubers of significance arrived, the outstanding exception being the Blue Lily (*Agapanthus africanus*) from the Cape, already being grown at Hampton Court in 1692. The Paris Daisy (*Chrysanthemum frutescens*) from the Canaries was here by 1699, as was the almost hardy Passion Flower (*Passiflora caerulea*) from Southern Brazil.

Some flower gardens

Quite a lot is known about the gardens made by royalist gentlemen who returned to England during the Commonwealth including the gardens of John Evelyn and his friend Sir Thomas Hanmer. Hanmer's book describing his garden at Bettisfield, in Flintshire, was written before 1660, though not published at the time. Sir Ralph Verney, returning to Claydon, in Buckinghamshire, in 1653 had his son send him from Holland 'Persian tulips and ranoncules' and, later, as well as obtaining 300 asparagus plants, bought red roses, double violets, '100 goodlie Julyflowers' (carnations) for the garden which Celia Fiennes found 'exact fine' when she saw it in 1694.

There is a very interesting list of the plants growing at Ham House in 1682, made presumably immediately after the death of the owner, the Duke of Lauderdale. As well as large numbers of orange and lemon trees in boxes and pots, and various 'greens', including gilded *Phillyrea*, there were 150 gillyflowers in pots and 50 in the borders, 50 double rocket plants, 100 striped and double auriculas, 200 plain auriculas, 200 'poliantheys' as well as other flowering plants.

Alexander Marshal lived for some time at Ham, where he painted a portrait of the Countess of Dysart, mother of the future Duchess of Lauderdale, and also some flower pieces. Later he lived at Fulham Palace, the home of Henry Compton, Bishop of London, dying there in 1681. Amongst the very many flowers Marshal painted were large numbers of striped, and even some double-striped, auriculas, and over 60 kinds of both tulips and carnations.

A feature of this age, even up to the time of Linnaeus, was that those who delighted in growing the fine exotics arriving from various parts of the world were also happy to grow old-established garden flowers and their cultivars. This was certainly true of Queen Mary and the Duchess of Beaufort, who both had superlative collections of succulents, but who grew many auriculas too. The *herbarium* of the duchess's plants contains over 60 named auriculas, dating from 1711 to 1713. The florets, carefully pressed, were of a good size and often showed a dusting of meal and, though their colours have faded, clearly these varied and many were striped. The two-volume *florilegium*, made at Badminton in the early years of the eighteenth century, contains what must be the earliest coloured illustration of a polyanthus and also some of polyanthus florets exhibiting early stages of lacing. In this the light edging also dipped into the middle of each petal to meet the eye and this was to become the characteristic feature of the gold-laced polyanthus of later times.

Jacob Bobart, the younger, curator of the Oxford Physic Garden, who also had a great collection there of plants both native and foreign, provided the duchess with many fine specimens and also some named auriculas and a 'Primula polyanthos limbis argenteis', the earliest reference to an edged polyanthus, here of the silver-laced kind. There is ample evidence that tulips and carnations were the most widely grown of all plants in such fine gardens and if the Duchess of Beaufort would seem to have preferred the two kinds of *Primula*, this may have been because they were still more of a novelty.

Even very large gardens such as those of Blenheim Palace had areas for flowering plants. In 1708, for the Duchess of Marlborough's personal garden, thousands of *Iris*, hyacinths, daffodils, *Ranunculus* and '4,600 tulips and 18,500 Dutch yellow crocuses' were bought, while in the following spring striped Brompton stocks, polyanthuses, carnations and 'Poppy Emmoneys' were obtained.

What the gardens looked like

There are, unfortunately, fewer detailed representations of flower gardens at the end of the seventeenth century than of those of an earlier date, such as in the engravings of Crispijn van der Passe in *Hortus Floridus* (1614), where recognisable flowers are shown growing in beds of a spring and of a summer garden. Of course, there are the many bird's-eye-views of gardens made by Kip which show patterns of the *parterres* but they show nothing of what was grown in them.

Since Queen Mary had an 'auricula quarter' at Hampton Court it would be useful to know more about this, and the other kinds of flowering plants which she might have grown in the quarters of her formal garden, and of how the plants might have been arranged in them. We know that the old Pond Yard lost some ground to the Privy Garden western terrace in 1689, but that, in its new form as the Glass Case Garden, it remained largely the same in general layout as it had been since Henry VIII's time. The *Narcissi*, auriculas and polyanthuses would have been similar to those grown by the Duchess of Beaufort. However, the detailed look of the remarkable botanical activity in the Glass Case Garden between 1689 and Queen Mary's death in 1694 has gone unrecorded.

A very Dutch-style, though much more modest, garden was created at Westbury Court from 1686 by Maynard Colchester. Clipped evergreens can be spotted in the Kip engraving. Contemporary practice was to have an edging of clipped box, while at regular intervals would have been planted neatly cut pyramids and balls of box, holly, yew or *Phillyrea*. We know that in 1702 Colchester bought '4 perimid hollys, 1 perimead yew, 6 lawrestinus headed [i.e. ball-shaped], 6 headed phillereys, 2 perimyd phillereys, 2 headed honeysuckles, 30 plain phyllereys and 5 mizerean trees (*Daphne mezereum*)'. Such small clipped bushes would have been used in many parts of the garden and not confined to flower beds, for they would have provided interest in winter.

11.4 Clingendaal, the *parterre*, by Leonard Schenk (c. 1700), showing how *plates-bandes* were stocked with flowering plants. Gardens purely for flowers are less well illustrated

Colchester's account book shows the garden to have been well supplied with flowering plants; for instance on 7 November 1702 he paid £3.17s.0d. for '100 iris's, 100 crocus, 50 junquills, 50 hyacynths double, 50 double narcissus's, 50 anemonys, 50 ranunculus's, 150 tulips and 1000 ews'. Colchester referred to the planting of 'the knot', by which he must have meant the four squares of straight-sided beds shown close to the house by Kip. Such simple quarters, typical of Dutch gardens and so different from elaborate French-style *parterres*, were well suited for growing Colchester's flowering plants. It is possible that he received some advice on his garden from his Dutch neighbour, Catherine Boevey of near-by Flaxley Abbey, the daughter of an Amsterdam merchant; she was certainly known to him as she joined Colchester in the founding of the Society for the Propagation of Christian Knowledge.

Many of the plants grown in these simple *parterres* would have been lifted and stored after flowering so a record would have been made of where and what was planted each year. Some idea of how the position of the plants could be recorded is shown in the little sketch made by John Evelyn for a section of his 'Coronary garden'. A record would have been kept of what was planted at each numbered position. Samuel Gilbert in his *Florist's Vade Mecum* (1682) made a plan of a large tulip bed in which each square was to

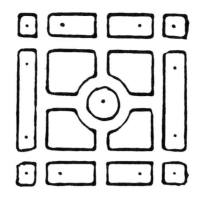

be filled with a different cultivar arranged according to height and contrasting colour.

Some idea of the general appearance of small *parterres* such as those of Evelyn and Colchester is provided by rare glimpses in paintings of mansions and their surroundings. Yester House, in East Lothian, then belonged to the Earl of Tweeddale, a close friend of the Duke of Lauderdale. A view of Yester House made before 1685 shows fenced-in areas with zig-zag beds filled with some kind of white-flowered plants and making a pattern like some of the 'frets' illustrated by John Rea in his *Flora* (1665), whose planting he described very fully.

Again, a view of Pierrepont House in Nottinghamshire painted about 1705 shows flower-filled beds and borders and also pots of plants standing by decorative railings. Carnations, as at Ham House, were frequently grown

11.6 Sketch of positions of plants in a bed, by John Evelyn, from the unpublished *Elysium Britannicum* (c. 1655)

190

in pots and always portrayed with some kind of supporting frame. This growing in pots seems to have been a fairly common practice in Britain, an early instance being on the terrace at Hadham Hall in the 1640s. In the Netherlands too, Van der Groen advised his readers to place plants in pots as ornaments, such as *Acanthus mollis*, *Aeonium arboreum*, *Capsicum annuum*, *Dianthus caryophyllus*, *Tropaeolum minus* and *Yucca*.

12

The Kitchen Garden and Orchard

12.1 *Previous page*:
Idealised garden scene by
A. Bleiswyk for the title
page of *De Nieuwe en
Naaukeurige Neederlandse
Hovenier* (1716), showing
dwarf and espaliered fruit
trees

The gardener's year

Each month's work in the kitchen garden and orchard were scheduled by P. van Aengelen in his *Herbarius: Kruijt en bloemhof* (1663), and in P. Nijland's *Den verstandigen hovenier* (1669). British readers would have been familiar with Evelyn's 'Kalendarium Hortense' printed in his *Sylva* (1664) and John Worlidge's *Gardener's Monthly Directory* printed in 1688.

'Good tools make half the work' declared Jan van der Groen in *Den Nederlandtsen Hovenier*. He advised the gardener to use the following tools in the kitchen garden: a rake, a hoe for the weeds, shears for box hedges, a trowel to dig out small plants, a three pronged fork to break up the beds under the trees whilst not damaging their roots, a shovel, a watering can, cloches to protect delicate plants, a wheelbarrow, an earth drill to lift plants without shaking earth off their roots, pots, trays, tubs and traps to catch moles, rats and mice.

Vegetables available

The vegetables and herbs available at the outset of the second half of the seventeenth century were catalogued into four classes by Van Aengelen. First, in the cabbage and carrot garden, grew artichokes, asparagus, beetroot, all kinds of cabbages, radishes, pumpkins, melons and cucumbers. Then, in the salad garden, were found kitchen herbs and the salad vegetables – spinach, endive, beetroot, sorrel, garden cress and chives. Third, amongst those in the medicinal garden, blessed thistle, *Aloe vera*, real camomile and marshmallow. Last, in the aromatic herb garden, were basil, hyssop, camomile, laurel, lavender, wild marjoram, mint, rosemary, sage, thyme and rue.

Many of the better Dutch varieties found their way to Britain. This is clear from the epithet 'Dutch' being applied to an odd assortment of vegetables and fruits; there were, for example, a Dutch lettuce, cabbage, gooseberry, asparagus and currant. Other Dutch or Flemish varieties growing in England in William and Mary's time included the Dutch Admiral pea, the long Orange carrots (which were later developed as the Horns and Amsterdams); the Windsor broad bean (introduced to that area by Dutch émigrés after the Revolution); the Flanders cherry; corn salad (which is an English native though the eating of it was a Dutch idea) and the large red and white Antwerp raspberries.

By this time the Englishman's passion for the kind of fruit and vegetable garden more usually seen on the Continent was aroused. Nervousness about the dangers of eating raw salads and fruit had been allayed by enthusiasts such as John Evelyn and Sir William Temple. Evelyn, in his *Acetaria* (1699), recommended the eating of 'salladings' and raw fruit to anyone who aspired to a long life. His book is one of the earliest to extol the virtues of an exclusively vegetarian diet. Temple, who knew the Netherlands well, and who had a fruit garden at Sheen, in Surrey, had a slightly more earthy attitude to the pleasures of the table. He claimed to be able to eat 30 to 40 cherries a day or 'a like proportion of strawberries, white figs, soft peaches or grapes' without feeling any ill effects.

Artificial heat

Progress in artificial heat at this time had not gone much further than hotbeds, while greenhouses were without glazed roofs but sometimes with underground flues. Bearing in mind that the English gardener had not yet discovered the advantages of heated walls or hothouses with glazed walls and roofs, it is hard to believe that fruits more suited to the climate of southern Europe could have been grown in England out of doors with much success, and the nursery gardeners' lists full of vines, figs, peaches and apricots should perhaps be treated with scepticism.

All authors did, however, recommend the warmth of a house wall by a fireplace (precursor of the heated wall) for the tenderest fruit, or at least a south-facing wall. One or two ingenious minds suggested the use of sloping

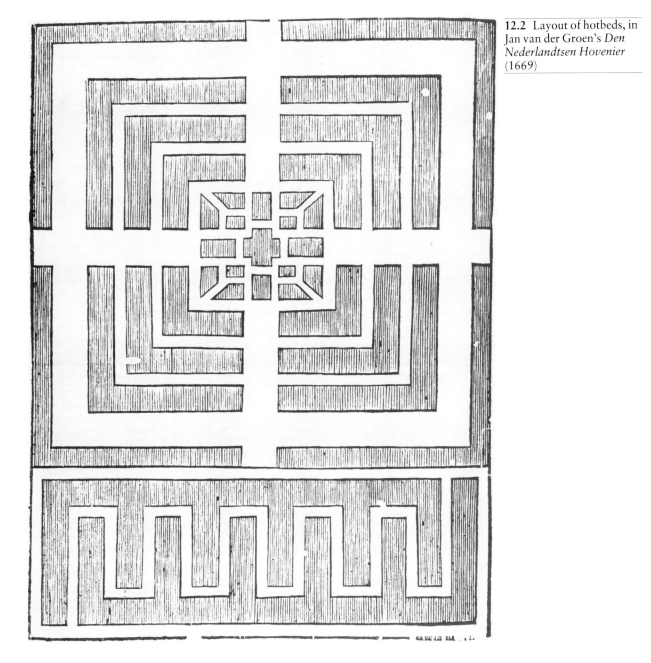

12.2 Layout of hotbeds, in Jan van der Groen's *Den Nederlandtsen Hovenier* (1669)

and 'niched' fruit walls as a way of increasing the benefit of the sun's rays; the one was to divide the rectangle or square by two diagonals, and after that to lead to the development of sloping glazed walls, which were incorporated in glass cases for exotics, and subsequently built by Boerhaave at Leiden and by Switzer at Belvoir; the other is no more than another version of the crinkle-crankle wall, as familiar in the Netherlands as in eastern England.

The hotbed owed its existence to the heat given off by rotting vegetable matter. It provided a suitable environment for those seeds from tropical countries which need warmth to get them to germinate, grow quicker or flower. Van der Groen advised hotbeds for the seeds of melons, cucumbers, green amaranths, Spanish pepper and also the roots of passion flower. They were made as follows: first a deep pit was dug, and this was filled with fresh horse manure. Then, a layer of good earth, thick enough to suit the plant, was laid down in which the seeds or seedlings were laid. Moveable frames, without bottoms and with a sloping glass top to protect plants against the elements, were placed with the sloping glass facing south on top of the earth. The glass formed a small greenhouse, and could be opened in good weather.

In the course of the seventeenth century the techniques of hotbed culture improved, and by 1700 much larger non-moveable frames such as in the Amsterdam *Hortus* or at William's hunting lodge at Soestdijk were to be found.

The English used hotbeds for raising cucumbers, melons and certain exotic flowers such as amaranths from seed; they also forced 'Indian bulbs' and *Narcissi* on them. However, they were apprehensive about the unwholesome heat, and also the unnaturalness of forcing *Praecoces* such as early salads, asparagus, and other 'forward Plants and Roots for the wanton Palate' on a heap of fermenting dung, 'which being corrupt in the original, cannot but produce malignant and ill effects to those who feed upon them'.

New fruits from far away foreign places engendered considerable excitement, with prices to match, both on the Continent and in England, none more so than the orange and the pineapple. Orange trees from Brompton Park cost £1.10s.0d. each in 1705, as compared to a mere 2s. for a peach tree, 1s. for an apricot and 6d. for a pear. Pineapples did not appear in nurserymen's lists as no one had yet succeeded in growing one in Europe.

For a pineapple to fruit and ripen can take as long as 2½ years. To achieve even this, the secret, discovered by the Dutch, is to start them on special hotbeds. A steady temperature of 75 degrees Fahrenheit needs to be maintained. This was almost impossible with the usual material for hotbeds used then, fresh horse dung, because it lost its heat quickly and was very variable in temperature. The trick the Dutch discovered was that heat from fermenting tanner's bark was far more even and long lasting. In other respects — the pits, mounded earth, and protective frames — the technique was similar to ordinary hotbeds.

The Amsterdam *Hortus* developed the practice of using tanner's bark from oak trees very early. Hans Sloane said that large and ripe pineapples were being grown in Amsterdam in 1687, and that they had been growing there since 1682. At a slightly later date the best known pineapple grower in the Netherlands was Pieter de la Court van de Voort, who lived at Allemans-gees't, near Leiden, and who published an account of pineapple growing in 1737.

The English might well have made the tanbark discovery for themselves if they had been altogether less puritanical about the use of hotbeds. England was, in fact, somewhat slow in learning from the Dutch. In 1722 Henry Wise, 'the Great Gardiner of Brompton Park near Kensington', told the

Reverend George Harbin that 'Tanners bark had not been used in England above ten years, & that we first learnt the use of it from the Dutch'. Likewise, it was not until 1702 that Sir Matthew Decker of Amsterdam settled in England, took up gardening, and was said to have first successfully ripened pineapples in 1714.

The famous picture by Hendrik Danckerts which is supposed to show John Rose presenting a pineapple to Charles II is an enigma both in respect of the house depicted and the possibility of Rose being able to grow a pineapple at the date of the painting, perhaps the 1670s. The pineapple was probably a present, or possibly imported, as there is no record of a pineapple being grown in England before 1714. Hans Willem Bentinck is said to have taken pineapple plants from the Netherlands to Hampton Court in 1690, where they might have survived in a glass-case, but not for long enough (if they were imported as suckers) to produce fruit and ripen.

Orchards

The distinction between fruit trees and soft fruit bushes was made as early as Van Aengelen's *Herbarius*. The most common orchard trees were apple, pear, sweet cherry, morello cherry, plum, peach, apricot, almond, dwarf almond, black mulberry, quince, medlar, dwarf medlar, walnuts and hazel,

12.3 Dieren, vineyard, by Pieter Schenk (c. 1700). The vines are protected by a high espalier hedge above

12.4 Espaliered fruit trees, in *De Nieuwe en Naaukeurige Neederlandse Hovenier* (1716)

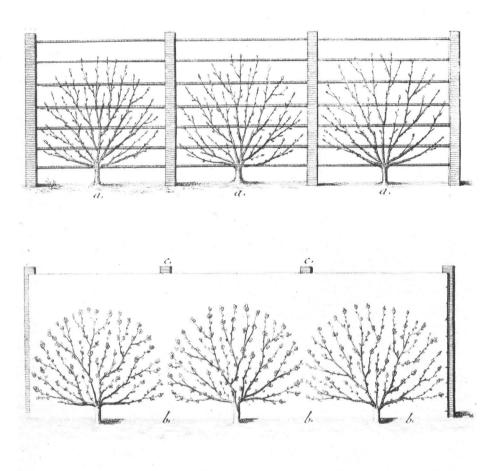

a. a. a. Model, hoe laage Boomtjes, so Appel als Peer aan Lattingen moeten geleid worden, booven-van alle swaare looten bevrijd. *b.b.b.* Model, hoe Perfikken of Abrikoofen aan Schuttin̄gen of Muuren moeten aangebonden werden. *c. c.* De Paalen van agter de Schutting ftaande, by haar top-enden aangeweefen.

while fig was also grown. The most common soft fruits were raspberry, redcurrant and gooseberry.

The already well-developed skills of taking cuttings, grafting and inoculating to improve the quality of the trees and fruit were described by Jan van der Groen. Preferably one species was grafted onto the stock of the same species, except for medlar and quince which were grafted on hawthorn. The tools which one used for these techniques were a grafting knife, a grafting saw and a wooden hammer.

The Van Oosten family of nurserymen of Leiden was well known for its fruit trees. Hendrik van Oosten, author of *De Nieuwe en Nederlandse Bloemhof* (1700), advised his readers to be careful that branches did not grow over each other, and that the first trees to be pruned should be the apricots and peaches because these sprout first. After that the winter pears are dealt with, then the summer and autumn pears and quince, and, lastly, the plums and apples. In the second edition of *De Nieuwe Naauwkeurige Neederlandse Hovenier* (1716) there is a 'Register of all sorts of pears and apples' of 1717. The introduction to this register states that most of the fruits could be obtained from Van Oosten, so perhaps this register was his nursery catalogue. The larger part of the trees on the register was most probably already present at the end of the seventeenth century.

The English too had their specialists; John Beale and Anthony Lawrence put together *Nurseries, orchards, profitable gardens, and vineyards encouraged* (1677), which was influential in a practical way. However, English gardeners, although skilled in the grafting, training and pruning of fruit trees, whether as standards, espaliers, fans or dwarfs, were clearly less advanced in this branch of horticulture than their counterparts on the Continent. The best books in English on the subject were the translation by Evelyn of De la Quintinye, the intendant of the *potager*, or kitchen garden, at Versailles, and the English edition of Van Oosten's *The Dutch Gardener*.

The ranks of vines on the slopes at Dieren were rather unusual in the time of William and Mary, though some people grew vines in baskets placed high up, say on top of a wall. The vine was usually propagated by cuttings.

Dwarfs

Dwarf fruit trees were produced by grafting low down onto stock of a low-growing variety. They were highly popular in the Netherlands and are seen on prints of Rosendael, Heemstede and Soestdijk and other places. At

12.5 Dieren, eastern fishpond flanked by an orchard of dwarfs and kitchen garden, by Pieter Schenk (c. 1700)

12.6 Rijswijk, *parterre* planted with dwarf fruit trees, by Van Vianen (c. 1700)

Heemstede the dwarf apple trees were said to be the *Malus aurantia humilis* of Bauhinus and Clusius.

Dwarf fruit trees were popular in England, too, especially for planting in the borders of garden walks. Instructions for their grafting on to paradise apple or quince stocks, and the subsequent pruning of both roots and branches and their training into cup, globe or pyramidal shapes are all to be found in fruit tree manuals of the time. None of them draw attention, though, to the fact that the 'new order of dwarf-trees' which 'have of late been much coveted and affected' was largely perfected by the Dutch. English writers on gardening were curiously reluctant to attribute anything new, improved or useful to the Dutch, though they were quick enough to credit the French or Italians.

Layout of the kitchen garden and orchard

Jan van der Groen described the layout of the kitchen garden in some detail, defining the 'Dutch' way of layout as that in which a square or rectangular plot or quarter was divided into four equal parts by paths at right angles passing through the centre. At the foot of the enclosing wall or fence there would be a border bed, inside which there would be a path. The four equal plots were divided up into a pattern of beds. Van der Groen's 'French' way of laying out was to divide the rectangle or square by two diagonals, then to fill the triangles with beds parallel to the surrounding walls or fences.

In an engraving of an 'ordinary' or commoner's garden as seen from the house, Van der Groen describes the garden as set out in four quarters, of which the right-hand one of two nearest is set aside for flowers and as a *parterre*. The left-hand quarter is for salads and culinary herbs and the two furthest quarters are for ordinary vegetables such as asparagus, cauliflowers, peas and beans. The garden is surrounded by a wooden fence, on which cherries, apricots and peaches are grown. Van der Groen suggests planting strawberries along the fenced borders. Roses and currant bushes are planted round each quarter. He also says that apples, pears and other large fruit trees may be planted 'here and there, as long as one is in line with the other'. In the engraving, the gardener's cottage seen at the far end has a vine growing on its south or south-west facing walls.

According to Van der Groen, a choice similar to that for kitchen gardens existed for laying out the square or rectangular orchard. Trees could either be planted in diagonal rows at right angles to each other or in straight rows parallel to the enclosing wall or fence. To make an orchard fertile it should be planted with cabbage in the first year. During the planting of the trees a lot of manure should be mixed with the earth. The trees were planted at distances of about 6 to 9 m. Cherry, morello and plum trees were commonly removed as soon as the apple and pear trees were fully grown. Meanwhile redcurrants and gooseberries could be planted under taller fruit trees since they can tolerate shade.

An orchard is illustrated as a bird's-eye-view in Van Oosten's *De Nieuwe en Naauwkeurige Neederlandse Hovenier*. Peaches and apricots were the sort of trees found against the warm south-facing walls. A wooden trellis is shown along the length of the garden between the fence and the tree plots, and cherries, plums, peaches and apricots are trained against it. At the corners and at regular distances along edges there were yew trees cut into pyramids. The tree plots are planted in three rows: the outside rows are grafted and pruned so that they stay low, at 1.5 to 2 m, while the middle row is grafted higher so that its foliage rises above the other trees.

The kitchen garden and orchard in the garden layout

It was thought desirable to keep, as far as possible, the sight of beds – made disorderly by the cutting, picking and digging of crops – and the smell of the dung for hotbeds and manuring well away from the drawing room, parlour or library. On the other hand, the suitability of a site for a kitchen garden was of prime importance: if it was to be of any use it should have a southerly aspect, good, well-drained soil and protection from bad weather, animals, thieves and small boys. As if in recognition of this, the owners of middling-sized or ordinary gardens were not judged too harshly if they made their gardens all-purpose in design, providing both pleasure and utility in one.

As far as the owners of large estates were concerned, it was usually easy enough to separate the ornamental and the useful at a price. In the more refined English gardens the view from the main rooms was over the 'Best Garden', containing only flowers, knots, fountains and *parterres*. Meanwhile, if the ground was suitable, the kitchen gardens were sited as close as could be managed to the side of the house containing the kitchens. Hence they were often found in the region of the offices and stables.

In Britain a number of options along these lines were tried. Places like St James's Palace and New Park had their kitchen gardens close but to one side. The Brompton Park layout for Longleat included the kitchen gardens and orchards at the sides and further parts of the great rectangle of the garden layout, while at Wimpole they were not in the walled rectangle but immediately alongside. In a few cases the kitchen garden was becoming slightly detached, within its own walled enclosure, as at Althorp. The 8 acre Hampton Court kitchen gardens were formerly the Tiltyard, but were convenient for the kitchens. The area was divided into six quarters by internal walls in 1690. In a few cases the orangery was placed in the kitchen gardens.

In their great layouts such as Zeist, Heemstede and De Voorst the Dutch, it seems, were less concerned with the convenience of a kitchen garden close to the house. At these places they were situated beyond the *parterres* and on both sides of the main axis. Sometimes they were within the main garden wall, but hidden by espaliers, but at Het Loo the kitchen gardens were situated beyond the walls, behind the re-sited colonnades, and so were completely invisible.

Many orchards were little more than fields with fruit trees, as at Badminton, but they could be incorporated in an ornamental layout, as Mollet had suggested. Such were the orchards at Honselaarsdijk, before being converted to *bosquet*, and the wilderness at Wollaton. An extraordinary feature of William's palaces is their use of dwarf apple trees on the *parterres*. At Soestdijk dwarfs flanked the *parterres*, but at Dieren dwarfs were planted instead of the *parterres*. So also the *parterres* at Rijswijk were replaced with dwarfs about 1700.

A modest country house garden

The garden designed for Herriard Park by George London in 1699 is a perfect example of the way in which the compromise between pleasure and utility was dealt with. London's client was an English country squire named Thomas Jervoise. Herriard is a small country estate not far from Basingstoke in Hampshire. In comparison with Melbourne Hall, Longleat, Chatsworth and Hampton Court, Herriard is very small. On the plan its garden walls include an area no more than 300 by 380 ft, but within this space is provided everything in keeping with the latest fashion.

The garden side of the house faces south-east. It is flanked by two large ornamental Pond Courts and it stands upon a broad, 17 ft wide terrace walk which runs the width of the garden and has a palisade at each end giving views over the estate. Below the terrace were three walled or hedged enclosures, the middle one being two cut-work *parterres* surrounded by *plates-bandes* with topiary at 12 ft intervals and divided by a gravel walk. The 120 ft wide space was narrowed down to half its width at the end by curving walls or hedges, behind which were two gardener's 'houses'. The left-hand enclosure was perhaps a small orchard with diagonal camomile walks surrounded by borders. The right-hand one consisted of 'sparagras' (asparagus) beds edged perhaps by lavender or rosemary, and quartered and surrounded by camomile paths. Outside these paths were borders with a grass walk down the centre.

Beyond these enclosures was a grass cross-walk flanked by more borders

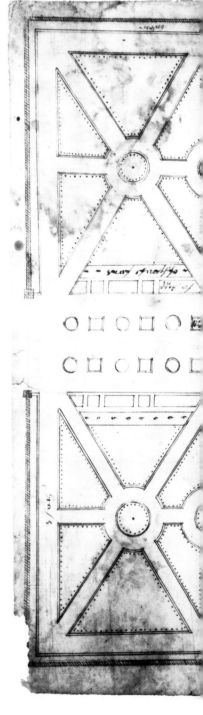

and with a sizeable greenhouse at one end and a gate at the other. At right angles, along the main axis, was a 60 ft wide grass broad walk with alternating square and round stone bases for setting out the 'greens' in their tubs and pots in the summer. This walk was enclosed by an 'espalyar of spruce firrs', behind which was an elegant arrangement of the 'quarters for ketching stuff', occupying almost half the walled area. At the far wall of the garden there must have been an ironwork palisade the width of the broad walk allowing views out over meadowland.

12.7 Herriards, in Hampshire, a design by George London (1699) for a modest country-house garden

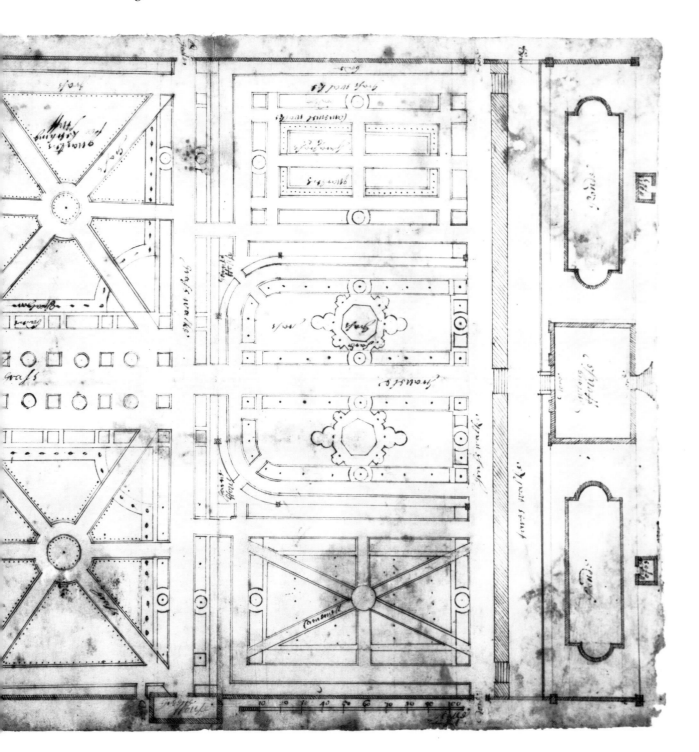

The *parterre* and broad walk beyond were the spine of the gardens, to which the various parts of the garden were united by cross-walks and diagonal vistas. The kitchen garden quarters lie furthest from the house, but London does not allow them to look like a separate garden; whilst hidden from the house, they are carefully integrated into the layout and easily discovered by anyone walking around the gardens.

Thomas Jervoise seems to have made his own plan of the house, garden and surrounding fields, and this confirms most of London's layout, though it suggests that the arrangement of the kitchen garden quarters was slightly simplified.

Bills sent to Herriard from London and Wise's nursery mention yews and variegated hollies. The greenhouse, measuring 35 by 14 ft would have been heated, if at all, in the old-fashioned way with pans of charcoal or small portable stoves. One might have expected it to house bays, myrtles, oranges and lemons. When set out along the broad walk in summer these would have continued the lines of the permanently planted yews and hollies to give the effect of an *allée* the whole length of the garden.

Fruit lists and bills dated 1703 and 1705 show that London and Wise supplied huge numbers of fruit trees; 20 standard and 24 espaliered apples on one occasion, with a further 52 espaliers later. However, the lists are mainly of peaches, apricots, nectarines, cherries, pears and plums of the kinds that would have been grown on walls. One of the lists was headed 'fruit trees planted in two of my new gardens' and contains 59 trees. The internal length of Jervoise's kitchen garden walls, if the internal divisions were walls too, was about 1,600 ft, enough for more than 100 fan-trained trees planted at the usual distance of 15 ft.

Dozens of different kinds of vegetable seed were also sent: there are all the usual salads, peas, beans and herbs as well as two kinds of flowers (larkspur and marigold) and, proof that somewhere at Herriard there must have been hotbeds, 'cowcumber and million seed'.

The 'quarters for ketching stuff' do not provide space for melon beds or forcing grounds, nor are they laid out in the square or oblong beds that a serious kitchen gardener might wish for. In fact, if it were not for the combined area of 1¼ acres, this kitchen garden would appear to be hardly serious at all, but merely decorative. The quarters were formed by diagonal paths, with circular beds at the intersections, crossing rectangles 100 ft across. The paths were 8 ft wide, which is generous for a kitchen garden, though made of grass so not very practical. The circular beds, large enough for each to contain a standard fruit tree, are 15 ft in diameter. The edges of the kitchen quarters were marked with dots less than 2 ft apart, indicating some sort of edging plant such as box, lavender, rosemary or thyme.

The idea of ornamenting herb and vegetable plots was an old tradition prevalent in major European gardens of the sixteenth century. The London plan is ample evidence that he practised what he preached for, in 1699, the same year as the Herriard plan, he and Wise published their abridgement of De la Quintinye, in the *Compleat Gardener*. In it they advise those 'with one garden' to 'employ it with Fruits and Legumes', rather than with 'Box and gras-plats' or at least to make only the part nearest to the house into a *parterre* and to set aside the rest 'for use and necessity'.

Appendix A
The Common Lime

Two species of lime are native in central and western Europe – *Tilia platyphyllos* & *Tilia cordata*. They hybridise naturally to give the common lime (*Tilia x vulgaris*), though this has not been reproduced artificially. Both species are variable, which means that almost every clone is morphologically distinct, though examination of a large number of common limes planted before 1750 shows that most trees belong to two distinct clones.

The more widespread clone in early avenues, and as single trees in parklands, has distinctive buttresses at the base of the tree. Although cylindrical and smooth-barked when young, with age the trunk becomes strikingly expanded at the base by the growth of narrow-flanged spurs. Groups of epicormic buds develop on the trunk to form hemispherical masses and these may produce dense clusters of sprouts. Sprouting sometimes also takes place within the lower part of the crown to form a dense tangle like an enormous witch's broom. It is not clear whether this has an extraneous cause, such as pruning when the tree was young, or is, in fact, evidence that there are two similar clones, one prone to sprouting and the other not. The exposed twigs develop a red bark.

The main axis is vertical, or it may be replaced by two or three almost parallel and vertical axes, which is probably the product of topping the young tree. The branches of the first order are short and in the lower half of the crown they arch over to give a parabaloid form in the open, but in avenues a narrow crown with a parabaloid top. In autumn the leaves turn distinctively yellow. The trees of this clone flower profusely. The inflorescences almost all have seven flowers.

The form of the crown and trunk, the bright green and dense foliage and the profuse flowering make this tree particularly attractive and suitable for

A.1 Silhouettes of trees of common lime, showing the parabaloid form and vertical limbs of the buttress-trunked clone whether a young untopped tree (left) or a 260-year-old tree (centre), as compared to the divergent branching and broad upper crown of a cylinder-trunked clone of 125 years old (right)

avenues, but the large burrs on the trunk and, in the absence of browsing by cattle or deer, the tendency to produce dense clusters of sprouts from the base of the stem are disfiguring. Eventually these sprouts become so large and vigorous, as in the old avenue at Kingston Lacy in Dorset, that the top of the tree becomes stag-headed and even the main limbs die back.

There is another clone, or possibly a group of two or three very similar clones, which is present in several of the oldest avenues and can readily be distinguished from the first by, amongst other features, the cylindrical form of the trunk being maintained in old age. The bark is initially smooth, but gradually it becomes regularly and deeply fissured with narrow ridges and in this respect resembles *Tilia platyphyllos*. Although sprouts may arise from just below ground level, clusters of epicormic buds are weakly developed or absent.

The axes of trees of this clone often depart from vertical, and the main branches, probably also resulting from topping the young trees, diverge, particularly in the upper part of the crown. The whole crown tends to become wider and the top irregularly hemispherical in outline. The lower branches are proportionately longer and less abruptly arched over. The leaves on the exposed part of the crown are typically larger than those on the buttress-trunked clone. In autumn they do not turn yellow, and tend to stay green before turning greyish-brown. The trees of this clone normally flower rather sparsely, and the inflorescences each consist of no more than five flowers.

At the same age the tree is taller and, when mixed, overtops trees of the buttress-trunked clone by at least a tenth of their height. In mixed plantings, the taller, broader crown of this clone is at once distinct. At Hatfield, for example, the two clones are distinct in all the avenues, even those of different ages. Very old trees of the two clones, probably planted in 1672, are mixed in the avenue at Cassiobury, in Hertfordshire, where the two types of trunk are strikingly distinct.

The buttress-trunked clone is sometimes mistaken for *Tilia cordata*, but the hanging inflorescence and the thick-walled fruits are distinct from the erect inflorescence and thin-walled fruits of that species. The cylindrical-trunked clone has been confused with *Tilia platyphyllos*, but the form of that species which was planted in early avenues has numerous simple hairs present on the young twigs, the leaf-stalks and along the veins on the underside and, to a lesser extent, on the upperside of the leaves.

Both of these clones of common lime have continued to be planted in avenues and have been perpetuated by using vegetative means of propagation. In the early nineteenth century, when avenues once again became fashionable after a period of neglect, several more clones of common lime were planted, possibly because by then seeding was common and trees were raised from seedlings. Certainly there is a much wider range of variation present in some younger avenues and this has tended to obscure the distinction between the older clones.

So distinct are the original clones, however, that they impart quite different visual characteristics to avenues. The broader crown and divergent branches of the cylindrical-trunked clone give a very different structure to a narrow avenue, but the dull green foliage, which is often heavily infested with lime aphids and lost early, and the sparse flowering, make the tree less attractive. This is, however, counterbalanced by the fine cylindrical, rough-barked, trunks which are scarcely disfigured by burrs. It is important that the differences should be recognised when selecting appropriate trees with which to restore, or replant, in an historical setting.

Appendix B
Trees and Shrubs for the Bosquet and Wilderness

The following sources have been analysed for the tables below:
John Evelyn (1664) *Sylva, or a Discourse of forest Trees*
Jan van der Groen (1669) *Den Nederlandtsen Hovenier*
John Worlidge (1677) *Systema Horti-culturae: or, The Art of Gardening*
George London and Henry Wise (1706) *The Retir'd Gard'ner*
John James (translator) (1712) *The Theory and Practice of Gardening*
Stephen Switzer (1718) *Ichnographia Rustica*
Where the species was not clear, or the use of the plant not mentioned, it has been omitted.

In hedges

species	Evelyn 1664	Van der Groen 1669	Worlidge 1677	London & Wise 1706	James 1712	Switzer 1718
Abies alba	■	–	–	–	–	–
Acer campestre	–	–	–	–	■	□
Alnus glutinosa	–	□	–	–	–	□
Berberis vulgaris	■	–	–	–	–	–
Buxus sempervirens	–	■	–	■	■	–
Carpinus betulus	□	■	–	□	■	□■
Castanea sativa	■	–	–	–	–	–
Cornus mas	–	■	–	–	–	–
Cornus sanguinea	■	–	–	–	–	–
Crataegus monogyna	■	–	■	–	■	■
Cupressus sempervirens	–	–	■	–	■	–
Euonymus europaeus	■	–	–	–	–	–
Fagus sylvatica	■	–	–	–	■	–
Ilex aquifolium	■	■	■	–	■	■
I.a. 'Ferox'	–	■	–	–	–	–
I.a. 'Aureomarginata'	■	–	–	–	–	–
Juniperus communis	■	■	–	–	■	–
Juniperus sabina	■	■	–	–	■	–
Laurus nobilis	■	–	–	–	–	–
Ligustrum vulgare	■	■	–	–	–	■
Malus domestica	–	–	–	–	–	□
Philadelphus coronarius	–	■	–	–	–	–
Phillyrea angustifolia	■	–	■	■	■	–
Phillyrea latifolia	–	–	■	–	–	–

species	Evelyn 1664	Van der Groen 1669	Worlidge 1677	London & Wise 1706	James 1712	Switzer 1718
Pinus sylvestris	–	–	–	–	–	□
Prunus laurocerasus	–	–	–	–	–	■
Prunus spinosa	–	–	–	–	–	■
Pyracantha coccinea	■	■	■	■	–	–
Pyrus communis	–	–	–	–	–	□
Rhamnus alaternus	■	–	■	■	■	–
Rhamnus catharticus	■	–	–	–	–	–
Rosa damascena	–	–	–	■	–	–
Rosa foetida	–	–	–	■	–	–
Rosa gallica	–	–	–	■	–	–
Rosa gallica versicolor	–	–	–	■	–	–
Rubus idaeus	–	■	–	–	–	–
Sambucus nigra	■	–	■	–	–	–
Sorbus aucuparia	–	□	–	–	–	–
Taxus baccata	–	■	■	■	■	■
Thuja occidentalis	–	■	–	–	–	–
Tilia x vulgaris	–	–	–	□	–	□
Ulmus glabra	–	–	–	–	–	□
Ulmus x 'Hollandica'	–	–	–	–	–	□
Ulmus procera	■	–	–	■	–	□

□ = tall hedge, ■ = low hedge or topiary

In the bosquet

species	Evelyn 1664	Van der Groen 1669	Worlidge 1677	London & Wise 1706	James 1712	Switzer 1718
Acer campestre	C	–	–	–	C	BC
Aesculus hippocastanum	–	–	B	–	–	–
Alnus glutinosa	–	–	–	–	–	B
Carpinus betulus	–	–	–	–	–	BC
Cercis siliquastrum	–	–	B	–	C	–
Clematis viticella 'Plena'	–	–	B	–	–	–
Colutea arborescens	–	–	B	–	C	–
Cornus mas	–	–	–	–	C	–
Corylus avellana	B	–	–	–	B	–
Crataegus monogyna	–	–	–	–	C	–
C.m. 'Biflora'	–	–	B	–	–	–
Daphne mezereum	–	–	B	–	–	–
Daphne mezereum 'Alba'	–	–	B	–	–	–
Diospyros lotus	–	–	–	–	C	–
Euonymus europaeus	–	–	–	–	C	–
Fagus sylvatica	–	–	–	–	–	BC
Ficus carica	–	–	–	–	C	–
Hibiscus syriacus	–	–	B	–	–	–
Ilex aquifolium	–	–	–	–	C	–

species	Evelyn 1664	Van der Groen 1669	Worlidge 1677	London & Wise 1706	James 1712	Switzer 1718
I.a. 'Aureomarginata'	–	B	–	–	–	–
Juniperus communis	–	–	–	–	C	–
Juniperus sabina	–	–	–	–	C	–
Laburnum alpinum	–	–	B	–	–	–
Laburnum anagyroides	–	–	B	–	–	–
Lonicera caprifolium	–	–	B	–	–	–
Lonicera xylosteum	–	–	B	–	–	–
Mespilus germanica	–	–	–	–	C	–
Morus alba & nigra	B	–	–	–	C	–
Paliurus spina-christi	–	–	B	–	–	–
Phillyrea angustifolia	–	–	–	–	C	–
Picea abies	–	–	–	–	–	BC
Platanus orientalis	–	–	B	–	–	B
Populus alba	–	–	–	–	–	BC
Prunus avium	–	–	–	–	C	–
Prunus cerasifera	–	–	–	–	C	–
Prunus cerasus 'Rhexii'	–	–	B	–	–	–
Prunus dulcis	–	–	B	–	–	–
P. persica 'Roseo Plena'	–	–	B	–	–	–
Pyracantha coccinea	–	–	–	–	C	–
Quercus robur	C	–	–	–	–	B
Rhamnus alaternus	–	–	–	–	C	–
Robinia pseudoacacia	–	–	–	B	–	–
Salix alba	–	–	–	–	C	C
Sorbus domestica	–	–	–	–	C	–
Spartium junceum	–	–	B	–	–	–
Spiraea hypericifolia	–	–	B	–	–	–
Syringa x persica	B	–	B	–	–	–
Syringa vulgaris	–	–	B	–	–	–
Tilia x vulgaris	–	–	–	B	BC	–
Ulmus glabra	–	–	–	–	–	C
Ulmus procera	–	–	–	BC	BC	–

B = in the *bosquet* or grove, C = as coppice or underwood

Appendix C
Selected List of Exotics Imported to the Netherlands Between 1685 and 1700

An impression of the numerous new introductions via the Dutch East India Company and the Dutch West India Company in the years following 1685 can be gained from the following selection:

Japan: *Rhododendron indicum, Cycas revoluta, Cinnamomum camphora, Camellia sinensis, Broussonetia papyrifera, Camellia sasanqua, Hibiscus mutabilis.*

East Indies: *Proiphys amboinensis, Cassia javanica, Kalanchoe ceratophylla, Clitoria ternatea, Pterocarpus indicus.*

Ceylon: *Crinum zeylanicum, Pancratium zeylanicum, Amorphophallus paeoniifolius, Typhonium trilobatum, Cyanothis cristata, Gloriosa superba, Pentapetes phoenicea.*

India: *Trichosanthes cucumerina, Euphorbia antiquorum, Euphorbia nivulia, Hibiscus cannabinus, Ficus benghalensis.*

Mauritius: *Momordica charantia.*

Eastern Cape: *Scadoxus puniceus, Sansevieria hyacinthoides.*

Cape of Good Hope: *Orbea variegata, Stapelia hirsuta, Lobelia erinus, Roella ciliata, Arctotheca calendula, Arctotis acaulis, Athanasia trifurcata, Castalis nudicaulis, Chrysocoma coma-aurea, Cineraria qeifolia, Felicia fruticosa, Helichrysum foetidum, Hippia frutescens, Kleinia ficoides, Othonna heterophylla, Polyarrhena reflexa, Senecio elegans, Ursinia paleacea, Cotyledon orbiculata, Crassula perfoliata, Euphorbia mammillaris, Orphium frutescens, Pelargonium peltatum, Pelargonium zonale, Antholyza ringens, Gladiolus gracilis, Homeria flaccida, Moraea vegeta, Aloe variegata, Aloe plicatilis, Aloe succotrina, Drimia capensis, Gasteria disticha, Haworthia retusa, Kniphofia uvaria, Anisodontea scabrosa, Melianthus major, Polygala myrtifolia, Leucadendron argenteum, Diosma hirsuta, Hebenstretia dentata.*

Ghana: *Dracaena fragrans.*

Cape Verde Islands: *Lotus jacobaeus.*

Canary Islands: *Justicia hyssopifolia, Convolvulus canariensis, Aeonium canariense, Euphorbia canariensis, Hypericum canariense, Lavandula canariensis, Teline canariensis, Isoplexis canariensis.*

Azores: *Jasminum azoricum.*

Morocco: *Aeonium arboreum, Euphorbia officinarum, Argania spinosa.*

Peru: *Tropaeolum majus.*

Brazil: *Caladium bicolor, Ananas comosus, Neptunia plena, Eugenia uniflora.*
Surinam: *Bixa orellana, Epiphyllum phyllanthus, Abelmoschus esculentus.*
West Indies: *Agave vivipara, Crinum americanum, Furcraea foetida, Hymenocallis caribaea, Mammillaria mammillaris, Pereskia guamacho, Verbesina alata, Hura crepitans, Pedilanthus tithymaloides, Phyllanthus epiphyllanthus, Capraria biflora, Zamia pumila, Guajacum sanctum.*
Mexico: *Crescentia cujete, Acacia corniqera, Rhynchosia americana.*
North America: *Aralia spinosa, Euonymus americana, Coreopsis grandiflora, Ipomoea coccinea, Liquidambar styraciflua, Lindera benzoin, Helenium autumnale, Ceanothus americanus, Physocarpus opulifolius.*

Besides the above exotic plants new species were also imported from the Mediterranean such as *Lathyrus odoratus,* and from Turkey *Lallemantia canescens, Origanum sipyleum, Lysimachia atropurpurea* and *Papaver orientale.* Also there was a lively interest in indigenous flora especially for orchids.

Principal Sources and Reference Works

Chapter 1

Hopper, Florence 'The Dutch Classical Garden and André Mollet' in *Journal of Garden History*, Vol.2, No.1 (1982)

Hopper, Florence 'Netherlands' in *The Oxford Companion to Gardens* (1987)

Mollet, André *Le Jardin de Plaisir* (1651)

Chapter 2

Britannia Illustrata (1707)

Green, David *Gardener to Queen Anne: Henry Wise and the Formal Garden* (1956)

Karling, Sten 'The Importance of André Mollet and His Family for the Development of the French Formal Garden' in *The French Formal Garden* (1974)

Land Use Consultants 'Royal Parks Historical Survey: Greenwich Park' (1985), for the Department of the Environment

Strong, Roy *The Renaissance Garden in England* (1979)

Travers Morgan Planning 'Royal Parks Historical Survey: Hampton Court and Bushy Park' (3 Vols.) (1982), for the Department of the Environment

Chapter 3

Bienfait, Anna G. *Oud Hollandsche Tuinen* (1943)

Fremantle, Katharine 'A Visit to the United Provinces and Cleves in the time of William III, described in Edward Southwell's Journal' in *Nederlands Kunsthistorisch Jaarboek*, Vol.XXI (1970)

Kuyper, W. *Dutch Classicist Architecture* (1980)

Ozinga, M.D. *Daniel Marot, de Schepper van de Hollandsche Lodewijk XIV stijl* (1938)

Van der Wyck, H.W.M. *De Nederlandse Buitenplaats* (1983)

Van Everdingen-Meyer, L.R.M. (ed.) *Een Beschrijving van's Konings Paleis en Tuinen van Het Loo* (1985)

Chapter 4

Britannia Illustrata (1707)

Green, David *Gardener to Queen Anne: Henry Wise and the Formal Garden* (1956)

Land Use Consultants 'Royal Parks Historical Survey: Kensington Gardens' (1984), for the Department of the Environment

Mitchell, Anthony 'The Park and Garden at Dyrham' in *The National Trust Yearbook* (1977–8)

Strandberg, Runar 'The French Formal Garden after Le Nostre' in *The French Formal Garden* (1974)

Travers Morgan Planning 'Royal Parks Historical Survey: Hampton Court and Bushy Park' (3 Vols.) (1982), for the Department of the Environment

Urwin, A.C.B. 'The Houses and Gardens of Twickenham Park, 1227–1805' *Borough of Twickenham Local History Society Paper Number 54* (1984)

Chapter 5

Batey, Mavis *Oxford Gardens* (1982)
Britannia Illustrata (1707)
Country Life, Vol. 4, p. 756; Vol. 5, p. 522; Vol. 10, p. 272
Defoe, Daniel *A Tour through the Whole Island of Great Britain* (1st edn 1724-6)
    (3rd edn 1742)
De Beer, E.S. (ed.) *The Diary of John Evelyn* (1959)
Gardeners Magazine, October 1828, p.435
Garden History, Vol.13, No.2
Harris, Walter *A Description of the King's Royal Palace and Gardens at Loo* (1699)
Honour, Hugh 'Leonard Knyff' in *Burlington Magazine*, Vol.XCVI (1954)
Hunt, John Dixon, and Willis, Peter *The Genius of the Place* (1975), pp. 148–50
Johnson, J. (ed.) *Excellent Cassandra*, p. 45
Law, Ernest *Hampton Court Gardens Old and New* (1926)
Loggan, David *Oxonia Illustrata* (1675)
Morris, Christopher (ed.) *The Journeys of Celia Fiennes* (1949)
Switzer, Stephen *The Nobleman, Gentleman and Gardeners' Recreation* (1715)
Temple, Sir William *Upon the Gardens of Epicurus* (1692)
Williams, William *Oxonia depicta* (1733)

Chapter 6

Alberti, Leone Battista *Ten Books on Architecture* (1755)
Country Life, 28 Jan & 4 Feb 1971
*Diedenhofen, Wilhelm 'Die Klever garten des Johann Moritz' in Soweit der Erdkries
    reicht, Johann Moritz von Nassau-Siegen* (1979)
Evelyn, John *Sylva: or a Discourse on Forest Trees* (1st edn 1664) (2nd edn 1679)
    (3rd edn 1706)
Favero, G.B. *Corpus Palladianum*, Vol.V
Hopper, Florence 'De Nederlandse Klassieke Tuin en André Mollet' in *Bulletin
    KNOB, jrg.82, Nr.3 & 4, pp. 98–115*
Gardner, J. Starkie English Wrought Ironwork of the XVII & XVIII Centuries
    (1911)
Hoppenbrouwer, O.S.B., Jansen, G.B., & Woerdeman, Trudi *De Slangenburg,
    Kasteel, park en bewoners* (1984)
Scamozzi, Vicenzo *L'Idea della Architettura universale* (1615)
Tijou, Jean *A New Booke of Drawings invented and designed by John Tijou* (1693)
Van der Groen, Jan *Den Nederlantsen Hovenier* (1669)

Chapter 7

De Vries, Hans Vredeman *Hortorum viridariorumque* (1583)
Dezallier D'Argenville, Antoine-Joseph *La Théorie et la Pratique du Jardinage*
    (1709)
Mollet, André *Le Jardin de Plaisir* (1651)
Stainton, Lindsay, and White, Christopher (eds) *Drawing in England from Hilliard
    to Hogarth* (1987), pp. 127, 170
Van der Groen, Jan *Den Nederlandtsen Hovenier* (1669)

Chapter 8

Bertrand, J.E. *Descriptions des Arts et Metiers . . . Nouvelle Edition* (1781)
Dezallier D'Argenville, Antoine-Joseph *La Théorie et la Pratique du Jardinage*
    (1709)
Van der Groen, Jan *Den Nederlandtsen Hovenier* (1669)

Chapter 9

Britannia Illustrata (1707)
Dezallier D'Argenville, Antoine-Joseph *La Théorie et la Pratique du Jardinage*
    (1709)
Evelyn, John *Sylva: or a Discourse on Forest Trees* (1664) (1679) (1706)
Johnson, J. (ed.) *Excellent Cassandra*, pp. 66 & 69

London, George, and Wise, Henry The Retir'd Gard'ner (1706)

Matthews, W.H. *Mazes and Labyrinths, their history and development* (1922)

Mollet, André *Le Jardin de Plaisir* (1651)

Morris, Christopher (ed.) *The Journeys of Celia Fiennes* (1949)

Nourse, Timothy *Campania Foelix* (1700)

Phibbs, John, et al. 'Castle Bromwich Hall Gardens Historical Survey' (1985)

Switzer, Stephen *Ichnographia Rustica* (1718)

Van der Groen, Jan *Den Nederlandtsen Hovenier* (1669)

Woudstra, Jan 'The wilderness in seventeenth and eighteenth century gardens; History and conservation case studies' (1986), thesis at the University of York

Chapter 10

British Library, Sloane MSS 2928; 3370; 4062,f. 246; 4057, ff. 1–3

Camden Society New series, Vol. XXIII

Coats, Alice M. 'The Hon. and Rev. Henry Compton, Lord Bishop of London' in *Garden History* Vol.IV, No. 3 (Autumn 1976)

Cowell, John *The Curious and Profitable Gardener* (1730), pp. 34–5

Kuijlen, J., Oldenburger-Ebbers, C.S., & Wijnands, D.O. *Paradisus Batavus* (1983)

Correspondence of John Ray (1684)

Pulteney, Richard *Historical and Biographical sketches of the progress of botany in England* (1790)

Rowley, Gordon 'The Duchess of Beaufort's Succulent Plants' *Bradleya*, Vol. 5, pp. 1–16 (1987)

Sloane, Hans *A Voyage to the Islands . . . and Jamaica*, 2 Vols (1707, 1725)

Switzer, Stephen *Ichnographia Rustica* (1718)

Wijnands, D. Onno 'The Hortus Medicus Amstelodamensis' *Kew Magazine*, Vol. 4, No. 2 (1987)

Chapter 11

Apollo (1984), pp. 104–7

Colchester, Maynard 'Account Book', Gloucestershire Record Office, D36

Green, David *Blenheim Palace* (1951), pp. 68–72

Evelyn, John, manuscript of 'Elysium Britannicum', Christchurch College, Oxford

Harvey, John *Early Gardening Catalogues* (1972)

Harvey, John *Early Nurserymen* (1974)

Marshal, Alexander, 'Florilegium' in the Royal Library, Windsor

Rea, John *Flora, Ceres and Pomona* (1666)

Sloane MS 3343, in the British Library, f. 136, No. 7

Sloane 'Herbarium', in the British Museum, Natural History, HS 138, f. 8–11, HS 235, f. 9

Trew, Dr *Hortus Nitidissimus* (c.1750)

Van der Groen, Jan *Den Nederlandtsen Hovenier* (1669)

F.P. & M.M. Verney (eds.) *Memoirs of the Verney Family in the Seventeenth Century* (1925)

information from John Sales, Gardens Adviser to the National Trust

information from Mrs M.P.G. Draper, Archivist to the Bedford Estates

Chapter 12

Evelyn, John *Acetaria* (1699)

London, George, & Wise, Henry *The Complete Gardener* (1717)

Temple, Sir William *Upon the Gardens of Epicurus* (1685)

Van der Groen, Jan *Den Nederlandtsen Hovenier* (1669)

Van Oosten, Hendrik *De Nieuwe Nederlandse Bloemhof* (1700)

Van Oosten, Hendrik *De Nieuwe en Naaukeurige Neederlandse Hovenier* (1716)

Index

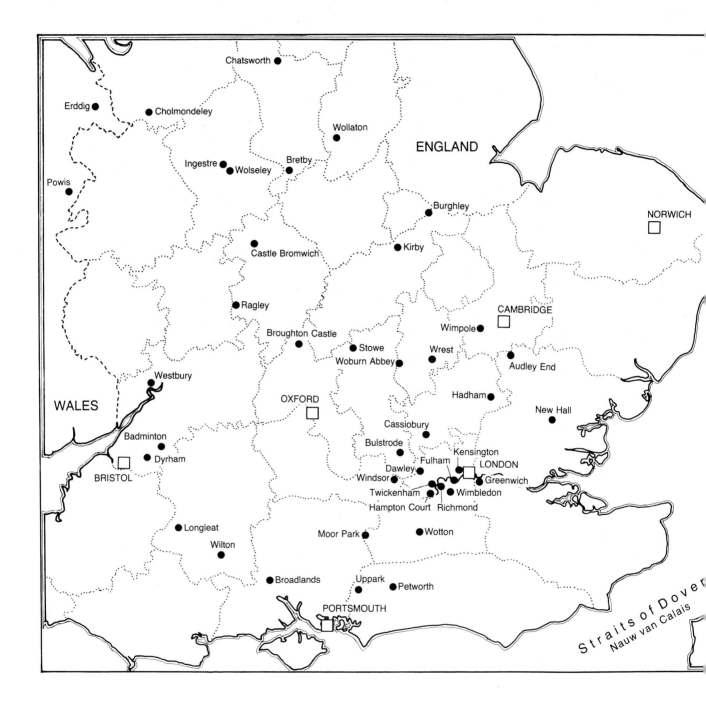

Map of the Netherlands
and south-east Britain
showing the location of
places mentioned